Figure It Out
Snapshots Of My Journey
With Multiple Sclerosis

Danica King

Acknowledgements

They say it takes a village to raise a child, if that is true, it also takes a village to manage a chronic disease. In this book, I will introduce you to some of the members of my village. Thank you Ma. Maybe this book is why you sent me to college. Thanks to my favorite brother, R-Jay, for always having my back, no matter how many times I threaten to punch you in the face. You probably won't believe that a large portion of this book was written before my 40th birthday.

Special shout-out to the entire MS community, especially those in Richmond, Virginia, including the MSers, the National MS Society and all of the other MS organizations, Neurologists and other medical professionals, and the DMT sales representatives.

Thank you to everyone who gave me permission to use their name, if I wrote a book about my MS journey. Thank you SD. I hope you see this book as a sufficient legacy for me to leave. Thank you P-Nut for assisting me with applying for disability. Thanks to Clyde who gave me suggestions and support throughout this process, if I wrote a book about my MS. Diane thank you for referring me to TJ. Thank you TJ for answering all of my questions along the way. Thank you Christine for your assistance with the title, if I wrote a book about my MS journey. Thank you to Tracie who listened to my over-excitement on Day One and gave me words of encouragement. Thank you Siarra for lending me your editing skills and thank you Tasia for the referral. Thank you Keshia for fixing my printer, remotely, when it decided to act up in the middle of writing this book. Thank you Kasharne and Regina for helping me compose an author bio. Thank you Phannetta for the last minute services you provided.

Thank you to the unnamed individuals who are referenced in the book. I apologize in advance to people whom actually know me and have heard some of these stories before. I promise there are several things in this book that no one knows about. I apologize if I forgot any MS related anecdotes. Give me a break, I have MS.

I am not claiming to be a medical professional or even a MS expert. This book is not intended to provide anyone with any medical knowledge. I am just sharing what I have been through, what works for me, my interpretation, and observations of things I have heard and seen.

I have so much more respect for indie authors. Writing a book is hard work.

Winning!

Chile.

The Look Back.

I wish I could individually name everyone who participated on the team MS King for Walk MS 2016 and 2017, but thanks to all of you and just know that your help was appreciated. I also want to thank everyone who helped me during any part of my MS journey.

Chapter 1

Let's just jump right into the crux of this story. I was diagnosed with Multiple Sclerosis on August 19, 2010. It is an autoimmune disease that attacks the CNS (Central Nervous System) which includes the brain, spinal cord, and optic nerve. Through a process called demyelination, the myelin sheath (protective covering) of your nerves is damaged. All future mentions of my disease will be referred to as MS. Now that I got that out of the way, we can go back.

I have a large family on both sides: several aunts, uncles, and a slew of cousins. Most are in Virginia or New York; a few in New Jersey and many are in other states as well. Having such a large family makes for a pre-made support system and I am thankful for that. Family over everything.

I was born in Hopewell, Virginia and moved to Poughkeepsie, New York with my parents, Roy and Sandra, when I was only five months old. I usually affectionately call my mother, Ma, but sometimes it's Sandra. When I was five years old, I was hospitalized for a week because I had a seizure; I have not had a seizure since then. While I was in the hospital, my grandmother and Aunt Marian came to New York to check on me. Aunt Marian, her husband, Uncle Wayne, and I all agree I may have had MS since then, especially now that I have learned some MSers have seizures. Some people call us MS warriors. That actually makes

1

sense since we have to keep several tools in our quiver as we battle this disease. I just prefer to say MSer, as opposed to MS patient.

Also, when I was five years old, one of my dad's brothers, Uncle Ralph, got a new motorcycle. I begged him and my dad to let me sit on it. They refused numerous times, but I never stopped begging. Sick of hearing me, they finally gave in and let me sit on it. As soon as I sat on it, I burned my leg on a pipe. I acted like nothing happened. Ma noticed it that night at bath time. That's the last time I got on a motorcycle.

As a kid, like many in my generation, I would spend the Summer down south at my grandmother's house. The house was always inundated with a bunch of cousins. Sandra, has six siblings: Aunt Elsie, Aunt Ann, Aunt Cat, Aunt Marian, Uncle Tee, and Uncle Frank, so my cousins were my playmates. I would hang out with Uncle Frank's daughter, my cousin, Tracie sometimes. I have fond memories of her making pork & beans. To be honest, I think the "secret ingredient" may have been a stick of butter, but I have never asked. My grandmother raised five really great mothers. I called her Grandma. I do not think there was ever a time Grandma was home alone. As someone that lives alone and is home alone most days, I can't even fathom that.

When I was eight years old, Sandra took me to get my first library card. It was from Grinnell Public Library in New York. Let me clarify, first "real" library card. I was certainly able to borrow books from my elementary school library. When I was in elementary school, I purchased a Lamborghini poster from a school book fair.

That began my Lamborghini fascination. I just always thought they were such cool cars.

When I was young, my parents took me almost everywhere with them, even places I was not supposed to be. I remember being the only kid going on a boat trip on the Hudson River. The boat staff put me downstairs with the bartender, who served me Shirley Temples the whole trip. I still am known for having them now even when everyone else has grabbed an alcoholic mixed drink.

On the rare occasion I was not with my parents, sometimes I would stay at Aunt Shirley's house. This was my father Roy's oldest sister. Being a girl, I had to stay in the room with her only daughter, Gloria. All I ever looked forward to was playing with her Fashion Plates when I was staying over there. Sandra claims she bought me some of my own, which she probably did, but I don't remember having my own.

When I was 10 years old, I remember seeing the movie *Jo Jo Dancer* with my father. It starred Richard Pryor who had MS. When I was diagnosed, I did not remember MS is what Richard Pryor was diagnosed with before he died. Also at 10, my parents and I spent Thanksgiving week at Walt Disney World and other theme parks. I had been on a plane several times before, but this trip to Florida was the first time I had ever watched a movie on an airplane. No, I don't remember which movie. I always relish the fact that I did those kinds of walking-extensive activities when I was young and able. On this trip, Sandra acquired a taste for what became her favorite animal, monkeys.

I went to some great schools most of the time, Arlington Elementary, Arlington Middle, and Arlington High School. On November 2, 1987, I met Regina. I had just started at Arlington Middle School. We were both in sixth grade. It was the Monday after Halloween and she was wearing a clown costume. She doesn't remember that, but I do. My long-term memory is on point, however, I experience cog-fog (brain fog) trying to recall more recent events.

The first school assignment Regina and I ever worked on together was creating a marketing campaign for a Greek Mythology figure. We had Poseidon, God of the Sea and protector of all things aquatic. Our product was Poseidon Pizza. We had Goldfish crackers covering French bread pizza. I made a rap and the plan was to play the song from a recording, but we were having technical difficulties with the tape recorder. We had to quickly come up with a Plan B or back-up plan. We had no choice but to recite the rap in front of the class. I still remember the rap. We also learned a helping verb song in that class. I still remember that too.

One of my favorite activities was to take pictures – no landscapes or anything deep like a professional photographer, mostly snapshots of friends and family enjoying themselves. I had been taking pictures since boys had cooties. I am such a shutterbug. I would put the pictures in chronological order, then put them in a photo album. I still do that today; I don't know anyone else that still does that. I received my first camera from my father. It was a Polaroid. I inherited the hobby of taking pictures from Ma. I used to either print pictures at the store or order them online and have them sent to a

4

store for me to pick up. Now I order the pictures online and have them mailed to my house.

My only sibling, R-Jay, was born June 4, 1989 when I was almost 13 years old. I had been asking my parents for a sibling since I was eight years old. Better late than never, I guess. He is a Junior, but I have never called him Roy. People think it's funny that he started Kindergarten the same year I started college.

When I was in the eighth grade, we went on a school field trip to New York City. The trip was in December, and we saw the most Santa Clauses ever. A portion of the trip was spent in FAO Schwarz toy store. I did not meet the rest of my class at the agreed upon time, so they had to call me over the loud speaker. That probably had more to do with me being enamored over the piano mat from the movie *Big* and looking at the massive LEGO exhibits, than anything related to MS. Now I have a hyper-sensitivity to hearing my name. I don't know if the two are related, but whenever I hear my name or think I hear my name, it grabs my attention, even if the person is not talking directly to me.

In high school, a lot of kids played sports. My friend, Tichanda, ran track and jumped hurdles. I was never on a sports team, unless you count ski club – most people don't.

When I was 15, I went on a vacation to Myrtle Beach. I had a pair of jeans airbrushed with a red Lamborghini on one leg and "Stylin' in the '90s" on the other leg. I suppose I thought airbrushing was going to stay in style until 1999. I was wrong. Later that year, Aunt Shirley's oldest son, my cousin Clyde, took me to see the Thanksgiving Day Parade in New York City. That is the only time I ever went to the parade, even though I grew up in Upstate New York. Like Disney World, I am so glad I got to experience that. I miss the days of being able to navigate a huge crowd like that.

On June 5, 1992, I had my Sweet 16 birthday party at my house. My birthday is in August, but this was long before social media and it was harder to stay in contact with people over the Summer. That in addition to people vacationing over the Summer were the reasons I had a party in June, the day after R-Jay's birthday and birthday party. Unfortunately, it rained so the party scheduled for outside was moved indoors. A DJ was hired and everything.

While in eleventh grade, I was in a Photography and Graphic Design program at BOCES (Board of Cooperative Education Services) Career and Technical Center. I went to Arlington High School for half of the day and BOCES for the remainder of the day. The BOCES program was a two-year program, which I was unable to complete. The Summer before I was to become a Senior in high school I was to move to Surry County, Virginia. Both of my parents were born and raised in Surry. It is a small town where most people know each other. Introductions are usually made by what year you graduated high school and your mother's maiden name.

I was lucky because Roy's sister, Aunt Rachel and her husband, Uncle Oliver, took me in for the Summer, so I could hang out with my friends in New York and take more snapshots a few months longer. Once I moved to Virginia, Aunt Shirley would mail me articles of my friend Tichanda's track accomplishments from *The Poughkeepsie Journal* newspaper. I guess she was doing her part to make my transition smoother. My graduating class went from almost 500 at Arlington High School to about 50 at Surry County High School. I was in the class of 1994. We had shirts made that read "Out the Door in '94." How did they know I like things that rhyme? I continue to keep up with a some of my Surry classmates via Facebook. After I graduated from Surry County High School, I attended Virginia Commonwealth University in Richmond, Virginia. I was a Marketing major and to think my marketing fascination all started with a Poseidon Pizza rap in middle school. While there, the photos continued. At VCU (Virginia Commonwealth University) on the same dormitory floor I met Kasharne, Keta, and Keshia, other freshmen who have all turned out to be some great friends. We were the foursome of Ks, Kasharne, Keta, Keshia, and King. Kasharne is the most optimistic person I know.

In 1996, Regina came to Virginia when I had my first surgery. I had my gallbladder removed. I didn't really think about it at the time, but maybe she thought I wasn't going to make it through the surgery and wanted to make sure she had the chance to see me first. I don't know, but I was glad she came.

When R-Jay was eight years old, I took him to his first concert at the Richmond Coliseum. We saw Busta Rhymes, Lil' Kim, and Puff Daddy (the name he went by back then), and a bunch of others. It made sense to take him to a concert at that age, since I went to my first concert when I was about nine years old. I saw the rapper, LL Cool J. Going to concerts has become me and R-Jay's Special Times event. Special Times is how I refer to bonding events or things I do repeatedly with the same person. Over the years, we have been to several concerts together. Before R-Jay could drive, Ma would buy tickets for the both of us for concerts he wanted to attend, so I could take him. Now we often buy tickets for each other for birthday or Christmas presents. It does not matter when the concert is, we use it as a gift for whichever of those two holidays comes next. It works out great because we both like all genres of music from all different time periods. Now that I require assistance navigating concert halls, I am glad that remains our Special Times activity.

In Summer 1999, I took my first trip to the Bahamas. I don't believe I would even be able to tolerate the severe Bahamas heat now. I'm certain I would sleep away my entire vacation. I went parasailing over the Atlantic Ocean while I was there. More than likely, I won't do that again. Sometimes I just like to try things just to say I did them and to have pictures of me doing a certain activity. I have plenty of pictures of me tethered to the back of the boat. Since then I have gone jet skiing in Myrtle Beach, now that one I would definitely do again.

In May 2000, I graduated from VCU. I had my graduation party at the clubhouse in my friend Kasharne's apartment complex where she was living at the time. Sandra's coworker and friend, Eileen, did all of the decorations for the party. That is the last time Regina and I did the Poseidon Pizza rap together in person. We performed it for my boss at the time. We were so lame. I still am.

Grandma's funeral was on June 1, 2000. Aunt Marian's son, Xavier, thinks he is a sibling rather than a grandchild. He wore black to our Grandma's funeral like the siblings did, rather than the cream adorned by all of us grandkids. I didn't like that, but he didn't ask for my input before selecting his wardrobe. At the funeral, Uncle James, Aunt Elsie's husband, recited a poem that he had written. I remember a small portion of the poem, "Did Tee get a plate? You best believe." Uncle Tee is Sandra's youngest brother. I see how Ma is with R-Jay, mothers have a weakness for those baby boys.

In June of 2002, Tichanda, her mother, and I went on vacation to Walt Disney World. I had been a few times, including once with Ma and R-Jay. I enjoyed it much more as an adult than I did as a child. Maybe that was just the kid that lives inside of me. A picture of me standing in front of Cinderella's Castle at Magic Kingdom is in a frame in my home office. Again, I was so happy I had done things involving big crowds and a lot of walking prior to my diagnosis.

Once I decided it was about time to buy a house in March 2003, Uncle James drove me to a house property listing. I said, "I don't need that big house." After viewing the house, it "talked to me." My friend, Kasharne, told me the right one would talk. I was very excited to make these my new digs. My first gray hair showed up during the home buying process. Roy's sisters, Aunt Shirley and Aunt Rachel, had gray hair as long as I can remember, so I always expected to go gray.

I was not worried about it when I saw my first gray hair at age 26.

On June 26, 2003, I was officially a homeowner. Unfortunately, I locked myself out almost immediately. When the locksmith came, he asked me to show him a piece of mail to confirm I was the homeowner. I told him I had just purchased the house, so I did not have any mail yet. I showed him my new house contract instead. I don't even think the ink was dry on the contract yet. After I purchased my house, I put up every single mini blind that is up in my house. I also put together the large bookshelf that is in my office, all by myself. I have moved the bedroom furniture around by myself. I even remember moving my bedroom furniture around by myself in my apartment I used to share with my former VCU roommate, Keshia. Doing things like that seem like a lifetime ago.

In August 2003, my Arlington High School friends George and Tichanda (and her now husband Vaughn), came to my housewarming party from New York. Regina (and her now husband Charles) even surprised me from New York when they pulled up in the driveway. Hands down, one of my happiest days. The getting locked out of the house on the first day made for a great housewarming party story.

On April 1, 2006, a few months before my 30th birthday I ran, okay partially jogged, the Ukrop's 10K (a 10K is 6.2 miles). I joined the YMCA training team to get ready for the event. This kind of activity was completely outside of my wheelhouse. Prior to this day, the closest I had ever come to running anywhere was watching my friend Tichanda's high school and college track meets. There was a lot of walking, but I did pick up the pace when I saw the cameras that were above us toward the end of the race. That picture is displayed on a corner wall shelf in my home office. Again, that seems like a lifetime ago. Now I'm struggling to walk one mile.

In Spring 2006 my friends, Kasharne, Keshia, Keta, and I attended a VCU Alumni party. We took a picture where we are all posing with four fingers up on our left hand, representing the fact that we all stayed on the 4th floor of the dorm. That was the only VCU Alumni party I ever attended. The next morning, we had breakfast at Cracker Barrel and we did the same pose from the previous night and stood in the same order. Both of these pictures are in a frame in my home office.

I was looking for something to do in my spare time. I had narrowed it down to three choices, cake decorating, bartending school, or Graduate School. In June 2006, I started attending Graduate School. Soon after I started, my cousin, Xavier, told me he started Graduate School after I told him I was going. He couldn't very well let his little cousin get a Graduate Degree and he not have one. Nothing wrong with a little friendly competition. I completed Graduate School with a 4.0 GPA. I have a MBA with a concentration in Management. I can't even imagine being able to come close to that scholastic goal now. Aunt Cat's children, Ta'Wane and Leticia, have both earned Master's Degrees after us. I'd like to think we inspired them.

In August 2006, my friends, Regina and Tichanda, (Tichanda's now husband, Vaughn), were all in Virginia again to help me celebrate my Dirty 30. That is what I called my 30th birthday party. There was nothing dirty about it. In fact, many kids were here at the house. I just called it that because it rhymed. My friend, Kasharne, is local so she is always present at my celebrations. Kasharne's gift was a Dirty 30 picture frame that she made. That is displayed in my home office. Regina made me a scrapbook of our entire friendship. The scrapbook was so good that even if you had never met me, you could look at it and you would know everything I liked or was into. The first page was our first picture together. It was the day we went on a middle school field trip – I don't remember where we went. All I know is that we showed up to school wearing the same vertical striped short set, in slightly different colors. The only other difference was I wore a tank top under my shirt. I had to add a pop of color to my outfit. We both had on sunglasses. She had previously had that picture made into a puzzle. Anyway, I cried like a baby and blamed it on my allergies for all of my party guests that were there watching me open my gifts. No one was buying the allergy attack story. My 30th birthday party, again, turned out to be one of my favorite days.

In November 2007, I rented a community center and had a baby shower in anticipation of the arrival of Kasharne and her husband Jay's 1st daughter. My friends, Tichanda and Vaughn even traveled to Richmond, Virginia for the occasion. Tichanda was a great help with the decorating of the baby shower hall. Even though I don't drink, we went to the Martini Kitchen & Bubble Bar that evening after the baby shower.

On January 20, 2009, my cousin, Leticia and I traveled to Washington, DC to see the Presidential Inauguration of our 44th President, Barack Obama. This is another thing that seems like a lifetime ago, me having the physical ability to attend such an event. Today I would not attend an event with such large crowds.

In May 2009, I traveled to New Orleans with play cousins (friends of the family – for anyone not familiar with the term) RonShai' and Sharna' and real cousins LaVita and Leticia. It was my first trip to the Big Easy and we had a great time. I think I gained four pounds on Bourbon Street.

In July 2009, my cousin, Leticia, moved to Alabama and I helped her drive her car there. We had about four carloads on that trip, but I was one of the few people that knew how to drive a stick shift (manual transmission). I ended up staying in Alabama for about a week. We walked up the steep hill in her apartment complex to rent a Redbox movie daily. I had not been diagnosed with MS yet, but the severe Alabama Summer heat wore me out.

In January 2010, I went blind in one eye, the left eye to be exact. In addition to enjoying rhyming, I tend to over-exaggerate things. I'm not over-exaggerating this one. Some may call it being a drama queen but that has a negative connotation, so I won't use that terminology. I went to work wearing sunglasses as I looked at the computer monitor. By the time I was able to get an appointment to see my Optometrist, in a couple of weeks my vision had been pretty much restored and she just updated my prescription.

In April 2010, I along with a few family members, participated in the Wakefield Community Walk for Breast Cancer along with Uncle Tee's daughter, Shardae. The walk in Wakefield, Virginia was in tribute to her late mother, Angela. The walk was only two miles long, but I was struggling, especially at the end. I used to wake up any given day and go to downtown Richmond, Virginia and do a five mile charity walk, no training required. Play cousin, Sharna', was more out of shape than I was and I couldn't keep up with her. I still didn't really think anything of it, maybe I was just hungry or something.

In May 2010, R-Jay and I travelled to New Jersey for Uncle Vernis' (actually Roy's uncle so our Great-Uncle Vernis) surprise 80th birthday party. He is the patriarch for that side of my family. I used to rip the line dance, Cupid Shuffle. Okay, maybe not rip, but it was the only one I did even halfway decently. I had to sit down halfway through the song. At the time, I thought it was because I was wearing really tall, high-heeled shoes. It is a shame I drove to New Jersey to see relatives that live right here in Richmond, Virginia. I need to do better.

Late May 2010, my friend, Kasharne, was on maternity leave with daughter #2, so we hung out a lot. Curbs had become the enemy. One day she made the comment, "If I didn't know better, I'd think you were drinking." That was from my stints of clumsiness and inability to walk straight. Keep in mind I don't drink, so she knew it couldn't be that. Okay, maybe I used to have one drink on my birthday every year. When I would tell doctors that, they say that didn't count when they ask me if I drink. Anyway, shortly after her comment, Kasharne gave me a card with cash in it. She claimed it was cash for me to go see the Jaheim concert, but we were already at the concert. I took it as my copay and went to the doctor. I never mind the guise that the money was for a concert ticket, but whenever I retell the story I let everyone know Kasharne gave me the copay to go see a doctor. Before I made it to the doctor, I would notice I had light sensitivity when I drove past The Shops at White Oak Village, a local shopping area. I thought I had a brain aneurysm. Keep in mind, I did not really know what that was, but that was my uneducated self-diagnosis. I knew my body and something just wasn't right.

On June 16, 2010, I went to Patient First, a walk-in doctor's office, which is open every day and has extended hours. I went in there feeling so stupid because I was at the doctor to tell them I was clumsy. I told the female doctor of my problem walking in heels, the struggles at the Breast Cancer walk a couple of months ago, and my light sensitivity issues. After listening to my story, without ever examining me or ever touching me, she said "I think you have Lupus or MS." Even though the letters M and S are in the world clumsy, there was no way that's what I had.

I took the doctors comment with a grain of salt and brushed it off like it was nothing. Clearly, she does not really know her stuff, that's why she works at this doc-in-a-box location. She referred me to a Rheumatologist and a Neurologist to confirm her suspicions. Despite my skepticism, I'll play along with this ruse. I went to the Rheumatologist first. After I went to the

Rheumatologist, my friend, Tichanda, called to check up on me. I let her know I was waiting for the doctor to call me back and I hadn't followed up yet, she said, "I can't be more concerned about you, than you are about yourself." I was driving and I broke down crying. She was right. I don't recall my exact course of action, but I'm certain I contacted the Rheumatologist shortly after our conversation.

The Rheumatologist said I didn't have Lupus, but I should move up my Neurologist appointment. It was then that I knew something was wrong. I do not remember the exact order of my guests, but Aunt Elsie and my friend, Kasharne, came over to help me cope with this news. Being the consummate optimist, Kasharne tried to convince me this wasn't such bad news. By now I knew better, nothing good could come of having to move up a doctor's appointment.

I bumped up the Neurologist appointment to July 29, 2010 and he agreed I might have MS. In order to confirm his conjecture, he sent me for an MRI (Magnetic Resonance Imaging) both with and without Gadolinium contrast (dye) used to find enhancing lesions. I was glad I was not claustrophobic. Though it does not give a definitive diagnosis, I was also sent for a Lumbar Puncture (Spinal Tap). Before the Lumbar Puncture, the nurse came in to say it's not that bad, it's just like an epidural before you give birth. That was not at all comforting since I have no kids. Clearly, she based her remarks on my age and assumed I had given birth at some point. The doctor, that I had never met before, asked me if I wanted to pray with him. That had never happened before. I did and it was then that I knew extracting spinal fluid was a big deal procedure. Luckily, it went off without a hitch.

After both of my procedures I went back to the Neurologist and on August 19, 2010 he confirmed my MS diagnosis. I don't think I will ever forget that date. In a nanosecond, my life changed. The news was completely traumatic. That was quite a defining moment in my life. Now I usually describe things as before or after my diagnosis. Okay, I have this debilitating, incurable, MonSter of a disease, now what? Actually, I later learned that I was one of the lucky ones to have been diagnosed so quickly. I have heard many horror stories that people have been told they were either crazy or a hypochondriac and have been misdiagnosed for several years before receiving the correct diagnosis. My Neurologist urged me to get on treatment quickly. He handed me color brochures of about five different injection medications and told me to pick one and let him know my decision.

"How am I supposed to do that?" was all I thought as I walked out of the office, not completely lucid, trying to suppress my tears. A few people knew I had a follow-up Neurologist appointment that day so the first person I remember calling me was my brother, R-Jay. I remember hanging up on him as I started to cry when I attempted to share the bad news of my diagnosis. R-Jay loves his big sister so I'm almost certain he immediately called Ma. My friend, Regina, describes R-Jay as all of the good parts of me. I think I should be offended, but I am not. I hung up on a few people that day – that was a bad day for me. Apparently, Ma got on the horn and called her four sisters to help her cope. That day, all five of the sisters called me to provide me with some solace. That had never happened before or since. I was definitely feeling the love, but I was still sad that day. Later that evening, I texted a few close friends, including my college roommate from VCU, Keshia. I texted "I have MS." She replied, "I have PMS." Normally, that would have cracked me up, but I was not in the joking mood on that occasion. Keshia and I lived together for several years both on and off campus so she knows me pretty well and knows I usually cope with things using humor, not that day.

Chapter 2

I was diagnosed on a Thursday. No time for a pity party, life had to go on. That Friday I was back to work, keeping my diagnosis to myself. I'm not sure if it was shame or embarrassment but I had only told family and very close friends. It's ridiculous, after my diagnosis people were listing a ton of people they knew or they had heard of with MS. It's kind of like when you buy a new car and then notice that car everywhere. I used to pack my lunch almost every day. I came home one day after work and was devastated I had left the deli meat for my turkey sandwich out all day. Of course, I had to throw it away. That was a bad day for me.

Sandra's sister Aunt Marian, also has MS. I was about 30 before I ever knew she had MS. She is one of the reasons I was not too worried when I was diagnosed. I have heard people say they have the preconceived notion of early death once they have the MS diagnosis. I see Aunt Marian at all the family functions carrying on as she always had done. She was even still wearing heels. Though I did not know the exact prognosis, because of her, I did not see MS as a death sentence at all.

Shortly after I was diagnosed, I resigned from my part time job with an event staffing company. It was a great job, I did not have to buy a ticket, get a new outfit, or get my hair done and I had seen some of the best shows and concerts that Virginia had to offer. I had been working there since August of 2002. Aunt Elsie and my cousin, Leticia, encouraged me not to quit. Leticia said that with every place requiring equal opportunity employment, they would not fire me for my physical limitations, as long as I told them about my diagnosis. That may have very well been true, but I did not want to always have to work on the elevator or work some other non-mobile assignment.

Lashi, another play cousin, worked at the store where Ma and I purchased the first few supplies for my initial DMT (Disease-Modifying Therapy/Treatment). She was helping from the start and she didn't even know it. About a month after my diagnosis, I started on injections. I chose to do mine in the evening after taking Aleve, to avoid any flu-like symptoms. I had never even heard the word titration before I began research for my injections. It is the process of gradually building up to the dose of a medicine until the desired dose is reached. I set up a refrigerator in my home office upstairs, which is where I would perform the injections. I think the refrigerator was from when my brother, R-Jay, was a Freshman at VCU. The injections had to be refrigerated and I just did not want to have to see the needles every time I went into the kitchen refrigerator. As a matter of fact, I did not want to have to think about the injections until it was time to inject.

They sent a nurse to my house to show me how to inject myself. Ma and R-Jay came over to learn as well. Moments before the nurse arrived, I was throwing mail that mentioned MS across the living room. Ma let me be and did not comment on my erratic behavior. I was fine before I checked the mail. As I look back, it may have been me exhibiting a mood swing, something often seen with MSers. All three of us learned the injection routine and with the assistance of the nurse, I gave myself my first medication dosage. At the time, I had a boyfriend that assisted with injections and took me to several MRI and Neurologist appointments. He also accompanied me to MS pharmaceutical company sponsored lunches and dinners. We have since parted company, but I am eternally grateful for his support.

I experience communication problems. Sometimes my thoughts are scattered and I struggle to articulate my point. Even with a speech impediment, it has not reduced how much I talk and I am quite loquacious. Sometimes I will say "One moment please," as a way to stall and figure out what to say next. Other times I will give a blank stare and remain silent when the person I am speaking to is waiting for a response, inadvertently creating awkward silence. Sometimes I feel like my brain is on a sabbatical._ Sometimes it takes a moment for me to process what has been said. I hear the words, but I don't always process them right away. I often misinterpret someone's meaning or am misunderstood myself. I will sometimes say month when I mean to say year. I experience a lot of confusion when it comes to opposites. I often say up for down and left for right. I also hit the up elevator button when I want to go down. This even happens when I'm writing. I will write "start" when I mean to write "stop."

When the doctor asks me to do something with a particular hand or leg, I have to take a moment and make sure I am using the correct side of my body. The same thing occurs when the massage therapist tells me we are going to start face up. I have to take a moment and think about which direction my body needs to lay on the massage table. This kind of mix up happens all the time. Things like that used to be so automatic. I tend to be more literal and I do not pick up on context clues like I used to be able to do. I also will sometimes put an erroneous "not" in a sentence I am reading, negating the entire meaning of the sentence. I have a tendency to change the tense of something I read, like inserting "had" when "have" is written. I don't always get it when someone is trying to be funny or use sarcasm. I also often have to tell people I do not understand something or ask them to clarify something. I often find myself prompting people to be more specific. They can then, dumb it down for me. For example, I may be referring to the size of something, when the other person if referring to the quantity. I find myself doing a lot more of my own bogus version of sign language to act out what I am talking about.

I find that I get easily sidetracked or find myself going off on a tangent. I often have random thoughts that have nothing to do with what is going on at any particular time. It is not just verbal communication, I have visual communication problems. I will walk down a hallway and not see the room number I am looking for. I will walk away and ask for directions just to be sent right back to where I came from. Miraculously the door I just left will be labeled with my desired room number. I have trouble with the visual processing of things. One time I was driving my brother's spare car and I had to put gas in the car. Both are things I had previously done. I had to call and ask him how to put gas in the car. Keep in mind, there is a picture of a gas pump on the lever. A picture I had seen before I called him. It is like my brain did not register the visual cue the first time. Sometimes I just do things out of order, like turn the bathroom light off, before I turn off the sink faucet.

There is another component to communicating involving memory. Sometimes MSers can only remember a portion of the word or a description of the word. Those of you who speak MS know exactly what I am talking about. My brother's girlfriend, Christine speaks fluent MS. My friend, Janene, does pretty well too. As you have probably already noticed, I have trouble staying focused. I hope everyone understands this book. There is often a disconnect between what I'm thinking and what I'm saying. I'm going to give it to you straight, MS sucks, but I am trying to manage the best I can. Some days are definitely better than others. Some people have told me some days they don't even realize that they have MS. I am jealous of those people. I am fully aware of my MS every single day. I don't feel like mine has ever gone into remission and I have no reprieve from my many MS symptoms. Not a day goes by where I don't drop something, knock over something, or have some kind of stumble. Sometimes unexplained bruises show up on my body, without me remembering hitting anything. Even getting up off of the floor is a challenge, even if I intentionally get down there. Sometimes people have to grab me to avoid me from tipping over like a teapot. If Ma or my brother, R-Jay, see me and other people are around, they will quickly snatch me up so no one is the wiser. This is usually a pretty good indication that it is time for me to leave the festivities.

23

My hearing is not as good as it used to be. Yet another MS symptom from the MS prize pack. I had a hearing test and though my hearing ability has declined, it is not bad enough to require the need of a hearing aid. Often, I say "Repeat that," "Excuse me," or "I'm sorry." In each case I am prompting the speaker to repeat themselves. Sometimes I even have to ask people to spell words. People may think I'm having a comprehension issue, rather than a hearing problem. Adversely, I tell someone I don't understand something and they repeat it, thinking I didn't hear them, when I actually didn't understand them. I can't tolerate some noises, like clanking bracelets sometimes irritate me. I have also noticed occasional tinnitus (ringing in my ears).

I also have a heightened sensitivity to some sounds. That would explain why I can no longer tolerate my cell phone ringer. I used to keep it on vibrate, but now even vibrate irritates me. Because of this, my cell phone ringer is always on silent. The downside to the ringer being off is if I misplace my cell phone, I can't call my number to locate it. If someone is really trying to reach me, they will call my house. Sandra always believes you should have a land line. R-Jay and I both have land lines, not many people do these days, especially not those Generation Y Millennials. My non-cordless land line is in my kitchen. I call it the pay phone. It is so antiquated, it doesn't even have caller ID, but it works though. I have it set up so the caller ID is displayed on the television, so I don't expel any energy getting to the telephone if it is not a call I want to take. My phone upstairs has three handsets, because it takes me a while to get from room to room. This way I can choose the closest receiver, expelling minimal energy. Most of the ringers on the handsets in my home are turned off too. The pay phone ringer is always on. The phone usually does not wake me if I am taking a nap.

One night I went to the movies with a bunch of my cousins and play cousins. I had purchased one of those kid snack packs to enjoy during the movie. Before I made it to my seat in the theater, I had dropped the whole box of snacks on the ground. I was devastated, but did not go get another one. That was a bad day for me. I remember one day I was lying in bed, and saw two huge, black spiders crawling on my bedroom wall. I am not sure if the MS had my mind playing tricks on me or if it was a side effect from some medicine I was taking at the time. There were no spiders. I never told my Neurologist about the mysterious spiders.

I ended up giving away all of my heels. It is hard enough trying to remain steady in flat shoes. I was devastated at first, but heels hurt. Clearly, I was only wearing them to attract men because it's not like they felt good to me. Aunt Elsie's youngest daughter, Jennifer, had a shoe charity event. It was a mutually beneficial arrangement. I was able to donate to a good cause and get rid of my obsolete footwear. I'd like to think I still have some cute shoes, even if they are all flats. Now when I go shoe shopping it is about finding the color I need in a flat shoe. The style is a tertiary issue.

I had noticed I had become jumpy and more on edge than I used to be. Noises that never bothered me before now startled me. I jump when the county picks up the trash and recycling, even though it is done on the same days every week. I have literally jumped when I hear someone knocking on the door or a delivery person leaving a package on the porch. Sometimes I don't even go to the front door if I'm not expecting company or I will just look through the peephole to see if a package had been left.

My emotions have been out of control since I moved to Virginia. This also leads me to think I had MS way before I was diagnosed. I did not cry this much when I was in New York. Regina says she has never even seen me cry in New York. Sandra attributes me crying to the fact that I wasn't around this much family and did not attend this many family events growing up in New York. She along with other family members call me a cry baby.

One thing in particular I noticed is the effect some movies have on me, a new effect. The movie *Marley & Me* had me wailing up severely and I am not a dog person. Pets are just not my thing. It is enough work just taking care of myself. I have met MSers that have dogs as support animals. I always thought the only kind of service dogs were seeing eye dogs for the blind. My favorite pet belongs to Aunt Elsie's oldest daughter, Jessica. It is a turtle named Squirt. Squirt is like 15 years old, but I digress. *The Game Plan* is another movie that has me in tears. When The Rock runs across the bridge with his daughter in his arms, man, that puts me in tears every time I see it. Another illogical thing is that I can't watch movies or television shows where the person is getting any kind of injection. I mean I can watch the movie or TV show, I just cover my eyes during those types of scenes. I also find myself laughing out loud more while watching TV shows and movies, even if I'm watching by myself.

Another problem has been navigating stairs, of course I would live in a two-story home. I have fallen down the stairs more times than I care to recall. When I told my Neurologist of my falls, he sent me to PT (Physical Therapy) at Sheltering Arms, a physical rehabilitation center. That was several years ago and I have rarely fallen down my stairs since then.

I have lists or at least reminders in my smartphone for everything, in fact, several every day. I even have a reminder to take a BM cocktail if I have not "gone" in a few days. Of course, the reminders only work if you remember to look at them, unfortunately I do not always remember. I try to write things down or put them in my cell phone right away, otherwise I am likely to forget my thought. If I happen not to have a pen or my phone near me, I have found that saying something out loud helps me remember until I get to a pen or my cell phone. Also, if I walk out of a room and forget the reason for my departure, walking back into the original room tends to jog my memory. I often have to create visual cues for myself to remind me of things. One example is putting a plastic bag around my front door knob. This reminds me that I need to remove something from the refrigerator or freezer and take it with me when I leave the house.

I used to carry a pretty large purse, then I started to carry one with a long strap going diagonally across my body. Now I carry a little one with a very short strap that rests beneath my underarm. I keep a pill organizer in my purse. Even with the pills on me and reminders in my phone, I still often forget to take my pills if I am away from home. Carrying such a small purse has cut into my ability to be a Girl Scout. Not a real Girl Scout, I haven't been one of those since the fifth grade, but I do try to make sure I have everything I may need at my disposal. I have a "just in case" mentality. It is better to be safe than sorry. Now I just keep all of my things in my car, which is usually close by. I've heard a lot of females name their cars. Mine doesn't have a name, maybe I'll name the next one.

One night I left the oven on all night. I was home, but I went to bed. Luckily, my cousin, Ta'Wane, was spending the night at my house so he turned it off when he got in. The next morning, he told me what I had done and I just started crying. That was a bad day for me. Unfortunately, that was not the last time I left the oven on, cooking nothing. Another time I had gone out for my friend Kasharne's birthday, so I got in late, well late for me. When I got home, I was devastated to see the oven was still on. It had been on since breakfast. I've also left the toaster oven on for hours after I have finished cooking. Other times I check the toaster oven after the allotted cooking time and it turns out I never turned it on to begin with.

At Aunt Ann's daughter, LaVita's baby shower, I was sharing a table with play cousin, Lashi. She was telling me she knew someone else with MS. She was telling me about resources available to me as a MSer. I was able to utilize those resources and I was grateful for her sharing.

When I was diagnosed, I did not even know about the National MS Society or that there were walks for this disease. A friend of mine asked me to join her employer's team for Walk MS in Richmond, Virginia. At first I declined, then I thought, "How can I expect people to walk for me and I'm not even walking for myself?" In March 2011, I completed my first Walk MS event. After the walk was my friend Kasharne's youngest daughter McKenzie's first birthday party. At the birthday party, one of Kasharne's friends suggested I start journaling as a way to help cope with my life with MS. I did not make my first journal entry until McKenzie was five years old. I just do not do stuff until I am ready. My friend, Regina, mailed me my first journal. Now journals have become a regular part of the pharmaceutical company SWAG (Stuff We All Get). Swag consists of a myriad of useful things including pens, cooling items, journals, lip balm, sunscreen, sunglasses, umbrellas, and bags – both the ones with handles and drawstrings. Pretty much anything the pharmaceutical companies can put their name on and use as a promotional item.

In April 2011, I visited Tichanda's family in New Jersey. She knew all I ever wanted to do was work and she knew I was unhappy at the job I had. She insisted I at least try to look for a new job. I did not start looking until June 2011. Sometimes it takes me a while to get ready to do something. Also in Spring 2011, the VCU men's basketball team made it to the Final Four. Go Rams! As a VCU alumni, I proudly wore a t-shirt celebrating the event.

I am still known for always being on time. Now tasks take a bit longer so I find myself running about 10 minutes late. I am told that is still considered on time, I don't agree. Because of my punctuality, Aunt Elsie asked me to pick up my cousin, Jessica, from a middle school event. I did not know ahead of time, but she performed at the event. I missed the dance performance, but was there in time for the ride home. Later that evening, my friend, Kasharne, took me to dinner at 3 Monkeys restaurant because I was terribly depressed. She told me I had to snap out of my depression. I just couldn't. She usually uses a much more gentler approach, so I must have been really bad back then.

In July 2011, I got my first handicapped parking placard. I say I'm in VIP Parking. There I go using humor as a coping mechanism. Even though I had the placard, I still did not tell people I worked with why I needed one. Back then I was still walking fairly well. I find myself moving my car closer if a VIP or another closer spot has become available after I have already parked. I never did that before MS. I will also circle the block several times searching for a close parking spot. Before MS, I don't believe I would have even had the patience to do parking space searches like the ones I do now. Sometimes the trip from the parking spot to the store entrance seems lightyears away, even if I am in a VIP parking spot.

Also in July 2011, my friend, Lona, told me about a job opening at her company. By mere chance, I had interviewed her for my Master's Degree thesis. She did not even remember that. Anyway, I used to work with her sister and could only surmise that she had heard positive things about my work performance. In August 2011, I was interviewed for that very job. I showed up and learned my interview was going to be on the second floor. For the first time, since my diagnosis, I was happy I had a two-story home. I hoped that navigating my stairs at home would be good practice for the trip upstairs. I prayed that I did not stumble. I successfully crushed the interview. Now that the interview was over and as I attempted to stand, I found out my knees had locked up on me. I did a few stretches and managed to successfully make it down the staircase. In case you're wondering, I got the job and worked there almost three years. Every day I had to climb that staircase.

After a while working there, I told Human Resources of my diagnosis and they were able to make parking accommodations. That daily trek to and from a far parking space and trying to navigate the stairs was beginning to take a toll on me. My employer started inviting me to the MS Women on the Move Luncheon sponsored by the National Multiple Sclerosis Society. I cried my eyes out the first two years. Any coworkers that attended the luncheon and didn't know I had MS, knew now. The MS Women On the Move Luncheon became one of my favorite MS events. Even after I was no longer employed with that company, I continued to attend the luncheons.

Chapter 3

I first started wearing glasses around 2002. Sandra has always worn glasses. I used to joke her when she would say she could not hear me without her glasses on, now I am the exact same way. I guess we are concentrating so hard on trying to see that we are unable to hear. Every time I go to the Optometrist my prescription has to be upped. My vision is so poor that I go to sleep with a pair of my glasses on since I fall asleep to the TV. Many healthcare professionals have suggested not having a TV in the bedroom at all to help you sleep. That may happen one day, but I'm not ready to make what I consider a drastic change yet.

I set the TV sleep timer every night. I wake up several times at night and the first thing I do is turn on the television, then go to the bathroom. When I return to my bedroom, I reset the sleep timer. I suffer from insomnia. I usually have no trouble initially going to sleep, it's staying asleep that is the problem. I only stay asleep a couple of hours at a time. I have stretches I do while I am in the bed. I often have leg spasms when I am in the bed. Those are uncontrollable, jerking movements. They don't occur every day, but every week. Sometimes I also experience numb limbs. I also sometimes wake up to cramping fingers and I feel discomfort when I try to bend my fingers on my right hand. It is not a result of sleeping on it or anything like that.

There are quite a few things I do differently from how I used to do them. I used to eat dinner upstairs every night, putting my plate on a folding bed tray, a gift from my play cousin, Sharna'. As soon as I walk into a restaurant or other building I am not familiar with, I usually search for the restroom sign or ask where they are located. Also, I often create Microsoft Excel Spreadsheets as a way to stay organized. I have always been a fan of Microsoft Excel, but I now make spreadsheets way more often than I ever used to do. I used to be able to iron a week's worth of work clothes, now I can only stand up long enough to iron a couple of pieces at a time. I have also left the iron plugged in, so I am grateful I have the kind that cuts off automatically. If I am out, I may have to use a port-a-potty. I never used them before, but now I lack the ability to hold in my urine for any real amount of time. It is easier to just wear a Depends and "go." Usually I just refer to it as I'm wearing a diaper. They are just like the diaper commercials claim, once you "go," you can no longer feel it. The usage of these items may seem taboo, but if the option is I don't get to go somewhere, then I'll wear one.

I usually am unable to just cough naturally like I used to do. It now usually has to be intentional and forced. It's the weirdest thing. I am no longer coordinated enough to use dental floss picks. I had my dentist show me a different way to hold my regular dental floss. If someone is around to assist me walk to the car or into the building, I will usually loop arms with them for assistance. I call it going to the prom. People automatically slow down when they are assisting me. I guess they figure I want to go slowly if I am requiring help. That is not the case, I'd rather get to my destination quickly. Sometimes when I intend to walk straight and end up hitting the wall I point in the desired direction and say, "Imma go that way." Again, humor has always been my coping mechanism.

I've always been extremely independent. Even after my diagnosis, I used to not ask for help. I did not want to burden anyone with my problems. Now if someone stops by my house, they already know they will have a project to do. A project is how I refer to anything I come up with that has to be done, including chores around the house. It can be anything from taking the baskets of folded laundry upstairs to carrying cases of bottled water from my car into the house. If I am taking the laundry baskets upstairs myself, it is a slow trek one or two steps at a time, resting the basket on each step until I reach the top landing. My brother, R-Jay, is the only one that fake complains about doing a project. Knowing full well he will have something to do before he stops by my house.

As a way to try to maintain some of my independence, I sometimes decline when a family member offers to fix my plate when we are in public at an event. My attempts to assert my independence tend to be unsuccessful. I usually end up wasting the food or drink, leaving me to wish I had taken them up on their initial offer.

R-Jay and his girlfriend, Christine, and my cousin, Ta'Wane, automatically check the mail whenever they come over for a visit. I check it by driving up to it when I get home and retrieve it through the driver's side window. It is so ridiculous how something as simple as checking the mail becomes this big ordeal. If I have to mail a bill, I will go to a mailbox that I can make a drop off from my car, unless someone is in the car with me that can easily make the trip to the mailbox. I have even gone as far as ask someone standing near a mailbox to come to my car and get a piece of mail and put it in the mailbox for me.

Things that never bothered me before, now give me anxiety. For instance, driving over a large bridge. It does not stop me from driving anywhere, but I am definitely more aware of them. It does not bother me to the point of a panic attack or anything like that. I just never really paid them any attention before I was diagnosed. I also notice things I would have not previously noticed, like if a restaurant or other kind of business does not have any close VIP parking spots or any VIP spots at all. I tend to notice this even if I am just driving by and not even visiting the establishment.

I leave a plethora of items out for easy access and ease of use. It can sometimes lead to clutter, but I would trade a little disorder for accessibility any day. Items that used to be in my attic, like luggage, now are housed on the ground. I have a bad habit of planning to do something on a particular day before I check my schedule in my cell phone. Some other things I do are open the refrigerator when I mean to open the microwave after it has beeped. I know many people occasionally make similar errors.

I gave up my regular gym membership because all of the cardio equipment was upstairs and they did not have an elevator. That was just a disaster waiting to happen. I used to do an hour on the elliptical machine, now I am tired after only three minutes. I purchased a recumbent exercise bike which is in my living room. I used to ride the bike for an hour. Then I went down to only being able to ride for a half hour and then stumble over and fall onto the couch which is just a few steps away. Now I can do a solid 30 minutes and walk decently to the nearby couch. While on the bike, I either read a book on my Kindle or read some paperback books I ordered from Amazon. I use a school picture of my brother, R-Jay, that was made into a bookmark. It is either from first or second grade.

As time passed, my physical abilities were deteriorating. My hooded hair dryer was sitting on a tray table in my living room. I had a fall, knocked over the tray table and broke the dryer. I also acquired a speech impediment. Sandra claims she has not noticed it, but she asks me to repeat myself often. I don't know, maybe that's just what mothers do, act like nothing is wrong. I also bite my tongue way more than I used to do. Sometimes it bleeds.

Aphasia (word finding) became an issue, and as if that is not bad enough, I had bladder dysfunction and bowel problems. These issues added to my growing list of doctors. I have 2 Neurologists – 1 of them is a MS Specialist, Primary Care, Optometrist, Gastroenterologist, Urologist, and a Gynecologist. I also developed a numb right hand. Well not really numb, but there is definitely a loss of sensation. There I go over-exaggerating again. Sometimes when I workout, I want to check on the increase in my heart rate. The first time I went to do this, I tried checking with my right hand, which had always been my dominant hand. After feeling nothing with the right hand, I quickly realized that is something I now have to check with my left hand. This has also created writing, typing, and texting difficulties. My Neurologist told me the only thing to remedy my right hand was an IV steroid. I chose not to subject myself to that treatment. I stated I didn't want any more medicine. The truth is, at that time, I did not know enough about MS to make an informed decision. Now the issue is chronic and nothing can be done about it.

Aunt Marian invited me to join her at a MS meeting in Williamsburg, Virginia. I was late, which is very rare for me. I blamed traffic, but I actually got lost. I get lost often even with a GPS. For some reason, sometimes I don't even look up when the GPS lady is speaking or when the GPS dings right before it is time to make a turn. On another occasion, Aunt Marian and her son, Xavier, met me in Williamsburg. Aunt Marian has not been to a MS meeting since I attended with her, that's not her thing.

I am now a part of the Richmond MS Community. I go to plenty of Richmond MS events. I average about two per week between pharmaceutical company sponsored events, support groups, and events put on by other MS organizations. I often hear newly diagnosed people say that do not know anyone with MS. I remember when I was like that. Now I see about 50 people every week with MS. If I am having a bad day, I have been offered to have people from the community follow me home and I have been checked on if I fail to show up for an event I was supposed to be attending. I have been asked if I get MS'd-out. I don't. I'm all about that MS life. They say if something is not going to matter in five years, don't spend more than five minutes thinking about it. Well MS is going to be with me forever, so I dedicate a lot of time to it.

In September 2011, I participated in my second Walk MS event. This time it was in Petersburg, Virginia. My aunts, Elsie and Rachel, my cousins, Frank, Jr., Shardae and a few other cousins participated. My friend, Kasharne, and her family were there as well. The walk started with a hill and I pushed the stroller holding Kasharne's youngest daughter, McKenzie, the entire time. I have not been back to participate in Petersburg's walk.

In October 2011, Ma's family took an outside family portrait in Williamsburg, Virginia. There were about 40 of us in the photograph. My cousin, Leticia, had coordinated it as part of her mother Aunt Cat's birthday celebration. There was no parking space near the place we were having dinner. My cousin, Ta'Wane, had to jump in my car and find a parking spot for my vehicle. I just hated having to inconvenience him like that. Now my brother, R-Jay, does that for me all the time. I no longer feel bad or embarrassed about needing this kind of assistance.

On January 23, 2012, Aunt Ann emailed me a very touching MS testimonial video. I must have really been going though it around that time. I remember she was present when I had an emotional breakdown at Uncle

Tee's house. Perhaps that email was in response to that breakdown.

If I meet six people at one particular event, I try to commit one of their names to memory, and I consider that a victory. I try to associate a person's name with someone else I know with the same name. Sometimes people help me come up with a trick or game to help me remember someone's name. A couple of people have even later quizzed me on those names. I usually don't ask people what medicine they are taking, chances are I won't remember anyway. My short-term memory is so bad I find myself forgetting conversations that I had recently. I am suffering from CRS. You know, can't remember…stuff. My friend, Kasharne, has commented that my long-term and short-term memory were always so good that now I have the memory of "regular" people. I don't know that I agree with that. On Monday I usually am unable to remember what I did the previous Saturday.

I remember being potty trained. I credit Ma for taking so many pictures when I was a kid. I am certain that's why I remember so many things. Even though all of the pictures only include me, I remember Uncle Ralph asking Ma to let Ms. Boo get off of the potty. She objected. Ma jokes that I was raised as *Three Men and a Baby*, this is a reference to a 1987 movie. The Three Men being my father Roy, his brother Uncle Ralph, and their nephew, Clyde. I also remember losing my first tooth and there are no pictures of that. I was five and walking up the stairs in an apartment building we lived in across the street from Mansion Square Park in Poughkeepsie, New York. Even I have to admit it's weird that I remember that. Maybe I'm just a freak of nature.

In April 2012, Roy's niece, Diane, had a birthday party. I had always heard Diane and Aunt Ann were best friends in high school. Aunt Ann couldn't make it to the party because her daughter, LaVita, was having a baby. A guy by the name of Kemel was doing his line dances at the party. That is what he is known for around the Richmond area. I discovered Kemel also had been diagnosed with MS a few years back when I had taken his class before I was diagnosed, and I couldn't keep up with him then. I certainly wasn't going to try now. R-Jay was on the dance floor the entire time Kemel did his routines. R-Jay is a big guy, but surprisingly, light on his feet. Boy, can he dance. He inherited that from our father. I got none of those skills.

Though I don't always know the correct lyrics, it is amazing how a particular song can conjure up a memory. Okay, I usually don't even know the correct cadence. That's how I feel about photographs. Pictures awaken memories for me. A photo of Sandra and me from that party is in a frame hanging on the wall in my living room. At Diane's party Uncle Vernis introduced me to my dad's first cousin, Dennis. He also has MS. Once Uncle Vernis learned of my diagnosis, he told me someone else on that side of the family also had MS. It was good to talk to someone going through the same tribulations I was experiencing.

In 2012, play cousin, RonShai', moved in with me. While staying here, she noticed I would boil water in a pot and transfer the hot water to a measuring cup. She suggested that I just measure the water ahead of time and only boil the amount I need. Why didn't I think of that? She only stayed with me for a couple of months. Looking back, I think I was depressed the whole time she lived with me.

I had gotten to the point where I would not go back in the house if I forgot my cell phone and I certainly was not climbing the stairs at work if I left it in my desk drawer. I didn't feel nearly as naked without my cell phone, as I have heard other people describe how they feel. Whatever shoes were at the door were the pair I was wearing that day if the pair I wanted to wear had been left upstairs. Hopefully, they somewhat matched. The same thing applies for a sweatshirt to wear over my gym t-shirt. I am not going back upstairs for that either. Good thing the coat closet is downstairs. My glasses are about the only item that will send me back upstairs. That doesn't happen very often. I can't safely do too much without them. If I don't check the weather and realize it is cold once I have locked the house door, I'm usually not going back inside. I have to sit down to put my sneakers on properly. I am no longer able to put them on while standing up against the front door. I used to have two potted plants in my house until watering them got to be too much of a challenge. Now my house only contains two fake floral arrangements.

In July 2012, I had a BM accident when I was working on the second floor. That day I tied my windbreaker around my waist and told my Manager I would return shortly. It happened to be a casual attire day at work, so I was wearing jeans. I went to Old Navy for a new pair of jeans. The Old Navy was the closest store to the parking lot at the mall I was near and they have shopping carts in the store. Then I went to Target for new panties. I returned to work, climbed those dreaded stairs, cleaned up in the restroom, and kept working. Unfortunately, that was not the last time I had such an accident. Now I always keep a change of clothes as well as underclothes in my car trunk. I never told my Neurologist about that incident. I did not want to give him a reason to take me out of work. As I continued to attend the pharmaceutical company presentations, I learned that I should share everything with my Neurologist. I do that now, we have an open dialogue. I believe I have a good rapport with both of my Neurologists. I have heard other MSers say they do not know why their Neurologist is taking a blood test. Me on the other hand, I question everything.

In Summer 2012, I had to pick my cousin, Leticia, up from the train station. I remember it was so hot that day and before I started keeping cooling items in my car. Nowadays I always keep a cooling item in my car. Some of them are "just add water, any temperature." I always have water in my car. Anyway, I woke up in the middle of the night and could not move my legs. I tried and my attempts were futile. Play cousin, RonShai', my cousin, Leticia, and another play cousin, Tasia, were all staying with me that night. I did not want to alarm anyone so I left them all alone. I was so worried that not being able to move my legs was going to be my new normal. When I woke up the next morning, thankfully, I was able to walk with no problems. It turns out the heat had affected me that dramatically.

In August 2012, my job on the 2nd floor had a Charity Bowl-A-Thon. Friends and family members alike were members of my MS team. That picture with us all wearing shirts containing the MS color of orange is displayed in a frame in my living room.

Whenever I go get a pedicure, I jump every time the pedicurist sprays on the nail hardening spray. That spray is very cold and I play it off like my feet are ticklish rather than sharing I have extreme temperature sensitivity. One day I'm going to kick them in their face, accidentally of course, and they will ban me from their shop. That is not the only time I notice extreme cold sensitivity. I notice it in my hands when I'm pumping gas. I keep a thin glove in my car that I only use for pumping gas in the wintertime. It is not just cold temperature sensitivity that I have in my hands. Sometimes I have to put a dish towel around a glass bowl or plate before removing it from the microwave.

I used to use an asthma inhaler often and I had bad allergies and had to get allergy shots. Since I was diagnosed with MS, I don't recall using my inhaler one time and I have stopped the allergy shots completely. I have always had a bad sense of smell. I always attributed it to allergies. I probably have been experiencing the MS symptom of hyposmia (reduced ability to smell). Silver lining – I don't have to put up with pungent odors. I don't have the sneezing, itching, and running eyes as severely as I used to have. I fully understand that having MS does not prevent you from avoiding comorbidity (simultaneously having more than one disease). It is like my body has stopped acting up in other areas to make room for all of the MS issues.

In addition to helping to diagnose MS, MRIs are a tool that offers the most non-invasive way to view the brain and spinal cord. I have heard MS described as a luxury disease, because of the availability of MRIs. Though the existence of MRIs has revolutionized MS, I personally don't think there is anything luxurious about it. My Neurologist would tell me each time it looked the same. He always said I had no new lesions (sometimes referred to as plaques) on my brain or spinal cord. I didn't believe him. I thought he was just saying that not to upset me. Not sure why I thought he would have a reason to spare my feelings. I don't know when I became so cynical. Anyway, I never wanted to look at my MRI, especially after learning my disease was aggressive. I had seen enough MRIs on slides to know what a bad one looked like and had no interest in seeing my own. I've met several people in the MS community and many have seen their own MRIs. At one point, I even had DVDs of all of my MRIs since diagnosis, in my possession and could not bring myself to view them.

In December 2012, R-Jay graduated from VCU. Ma's friend, Eileen, also did the decorations for his graduation party. R-Jay even had candy bars with his name on them – I didn't have that at my graduation party. This time I reserved the same venue I had rented for my friend Kasharne's first baby shower. A picture of R-Jay and me from that party is in a frame in my living room. Later that same month, I fell in my bedroom, tripping over nothing in particular. I started crying and called Sandra. She asked if I wanted Aunt Elsie to come over since she lived nearby. I refused. She told me she was on her way.

I said, "Don't come, I fall all the time."

Ma said, "Maybe, but you never called me crying before."

R-Jay was at my house in no time. I hadn't called him; Ma must have called him. I had calmed down by the time Ma arrived, her home in Surry is an hour away from my home. I do remember going to work the next day as if nothing had transpired.

I've learned many things during my MS journey. I've learned that reading, writing, and doing puzzles can help keep with mental clarity. Like a muscle, the brain needs to be worked out like the rest of your body. Using your brain can make it stronger. I have tried some online memory improvement games. I occasionally do Sudoku and Word Search. I don't do crossword puzzles. I couldn't do those before MS. I also play Candy Crush Saga with no volume. I use my mind to figure out the strategy to move on to the next level. While that may be true, I think I just like playing Candy Crush. If you are unable to proceed to the next level, it displays "Level failed!" and "You failed!" I think I take it personally when I see those words displayed on the game screen. Failure is not an option. Candy Crush has become my guilty pleasure. I play using my Kindle e-reader, I refuse to put it on my smartphone. Aside from the fact that the screen would probably be too small, I don't want to have that much access; I would play all the time. I also use the toy Bop It Extreme. Both of these games help with my hand dexterity and hand-eye coordination.

My right hand has been numb for about five years. You guessed it, I'm right-handed. My handwriting has never been too good anyway. Since I lost sensation over five years ago, I play Candy Crush, and sometimes scroll though Facebook using my middle finger. I seldom make comments on Facebook, but when I do it is usually done using the voice command. More often than not, I just select an emoji and keep it moving. If I do enter a comment, it is usually very short. I also either text with my middle finger or send a voice text message. In some instances, the words I think I'm saying aren't the words that are coming out of my mouth. It allows me to see what people hear when I say certain words. I know the voice texting technology is not perfect, I realize it may transcribe words incorrectly even for people with perfect articulation. Sometimes with voice texting it puts "your" when I intended to use "you're" or "whose" when I intended to use "who's." Sometimes predictive text technology betrays me too. I try to remember to read the text, doing any edits, before I hit send. As you might imagine, it takes me a while to send a text message. I have tried to text with my thumbs like I see other people do, but it is too confusing, like multitasking, which I am no longer able to do.

When someone responds to a text message, even if they respond immediately, more often than not I have to go back and see what I initially texted them for their reply to make sense. On the other hand, I type or verbalize a whole message and I'm waiting for a response and it turns out I never hit the send button. My communication skills are so bad that I am sometimes waiting for a response to a text, but I did not put a question mark or word it like a question, so the person never responds. I have sent text messages to the wrong person. It is often sent to the someone I spoke to recently, instead of the intended recipient.

I've noticed that I am unable to laugh and walk at the same time. People think I am being funny when I say that, but I am serious. In fact, I can't do much when I am laughing. That whole inability to multitask thing is real. People taking me to the prom will always stop and let me laugh. My brother, R-Jay, is the only person that does not stop every time. I am unable to do something else while I am on the telephone. Either I lose my train of thought, or miss all of the prompts telling which number to press to reach my desired destination. I used to do my homework while watching TV every night, and I was a pretty good student. Now I have to at least mute the TV in order to scroll through Facebook and turn it off completely to do things like pay bills.

I also experience trouble typing. Now I usually type while staring at the keyboard the whole time. I usually don't feel when the right hand touches the keyboard, so I tend to hit a lot of duplicate letters. Another thing that was happening with a numb hand is that I would not feel when I got a paper cut. I would get so upset when all of a sudden, I would just see blood on my finger. I also have trouble working pump action bottles, like those containing body spray. I have moved things like hair products into trigger spray bottles. Due to my poor hand coordination, I use a funnel to transfer these items into the spray bottles.

Chapter 4

In April 2013, it seems I had gotten a severe injection site reaction. I had the nurse that initially trained me to do my injections come back to the house. She instructed me to see a doctor because she feared I had an infection. Between the infection and the decreased physical ability, it was time to change medicine. I should have known it was time to change medicine. A couple that I had met at the very first MS meeting I ever attended in Richmond had to help me get to my car after a MS dinner. The car was only about a block or two away from the restaurant. We realized too late that the restaurant offered free valet parking. Anyway, oral medicine had been FDA-approved since I was initially diagnosed and had been on the market for a while. I was super hype. I would certainly prefer to medicate by swallowing a pill, rather than administering an injection. That hype was short-lived, my Neurologist informed me that he felt my disease was too aggressive for the oral medication that was available. I ended up taking a medicine that was out at my time of diagnosis, but it was so risky that it was not one of my five initial brochures.

I later found out not all medicine is always prescribed as a first line of defense. Decisions like that are usually at the doctor's discretion. I was at work, on the second floor, when I was told over the phone that I needed to change to this riskier medicine. Coincidently,

I had a MS lunch meeting that day. Oh, boy were the tears flowing at that lunch meeting. Fellow MSers Sharon and Edith comforted me. I later found out they did not know if I was having a MS issue or if I had just broken up with a boyfriend. It was the MS. Turns out they were both familiar with my new medicine and tried to reassure me everything would be fine. That day I was invited to my first MS support group. Prior to that, I did not even know there were MS support groups and even if I had known they existed, I certainly had never considered attending one. When I first started going to Sharon's support group, I remember voting on the name of the group. I didn't come up with the name, but I did vote on what became the winning selection. It reminded me of when I came up with the winning newsletter title for one of my former jobs. I was utilizing those transferable skills, a term often used in the working world.

In 2013, I was not up for going to Walk MS. My friend, Kasharne, did the walk on my behalf and collected some swag and brought it to my house. Hopefully I will be able to continue to walk for myself every year. Even if I am experiencing ambulation problems, I still plan to go out to the event and be with "my people." You know, other MSers not moving quite as well as they would like.

My friend, Kasharne, told me about something she saw on television. It was a story about a quadriplegic and how he would wash his hair by rubbing his head up against the shower interior. I have all my limbs, but I totally get the concept. When you face physical challenges you often have to find a new way to do things you once did extremely easily. I explained to her the concept that you just figure it out. That may sound aggressive, but that is what is required to navigate this tricky disease. I'm by no means saying it is always easy but with some trial and error as well as speaking to others facing similar challenges, you somehow find your way. "Figure It Out" has become my personal mantra.

I'm now going to take you on a tour of things I do around different rooms in my house and different parts of my life. During this book, I will try to cover how I handle things in all facets of my life. I am speaking specifically about MS, but many of these items can be helpful for anyone. I used to love my bed that sits up high off of the floor. Now getting in it each night and out of it each morning is a challenge. I have even figured out a way to easily get out of bed, a task that had always been so easy. I press the right-hand webbing between my index finger and thumb with the same webbing on my left hand, so the right thumb is in the palm of your left hand. I do this while pressing my left elbow into the bed. I would imagine it works with the right elbow too, but my television is on the left and I exit the bed on the left, so I have only done it one way. Many things that used to be easy before, are hard now. I am winded by the time I change the sheets on my bed. I also experience some slight dizziness when I roll over to the other side of the bed.

I have strategically placed tools all around the house to make my life easier. I have box cutters everywhere to help me open things. Some are even hidden-in-plain-sight. Inside my house, I have a nylon bag with a handle on the bottom stair railing and another one on the spare bedroom door knob upstairs. I put these in place so that I can easily transport things between floors. I tend to drop things if I hold things in my hand and try to hold onto the stair railing at the same time. I make sure that the banister is tightly secured to the wall since I use it every time I use the staircase.

Thanks to Ma, I have upgraded to a wireless printer that is in my home office. This way I don't have to take my laptop upstairs to print something. Now I can just wait until I go upstairs for the evening to collect my printed pages. Also, my brother, R-Jay, took a case of printer paper upstairs to my home office as one of his many projects.

Getting dressed is even sometimes a difficult task now. Something as simple as unhooking a bra can pose a challenge. If my hands are cold, which they usually are, that can be a downright dreadful experience. My hands are cold so often that I used to wear fingerless gloves at work. Anyway, I have even worn a bra without connecting the second clasp after attempting to secure it several times. I try to purchase shirts without those pesky small buttons. I have not been in a fitting room to try on clothes in forever, so I sometimes forget the small button rule until it is too late. That has turned out to be a downside to not trying on clothes ahead of time. I have a non-slip, soft grip button hook tool. This is used to assist me in securing those pesky buttons. It is ideal for people with limited fine motor skills, like myself. In some instances, I secure the arm buttons before I put the shirt on. This tool allows me to secure buttons even faster than before I had any hand dexterity issues. I also have a zipper helper dressing accessory. It is specifically to assist people who have loss dexterity in their hands. I usually don't even try on shoes. I just make the purchase and hope that my feet have not grown or shrank.

I have developed allodynia. It is when things pain or bother you that didn't bother you before or should not be painful. Specifically, if I pull up my shirt sleeves to my elbow or if I am wearing a ¾ sleeve shirt and there is any kind of elastic, that now will irritate me. The elastic does not even have to be tight. This has also become a negative aspect of not trying on clothes before I purchase them. I also am unable to wear the athletic socks or even slipper socks that fit snug around your feet. They don't even have to be compression socks. These are things I would not have even previously noticed.

I wear sneakers way more often than I ever have before now. Stockings and tights are difficult to get on. I have heard that some people purchase a larger size to make it easier, but I have not tried that. I keep my tights in labeled Ziploc bags by color. My socks are even sorted in the same drawer by color. I do anything I can to make things easier for myself. Pants that have a couple of strings that remain once you remove a tag are usually worn with the strings still on. Sometimes I don't even stress myself by even trying to remove them, especially if I am wearing a shirt that will hide them.

I have worn a skirt upside-down. Yes, you read that correctly, upside-down. I was around people all day. This is back when I was still working and I even went out to dinner that evening. I have put shirts on backwards and panties on inside out. Now that some articles of clothing are tagless, I need to pay closer attention when I am getting dressed. And who decided skinny jeans were a good idea? It takes me forever to get out of a pair of those. I also usually do not wear a belt with my jeans, even if I need to be wearing one. I don't need any additional barriers slowing up the process of me using the restroom. I have had more than a couple close calls. I have even changed the way I organize my clothes in my closets. I have a round, LED, Tap Light affixed to the wall in one closet. This makes selecting a piece of clothing much easier. Now that none of my shoes have heels on them, it even changes the way I put my shoes on the over the door shoe rack on the inside of my closet.

Part of my daily regimen includes taking my morning pills and vitamins. The bottles sit right on the end of my dresser, near the door that exits the room. This way I have a visual cue to remind me to take my medicine before I leave my bedroom. Sometimes I drop a pill and don't see it on the floor. I'm sure there is quite a supply of pills under my dresser. I currently leave my pill bottles and a bottle of water open on my dresser. I know it is not the most sanitary way to do things, but no sense in starting off the day being infuriated as I struggle to open the bottles. I also keep a second bottle of pills downstairs. That bottle has the top on it, since I don't take them often.

I have greatly reduced my stepstool usage because I have fallen off more times than I care to remember. I have a Grab it reaching tool, an As Seen On TV item. It is a lightweight tool with a no-slip grip handle that helps you grab things that you would not normally be able to reach. You can switch to ratcheting mode for heavier items. It even swivels 90 degrees to reach awkward places and it is foldable for easy storage. I upgraded to the deluxe model that has a LED light, magnet, and jewelry hook. I keep one on each floor of my house. I can now handle a few DIY (do-it-yourself) home repairs without using the stepstool as often. One project that does require the stepstool is changing the air filters. That used to be one of my cousin Ta'Wane's projects. Now I handle that one on my own. One of my tricks is I keep a coin on the top of the door ledge near the air filter that has to be changed in the ceiling. This allows me to easily open the trap door without having to remember to take a coin when I get on the stepstool each time.

I purchased blackout curtains for my en-suite, hoping that would help me sleep better. The light was impenetrable through my new curtains. Somehow the light was much brighter through my bathroom window than through my bedroom window. I got tired of trying to remember to close the bathroom door when I exited in the middle of the night.

I used to love to take a hot shower. I would make the water as hot as possible before stepping in the shower. That is no longer an option. I had the temperature reduced on my hot water heater. So now the water will not even get as hot as it used to in the shower or when I am washing my hands. Not only will the heat suck away all of my energy, my temperature sensitive skin just can't take it anymore. I got a bathtub bar. I don't know how I ever got in and out of the shower without it. I now leave my shower curtain open when I am not in the shower because sometimes I have to catch myself from falling towards the tub instead of onto the toilet. On more than one occasion, I have gotten into the shower wearing my glasses. I did not realize it, until my glasses would fog up. A warm soak in the bathtub is a thing of the past. Something I learned the hard way, after I needed a three-hour nap after soaking in a hot tub. I now know I was experiencing Uhthoff's phenomenon, which is a worsening of MS symptoms when the body gets overheated from hot tubs. I can joke about it now and I say I was being boiled. I tried taking a bath with cooler water, but I struggled to get up off of the tub floor. That's okay, I didn't really like the lukewarm temperature anyway. I also have a large shower caddy hanging in the shower. In fact, the largest one I could find. The items that were once housed under the bathroom sink are now readily available to me in the shower at all times. I have a removable shower head that makes for easier cleaning.

I also have a Tubshroom. This is an item you put in your shower drain to catch every single hair that sheds from washing your hair. Since the Tubshroom collects hair beneath the surface, it stays trapped and unseen. So, if you don't feel like you are able to bend over right after your shower, you can just leave it in the drain until later. Out of sight, out of mind. It replaced the hair stopper that collects the hair right on top of it. I have a long-handled loofah that stays in the shower and helps me clean the hard to reach center of my back. I also have a non-slip mat to step on when I climb out of the shower.

The information superhighway will instruct you not to cut your toenails when they are wet, but I have found cutting them when I step out of the shower works for me. I have taken Super Glue and attached a couple of magnets to the inside of my bathroom cabinet door to affix my toenail clippers for easy access. Since I have hand coordination issues, I am no longer able to paint my own toenails as well as I used to do.   In order for me to paint my toenails, I have a flexible, silicone nail polish bottle holder that you wear on your fingers. I also have a handle that attaches to my fingernail file for easier gripping.

I keep multiple plastic bags in my bathroom trash can all at once. This way when I tie the handles and remove one, there is another waiting to take its place. Some of my bathroom changes are very subtle, like buying the larger rolls of toilet paper so that I have to change them less frequently. I have started buying the toothpaste with a flip top, rather than the little cap that you have to screw on after each use. I have a toothpaste tube squeezer. This is used to help me get the toothpaste out of the tube. It is also a money saver and makes sure I don't waste any of the toothpaste. I sometimes have to use a grippie to remove the cap from the deodorant. They are those flat, non-slip gripper pads used to take the tops off of jars and bottles.   My friend, Kasharne, gave me my first one years ago. I still have it; it's white and square.   The round ones are now a common piece of pharmaceutical company swag.

I also have a Bowl Light. It is a motion-activated light that you put on your toilet rim, below the toilet seat, facing the entry way to the bathroom. Their slogan is "Turn Your Toilet Into A Night-Light!" It illuminates the whole bathroom as you approach, not just the area around the toilet. You can either select one of seven colors or choose color-cycle mode. The first time Sandra saw it, I had selected color-cycle mode and she called it my Christmas tree. The light automatically turns off after approximately one minute. This is another As Seen On TV item. I have upgraded my electronic scale to a lightweight one with a non-slip mat. I have an automatic car starter, I had that before I was diagnosed, but after I was diagnosed I was glad I had one. My extra automatic starter is posted on the wall in my en-suite, so that I can start the car from upstairs. The starter is affixed to the wall with a Command hook. This really came in handy when I was working.

I roll my laundry bag down the flight of stairs to do laundry since all the dirty clothes are upstairs and the laundry room is downstairs. To be fair, I was doing that long before I was diagnosed with MS. I keep a second bottle of stain scrubber upstairs for when I need to pretreat an item before it goes in the washing machine. The first bottle of scrubber is in the laundry room. I call it a stain stick. This way I don't have to worry about forgetting to pretreat a stained item once it is downstairs in the laundry room. I sit down on the ottoman that is in my dining room area to sort the dirty laundry. Sometimes I barely have the strength to select the water temperature or other button on the washing machine. Since my washing machine does not have an agitator, I can complete the laundry task with fewer loads. I move the laundry baskets that normally stay in the laundry room into the bathroom next to it, so that I am reminded I am in the process of doing laundry every time I go to the bathroom. I have reorganized the shelf in the laundry room to make the more frequently used items more accessible. Sometimes the door of the washing machine slams down, causing me to jump as if I didn't know it was going to make a loud noise. I also jump when the dryer signals that my load is dry. My bath towels are not as neatly folded as they used to be, but they are clean and in the linen closet unseen. I've learned that you just can't sweat the small stuff, at least I try not to.

I have a tray table that stays up in my living room. It houses frequently used items like pens, scratch paper, napkins, and a grippie. I keep those all around my house and even in my car. Most of the time I drink water when I am home. I often buy the small 10oz bottles because they tend to be easier to manage then the larger ones. I have to worry about losing less water when I knock over the bottle. When I am not drinking water, I enjoy an occasional Sprite. I was a fan long before I was diagnosed with MS. The caffeine-free soda has turned out to be a good choice since MSers are told to avoid it. I have a magnet on the side of my refrigerator that is to assist me opening those cans. Some days I barely have enough strength to open the refrigerator. I keep a dish towel around the refrigerator door handle to use as leverage on those days. I also have The Magic Tap. It is a hands-free beverage dispensing tool. I am able to avoid spills by eliminating the need to lift up a large drink container.

Even my grocery list is different. For a while, I had stopped buying grated parmesan cheese, because it was too difficult to open the plastic bottle. I have since figured that out. Those grippies are good for opening lots of things. I now use the Ziploc slider quart size and gallon bags, rather than the original pinch zipper bags. Sandra suggested that change. I use Glad Press'n Seal wrap in place of its plastic wrap predecessor. I also use it to secure bowls because it is difficult to get the plastic top off of my plastic mixing bowls. I buy bonelesss chicken tenderloins or thin chicken breast instead of the thick chicken breast I used to purchase, because the smaller pieces are easier for me to cut.

I don't cook often, but if I'm going to cook it will be during lunchtime, rather than dinnertime. My body nor my mind work as efficiently later in the day. Attempting to cook dinner, I have misread a recipe and burned my dinner. I still ate it. I try to always set my dry ingredients out long before I start to cook. Occasionally, even with the recipe right in front of me, I skip some of the ingredients. Sometimes I turn on the wrong burner on the stove, even though the stove has pictures. I think my visual communication issues account for these oversights. I now put the pots on cork trivets, so not to leave them on the wrong burner. Another thing I learned the hard way when I set the kitchen on fire. Okay, not the kitchen, but the stove did catch fire. I fell on the kitchen floor trying to retrieve the fire extinguisher from under the kitchen sink. It now sits on the countertop, just in case. You live and you learn.

There are plenty of gadgets that exist to make life in the kitchen easier. I'd like to now share some of the items I use. I replaced my small corn on the cob holders for larger ones that are easier to grip. I also have plastic clips that secure things like bags of frozen vegetables. I either use an electric can opener or purchase the kind of cans with the pull tab, not requiring a can opener. When my original electric can opener broke, I upgraded to one with an easy to open battery compartment. It's purple. That's my favorite color. I used to have to take the can opener along with some batteries to work and get my coworker, Janene, to replace the batteries. I have a can colander to easily drain liquid from canned vegetables. I use a citrus peeler to remove the peel from oranges. I also do not always have enough strength to use the apple corer and slicer, but I don't purchase many apples, so that is not too much of a problem. I also use that tool to make potatoes wedges. I experience trouble squeezing the garlic press. For that reason, I will use minced garlic in the bottle when recipes call for it. To avoid having to dice onions, I will use onion powder or frozen diced onions, depending on the recipe. Another thing I don't always have the strength for is emptying ice trays. I usually don't put ice in my drinks, but when I do, I use reusable, plastic ones.

I have researched an easier, less time-consuming way to remove the skin off of cooked potatoes. Anything not to be on my feet longer than I have to be. What did we do before Google? I have a rocker knife with a non-slip, large, soft grip. It offers assistance to people with weak grasps or limited hand coordination. I also have other bendable utensils, hopefully I won't ever need them, but like the Girl Scout I am, it is good to have them available just in case. One suggestion I received from a fellow MSer was to get a plastic 2-cup liquid measuring cup, rather than the glass one I was using. The plastic version is a lot less heavy and therefore much more easily manageable. I use flat, flexible cutting board mats, rather than the previously used wood or hard plastic cutting boards. I have silicone funnels, the benefit for them is that they fit into the utensil drawer without the struggle I experienced with the plastic ones. I still have plastic funnels. I just keep them in the cabinet now. I have mixed up flour and sugar, even though they are in see-through, glass canisters. Those were given to me by my late, Aunt Angela when I moved into my first and only apartment. I did not label the canisters right away, but they are now labeled with Post-it notes, so hopefully I won't make that mistake again.

I have Angry Mama, which is a device that uses steam to clean your microwave, eliminating the need for scrubbing. I have a dustpan with a stick on it so I don't have to bend over to pick up the debris, after I have swept the kitchen floor. That was suggested to me from someone outside of the MS community. I get tips from everywhere. My kitchen trash can has a step used to lift the lid. I usually just keep the top off of it altogether. My goal is to keep my feet on the floor at all times, if possible. Proper protocol dictates that I show off for company. You know, make things look nice for visitors. So, when I have company, the top is usually on. I know a lot of people that show off for company, just not everyone tells you about it like I'm doing. I have organized some of my kitchen cabinets to put the more frequently used items on a lower shelf. Unfortunately, not all the gizmos I have tried have made life easier in the kitchen. I have a cake cutter made out of hard plastic. It is supposed to allow you to cut a piece of cake, give it a slight squeeze, and transfer it to the plate in one quick and easy motion. It did not make cutting a slice of cake any easier than the normal cake cutter or butter knife I normally use. I also tried the short silicone oven mitts, but I prefer the regular, fabric oven mitts that go up your forearm.

In addition, I usually use disposable plates and flatware. I now buy disposable foil pans to cook easy meals in the oven. Even with the lightweight foil pan, I have dropped an entire casserole of baked spaghetti. It was a disaster. Both the bottom inside of the oven and the oven door were covered in cheese and pasta. I was so upset. Aunt Rachel told me how to go about cleaning the oven. That is an error I only made once. She was fully aware of my diagnosis. She had given me two books by Montel Williams early in my diagnosis. He is one of the celebrity faces of MS. The use of foil pans cuts down on the total number of dishes I have to hand wash since standing at the sink too long has become a challenge. Yes, I do have a dishwasher, but I still hand wash some items. The reduced heat on the hot water heater is good for this reason as well. I have forgotten whether the dishes in the machine are clean or dirty, so I purchased a magnet that has both clean and dirty imprinted on it. Since the dishwasher is not metal, the magnet does not stick to it, so I have it attached with some Velcro. The Velcro was a great idea, but even with the visual cue, I am not always prompted to turn the sign the other way. Now I use dishwasher pods, rather than try to pour the heavy bottle of dishwashing detergent into the machine. Even the task of unloading the dishwasher can be a challenge. I consider it a victory if I am able to unload it in one fell swoop. I realize there are also laundry detergent pods, but I am almost certain I have done a load of laundry forgetting to enter a pod. I don't believe I have forgotten to enter the bottle laundry detergent into the washing machine. Even though the largest detergent or other item container is usually the better value, I sometimes have to get a smaller size just to be able to handle it successfully.

I bought some very large bottles of dish liquid on sale. I kept dropping the large containers in the sink. My friend, Kasharne, suggested I buy a small dish liquid container and keep refilling it from the larger bottle. Why didn't I think of that? Now I only purchase the small bottles of dish liquid. I still drop the small bottles, but not nearly as often.

Chapter 5

It used to be such a struggle to clean the downstairs bathroom going up and down the stairs with the cleaning supplies. Aunt Elsie suggested that I keep a second set of cleaning supplies downstairs. That seemed so obvious. Again, why didn't I think of that? I now keep a second set of cleaning supplies in the laundry room downstairs. I leave the tops loose or off of my cleaning supplies, so I do not have to struggle to use them. I also keep my cleaning supplies in a college-style shower caddy to transport items between the two bathrooms upstairs. I have a second broom and dustpan upstairs for the bathrooms.

I used to have my own lawn mower, thanks to Ma and I would cut the grass myself. I also used to use the weed wacker and hedge trimmer to manicure my bushes. Uncle James came over to teach me how to mow the lawn and yes, I had him take pictures of me during my training. Now I have had to hire a company to maintain those types of services.

I usually have to lift my left leg up to put it in the car before I drive. I try to be careful, but I have hit my head on the top of the car more than a few times as I try to get in the car. If I'm having a really bad day. I may have to lift my right thigh to change from the gas to the brake pedal. I haven't had trouble rotating my foot between the two pedals. I have dorsiflexion, the ability to move my toes up at the ankle and plantar flexion, the ability to move my toes down. I am grateful for cruise control on those days. I used to self-medicate with retail therapy and a trip to the mall. Since that is no longer an option, sometimes I go to a convenience store and get some candy. As you might imagine, it doesn't help at all with the MS. Plain M&M's are my absolute favorite candy, but I like Starburst too. For a while, I hadn't purchased them because the wrapper on the individually wrapped pieces had become too much of a challenge for me. Now they make Starburst minis that are already unwrapped and those are just perfect for me.

My friend, Kasharne, showed me an easier way to get into her SUV. Unfortunately, this does not work to get into my brother, R-Jay's huge pickup truck. I have a small organizer bag that attaches to my car air vent. I use it to hold my cell phone. Even with the phone in view, I still leave it in my car sometimes. The bag has an extra pocket in the front. I use this to store parking passes. I have tint on my car windows to block out the sun. The sun visor usually does me no good. Short people problems. I also have a sun visor to use when the car is parked on a sunny day. Unfortunately, I usually forget to place it in the front windshield. I have a Car Cane that attaches to the inside of the car door, once the door is open. It allows me to grab hold and climb out of the car more easily. It doubles as a flashlight, seat belt cutter, and a window breaker. I don't have to use it every time I drive, but the Girl Scout in me keeps it in the car just in case. I also have a E-ZPass for the toll roads. Even though I had it long before diagnosis, it has helped since diagnosis. I'm almost certain I would not be successful in trying to throw my coins into the toll basket. Sometimes I put the car in park and try to get out with the seatbelt still attached.

When I go to the gas station I always pay at the pump. Walking all the way into the gas station convenience store just exerts too much energy. I sometimes have trouble tightening the gas cap after I have finished fueling up my car. Grippies can help with that too. Whenever my gas light comes on I always saw it feels like my car is pulling. It probably isn't, I might have made that up. I do that sometimes.

I usually drive my recycling bin to the end of the driveway, rather than walk it down the slight hill. If it is not time to put the recycling out and no one is coming over, then I check the mail myself, while I am at the far end of the driveway. I keep a nylon bag, with handles, in my car in case it is too much mail for me to carry inside. Sometimes I am able to walk the recycling to the curb, if I do it early. I call that, using my morning legs. This refers to the slightly enhanced amount of mobility I have before MS fatigue sets in. To my surprise, going downhill is a lot trickier for me, than going uphill. If I happen to be home when the recycling bin in dumped, I will see the bin from my porch, again in my rearview mirror and I have still forgot and run into it with my car by the time I get to the end of the driveway. In case you were wondering, the driveway is not that long, my short-term memory is just that bad. I will then put the bin in the back seat of my car and ride with it for who knows how long. If I am out when the recycling bin is emptied, the next time I arrive home, I stop at the bottom of the driveway, put the bin in the backseat of my car and drive it up to the house. Sometimes I forget about the bin during the short drive to the top of the driveway. Sometimes the bin will at least spend the night in my back seat.

Sometimes I throw my kitchen trash bag down the four steps onto the sidewalk landing in front of my house. The big trash bin does not go to the end of the driveway every week for the county to empty. It usually only goes when there is someone here to take it or when it is full and I have no choice but to take it down the hill. I have seen the large trash bin moved to the side of my house before and not known if maybe a neighbor saw me struggle down the hill and was kind enough to move it back to the side of my house or if I just forget pushing it back up the hill myself.

Whenever I arrive at home, I try to remember to pull the car up as close to the house as possible. I'm always conserving steps whenever possible. I have a sensor light that comes on as I approach the porch after the sun has set. This helps to avoid any incidents walking up the stairs and unlocking the door. I keep my keys either on a spring, spiral keychain or on a key fob attached to the outside of my small purse. If I am not carrying a purse, either of these items can go around my wrist. As soon as I walk in the house, I put my keys in the same place, so that I don't misplace them. Consistency is important. Okay, consistency is the key is what I wanted to say. I'm sorry, I like corny puns. Anyway, I also have a paper calendar hanging on the door in the foyer of my house. It is attached to the coat closet with a Command strip. Sometimes I am two weeks into the next month before I remember to change the calendar to that month. I have also had bladder and BM accidents on my porch or in my kitchen trying to make my way to my downstairs bathroom. It's amazing how the need to use the bathroom intensifies as you approach the front door.

As a way to extend my budget, I buy in bulk. Okay, that is not entirely true. Partially because items are on sale, more so because I inherited that behavior from my father. I used to say I would stock up on items if I was having a good MS day, because the next time it's on sale I might be having a bad MS day. Well now I have more good days than bad and I never stopped buying in bulk. Some people may refer to it as the beginning of hoarding behavior. I do not agree with that, but I have abundant supplies of household items. I also have stockpiled cases of bottled water, way more than a person living alone should have. All items are out of the way, so they do not cause a potential fall risk. I even purchase some food items in bulk if I catch a good sale. My cousin, Ta'Wane, and I made a project out of putting together a wood pantry for those items. I put one of my fake floral arrangements on top for decoration. Though I buy some items in bulk on purpose, I inadvertently ended up getting some duplicate items because I would forget I already had some at home. I have started keeping a running grocery list on my kitchen table. I will put the list in my phone if I am only picking up a few items. This has decreased the instances of me purchasing duplicate items by mistake.

I save empty tissue boxes. Some are attached to the tissue box currently being used as a way to dispose of the used tissues without having to get up and put the tissues in the trash can after each use. They are attached with large, colorful rubber bands. Anything to brighten my day. Others are used as storage containers to hold the extra plastic grocery bags that I repurpose as trash bags. I have it so the bags pop up like the tissues used to do.

In June 2013, my friend, Regina, and I met in Philadelphia, Pennsylvania to see a New Kids on the Block concert. That is one of our Special Times. We have each been to four NKOTB concerts, three together. We are such Blockheads. It was the first time we had seen each other since I was diagnosed in 2010. Regina asked me to say handicapped parking, instead of VIP when I asked the parking attendant where we needed to go, just so he would know what I was referring to. I couldn't help but smirk when the attendant referred to it as VIP parking. We both laughed as we pulled away. We had seats up in the rafters. Someone came up there and asked us if we wanted floor seats. Of course we did, so we moved. Boyz II Men was on the bill too. Hearing Motown Philly from Boyz II Men, while in Philly, is something special. As had become the norm, people assumed I had been drinking when I would stumble. I mean it was a concert. A picture of the two of us from that concert is in a frame in my living room.

On June 26, 2013, the Administrative Assistant from my job on the second floor was retiring. During her retirement party, folks were going around the table in the conference room sharing a special moment about their time with her. I even had my own share. Before it was my turn, I started crying and had to walk out of the room. It was humiliating. Don't get me wrong, I liked her but not to the point of me bawling like I was doing. Once I got my composure, I called my Neurologist. That was the second time, in a short time, I had inappropriately started crying. The first time was at Kayden's (Kasharne's oldest daughter) dance recital, right after her grandmother asked me how I was doing. I was so embarrassed that day. My Neurologist told me if it happens again, I need to talk to someone. I'm not opposed to counseling for everyone. I've heard some people have received great benefits. I just don't think therapy is right for me. I believe working out at Sheltering Arms has become a type of therapy for me as well as a place to socialize. I also chose not to go on medicine for my depression, though a couple of my doctors recommended I should. Though it was not funny at the time, now the running joke between Lona, Janene, and I is that every time I cry, it's time to go talk to someone.

Spring 2014 was the first time my Neurologist mentioned disability and I rapidly shrugged off the notion. I have always enjoyed working. I probably should have paid more attention to his suggestion back then. At work, I was holding onto file cabinets as I walked through the halls daily. Also during Spring of 2014, Aunt Elsie and I went to an event at The Jefferson Hotel. I invited her because it was sponsored by one of her former employers. It was a place that provided residential care to adults with physical disabilities. I had gone to work with her one day when I was a freshman at VCU. She did not remember that, so the symbolism was lost on her.

In June 2014, I had the front porch floor painted and wooden posts on my porch replaced with vinyl. During that time, I also had an accent wall and the downstairs bathroom painted. I'm glad I had it done when I was still working, because now that would be considered an unnecessary luxury item. Don't get me wrong, I'm not complaining about disability, Ma taught me that a half loaf of bread is better than no bread at all.

In July 2014, I asked my former coworker, Lona, to honestly tell me if she had told the hiring Manager that I had MS before my interview. She has known about my diagnosis since early on. I let her know I wouldn't be mad if she did, I just wanted to know. She confirmed that she had indeed told the hiring Manager. My cousin, Diane, had told me she probably had told them ahead of time, and she was right. I didn't work there anymore, so it was a moot point. I was happy to know they hired me, already knowing of my disease.

In August 2014, I drove to New York to stay with my friend, Regina, Charles and their family. My luggage for the trip was a MS duffle bag that I now keep in the trunk of my car filled with a change of clothes. Regina's oldest daughter greeted me at the car with a welcome picture she made. I keep that picture in a photo album along with Christmas cards Regina sends me. During the weekend, Regina planned a breakfast and a dinner where I got to see several of my old Arlington friends. One of the friends I had breakfast with was Aloma. She was one of my friends from the third grade at Arlington Elementary School. Growing up I spent many nights at her house. My friend, Randi, was also at breakfast. I met her at Arlington Middle School. A couple of the friends I had breakfast with had let's say "borrowed" cars from their parents. I wasn't borrowing a car from my parents, Roy and Sandra didn't play that kind of mess. I would happily catch a ride with someone else who had access to a car. Oh, to be young and stupid. I took old snapshots of the friends I knew I would see, they all enjoyed thinking back to the good old days.

After breakfast, I went to Regina's mother-in-law's house. I call her "my girl." She reminds me a lot of Ma. I jumped on a trampoline in her backyard. This was an item on my bucket list. Aunt Elsie used to have one in her backyard, but I never got on it. It is so illogical how you don't want to do things until you're not really able to do them anymore. I fell and hurt myself, but I just played it off like everything was fine. I was just happy Regina got the photograph when I jumped up in the air.

Next, I went to a cookout my friend, Aloma, was attending. My lime green pants were filthy from my trampoline fall, but I didn't care. I didn't eat, but I got to see her mother, youngest sister, and some aunts I had met when I was at her house all the time. That evening I had dinner with another couple of friends from elementary school. Aloma was at both the breakfast and dinner event. Even though I did not graduate from Arlington High School, the breakfast and dinner events were like a high school reunion. I also went to lunch with my cousin, Clyde. Having lunch when I am in New York is our Special Times.

During this visit, I went to Waryas Park in Poughkeepsie, New York. I lived my entire childhood in Poughkeepsie and never knew the name of that park. We used to just say we were going down the river. I had my 5th birthday party down the river. My cousin, Ta'Wana and my Aunt Elsie were both there. My gift was a Strawberry Shortcake bike. Prior to that, my mode of transportation was a Big Wheel. The bike had training wheels and streamers coming out of the handlebars. Anyway, that weekend I also saw the name of Arlington Elementary School had been changed. I also had Regina take a picture of at outside of Arlington High School. That trip was so nostalgic for me.

When I returned to Virginia, I purchased a Groupon to drive a Lamborghini. Groupon allows me to experience things I could not otherwise afford. Anyway, that was my birthday gift to myself. I'm usually into practical gifts, but I just wanted to treat myself and driving one was also on my bucket list. I never thought it would actually happen.

After driving the Lamborghini, I purchased a 1500-piece Lamborghini jigsaw puzzle. Until then, the largest puzzle I had completed was a 550-piece M&M's puzzle. That was purchased way before my diagnosis, but I thought it would be fun. I mean it is my all-time favorite candy. I don't want to even talk about how little I have done on the Lamborghini puzzle. Florine, Uncle Frank's wife, came to my house and inspired me by putting several pieces together. While working on the puzzle, she saw a picture of Regina, Tichanda, Kasharne, and me. It was taken at my housewarming party. She asked me who was most like me. I answered, Regina. Shortly after her visit, I finished the border at least. I also put similarly colored pieces in Ziploc sandwich bags.

On September 22, 2014, I went horseback riding for the first time. Another thing that was on my bucket list. The last time I was on the back of an animal was an attraction riding the back of an elephant at Catskill Game

Farm as a kid. Anyway, the horseback riding instructor was telling me to do things that my legs were unable to do. I should have told them I had MS when I called to redeem my Groupon, but I did not. The instructor thought I was being difficult, but I was truly physically unable to fulfill her requests. I have since learned that hippotherapy (therapeutic horseback riding) places exist specifically for people with physical disabilities. I need to try one of those places next time.

In Fall 2014, I met my friend, Keta, in Newport News, Virginia. We stayed at one of her nephew's houses for the weekend. This was still during the time I was keeping my diagnosis a secret from new people that I met. In preparation for a party on Saturday, all of the people staying at the house helped clean the house. I selected vacuuming, so that I could use it to lean against and would have the best chance to disguise my disability. Our friend, Keshia from VCU, also came to the party on Saturday. By Sunday morning, other people that were staying at the house had commented that I was still drunk based on me using the walls for support. The other people staying at the house did not know I did not drink, so I just let them believe what they were saying. The use of the walls wasn't from drinking, it was from a busy weekend and the MS showing in my movements. I left straight from the party house to attend a scrapbooking class. That was more my style.

Even with declining physical abilities, I continued to look for a new job. I have a Master's Degree. I am not married, no kids, all I ever wanted to do was work. To be honest, all I really wanted to do was make money, but I was certainly willing to work for it. My brother, R-

Jay and I both inherited a strong work ethic from Ma. I was in a lobby waiting for an interviewer. When the interviewer finally arrived, I pretty much stumbled on him and quickly said "I haven't been drinking." I know that wasn't the best choice of words, but I was so humiliated and didn't know what else to say or do. He had me sit with someone, but never actually interviewed me. The Human Resources recruiter called me later that day asking if I wanted to take the job. Apparently, he never even told Human Resources he never interviewed me. I told the recruiter what had happened. I certainly did not want to work there. That was a bad day for me.

In October 2014, I met my mom's family at a restaurant for dinner and I was so excited to share that I had been to four different places in one day. That was a big deal back then, considering I was struggling to make one stop in any given day. When I shared it, some people said, "That old story." That is just something I started saying a few years back. It sometimes can jokingly reference something that just happened moments before.

In November 2014, I went to Aunt Ann's house, my cousin, Leticia, was visiting her. I did my version of a happy dance when I announced to both of them I had just received a job offer. My new job was providing financial assistance to people with orphan (rare), chronic diseases. God has quite a sense of humor. You got to love the irony. This company had plenty of VIP parking. No special accommodations were necessary for my parking needs. They also had an elevator, no longer had to tackle the dreaded staircase.

In December 2014, during our support group holiday gathering, Sharon and I had a conversation about MS medications. I told her I just wanted to be able to go to the mall. I used to always enjoy roaming around the mall, even if I was not trying to purchase anything. When I was in the process of losing weight, my cousin, LaVita, took me to the mall to get some new pants. After our trip, she said "Never again," and she loves to shop. The day before our mall trip I had gone to see the Butterflies LIVE! exhibit at Lewis Ginter Botanical Garden, so I know my legs were tired. LaVita and I will take another trip to the mall, eventually. Also in December 2014, I traveled to Maryland to go to the college graduation party of my friend Tichanda's niece. I have basically known her for her whole life, and I was crying crocodile tears during the entire video tribute.

In January 2015, I started working my new job. I did not share my MS diagnosis with Management, but I did let them know I had some physical limitations and requested to be near the restroom. Management easily made that accommodation. I told one person at this job that I had MS. That was only because I almost fell on them during training. I felt that warranted an explanation. I think it is accurate to say I struggled through training, but with a pep talk from Aunt Elsie I managed to successfully make it through. I asked my more senior colleagues several questions a day, but I was doing pretty well. I had made it to 89 percent productivity, the goal was 90 percent.

In March 2015, R-Jay and I flew to our cousin Leticia's 30th birthday party in Alabama. I would normally not hang out with a male 13 years my junior, but that's my only sibling, so that's my hanging partner. The theme was Mardi Bras, that's not a typo. In lieu of gifts, she asked that all the party goers bring feminine products, bras, and panties to donate to homeless women. She also encouraged us all to find our passion. I thought about it, but I didn't have one. At least, I didn't think I had one at the time. Also in March 2015, R-Jay and I were traveling together again. We drove to New Jersey, then to New York. We went to see Tichanda and Vaughn's oldest son perform in an off-Broadway play.

By the end of March 2015, I noticed something was changing at work. I was having trouble remembering things. I experienced comprehension problems. I had about 100 Post-it notes all over my computer for my job duties. That number may actually be accurate, not an over-exaggeration this time. I had convinced myself that I was using them to work smarter not harder. It turns out I was using so many of them because I was having trouble just keeping up and processing information. I noticed in March and management noticed it April. I went from 89 percent productivity to 65 percent real fast. Needless to say, I was written up. That is actually what should happen if you can't do your job and the people in charge have no idea why you are unable to do it.

On April 24, 2015, I had a Neurologist appointment and told him of my job woes. He asked why I didn't tell my job I had MS. I told him because I didn't have to. He did not press the issue. He again suggested maybe we should consider disability and referred me to a Neuropsychologist. Great, another type of doctor to add to my list. My apprehension to going on disability was that I would be home every day and be bored. That was a time of severe depression.

On April 25, 2015, R-Jay had his own housewarming party. The person I referred to as my stupid little brother was a homeowner. What in the world? I should have been happy and believe me I was, but I was no fun at that party. In most of the pictures of me from that event I am dawning a saddy-bear face. Several friends and cousins, even play cousins showed up for his housewarming. Our cousin, Leticia, flew from Alabama to be at his housewarming party. Being his only sibling, not showing up was not an option. Sandra and R-Jay would not have accepted me as a no-show, but I was not feeling it.

On May 2, 2015, that morning was Walk MS. I was on a team with people from one of my support groups. I went to vendors to collect swag. Adorned with my personalized support group t-shirt, I took a team photo then sat at a table for the duration of the walk. My friend, Kasharne, and her daughters, Kayden and McKenzie, showed up and did the walk. After the walk, McKenzie gave me her keychain she earned for completing the walk since I couldn't do the walk myself. Certainly, a 5-year old doesn't need a keychain, but it was very sweet just the same. They were selling raffle tickets several feet away from where I was sitting with members of my support group. Normally I would not have ventured that far away on my own, but I was with "my people," so I walked all the way over there to purchase some raffle tickets. In case you're wondering, I didn't win anything.

Later that evening, my cousin, Frank, Jr., had a cookout for graduating from college. I must have been looking bad that day. Uncle Frank came over to my picnic table and we talked. It was the first time I ever bonded with Uncle Frank on that level. He apparently could tell something was wrong with me.

Chapter 6

On May 6, 2015, I went to Aunt Elsie's house. My cousins, Jennifer and Jessica, were both there as well. I shared with her then I thought I was going to get boxed (fired). You know, they put or allow you to put all of your belongings in a box and send you on your way. Anyway, I distinctly remember that I yawned the entire time I was there and neither of the three of them yawned once the entire time. Aunt Elsie suggested I try to go out on work disability. That would at least require me to inform my employer of my diagnosis and I just was not ready to share my diagnosis with my new employer yet.

On May 8, 2015, two weeks after my last Neurologist appointment, I was relieved of my duties. Okay, I got boxed (fired). I didn't blame them at all. At the time, my thought was, if you can't keep up with the pace of your job, you should get fired, especially if you haven't shared with the employer the reason for your diminished cognitive abilities. All kinds of accommodations can be made for physical issues, but not much can be done if you are losing your brain juice. Management provided ice pops earlier that day before I was notified I was getting boxed. Not a bad send off, if you ask me. I had so much candy in my drawer at work. Don't get me wrong, I like candy, but I later realized that was me attempting to stay awake and have energy every day. I had been prescribed medicine that was supposed to give me energy, but I stopped taking it since I didn't notice any energy increase. I also have an electronic back and neck massager that I would have to use every evening after work. I guess I was not working in an ergonomically correct fashion.

Since I was no longer working, I stopped taking Ambien to help me sleep. I did not sleep well, and I needed a good night's sleep to make it through the work day. When you don't have anywhere to be first thing in the morning, it really doesn't matter what time you get up and get started or how many times you wake up during the night. At least that is what I thought at the time. Even without sleeping all that well, I was still waking up early without an alarm clock. My body had been conditioned for so long to wake up early and go to work. Yes, I still have an alarm clock, no cell phone alarm for me. The last one I had lasted me 20 years. My friend, Regina, bought it for me. She didn't even remember gifting it to me, when I thanked her 20 years later. I made sure to purchase the same brand when I replaced it. I had a purple lunch bag that I used to carry my lunch in. I ordered a second lunch bag, but I had been boxed (fired) by the time I received it. I ended up giving the bag to Aunt Elsie so she could take her lunch to work.

I was also on medication prescribed by my Urologist to help with incontinence. Sometimes I feel like I have bladder urgency and barely make it to the toilet. Other times I have a false alarm, I get there, sit down, and nothing happens. Sometimes turning on the faucet or leaning forward can help the situation. I have had nocturia (getting up in the middle of the night to go to the bathroom) as long as I can remember and it doesn't matter what time I stop drinking something. My

Urologist sent me for Urodynamic testing, which analyzes how the bladder stores and releases urine, but no real problem was discovered. I now just need to make sure I am double voiding (completely emptying bladder). I was given Kegel exercises to help strengthen my pelvic floor. These were both useful tips from my Urologist.

I continued to attend MS events and learned applying for disability has taken up to 2 ½ years for some MSers. I was initially upset I didn't get approved for Unemployment. My cousin, Frank, Jr., informed me that I needed to handle this portion of my journey without Unemployment. How can I apply for Unemployment benefits while at the same time telling Social Security I needed to be on Disability because I couldn't work? When Frank, Jr. explained it that way, it made a lot of sense. But understanding was not going to keep the lights on or keep me able to reside in my home. I had to call Ma and let her know my dilemma and the possible 2 1/2-year delay. As always, she had my back. Taking words from one of my favorite sitcoms, *The Middle*, "You do for family."

Even with my cognitive issues, I'm pretty good with numbers, so I tend to remember dates, times, and amounts. Math was always my favorite subject in school, with the exception of Calculus at VCU. That subject was a struggle and almost defeated me. Operative word being almost. I know both me and R-Jay's birth time and birth weight. I plan to list several dates throughout this book as you go along with me on this journey. I even remember my first middle school locker combination. I know you can't verify this, but it was 36 – 26 – 32. I know that sounds a little *Rain Man-*

ish. That is a reference to a 1988 movie. Another thing I have learned from pharmaceutical meetings is to have items ready to discuss with your doctor. Remembering my appointment dates comes in handy for that purpose too. Anything I want to discuss with my doctor, I put it in my smartphone calendar under the date of my appointment. It has been suggested to prioritize and have two or three things to discuss with your doctor. I usually have more than that. He is happy to oblige, at least that's the impression I get. I think the fact that I talk fast helps.

On May 23, 2015, I called my cousin, Xavier. I didn't want anything per se, just needed a riding buddy. You know, someone to keep me company as I took an extended drive. I shared that I had recently been boxed (fired). He is always such a beacon of hope and inspiration. He suggested I write a book about MS. I told him I considered writing a book, not about MS though. My former coworker, Ta-Shima, told me her mother wrote a book and I immediately started writing, right there at work. That was the first time I ever considered writing a book. My novel from 2009 began and ended in Chapter One. Anyway, I told Xavier "I ain't writing no book" – I know double negatives are forbidden, but that was what I actual said at the time. I remember my friend, Tichanda, would keep journals when we were at Arlington High School. She was the writer, not me. Ironically, I won a cake decorating contest in high school and she owns a cake business, Sugar Puddin Cafe, and here I am writing a book. Who'd a thunk it? That's me once again taking liberty with the concept of Artistic License.

On May 26, 2015, I had a comprehensive neuropsychological evaluation. They put me through the wringer. I took a battery of test with the Neuropsychologist that took a couple of hours. During my initial consultation with the Neuropsychologist we talked about problems I had with following movies, balancing my checking account, problems with working that lead to my unemployment, and let's not forget the depression. The final results weren't great. No, I'm not clinically insane, contrary to what some people that know me may think. I may have been clinically depressed back then, but not insane.

Following Frank, Jr's instructions, I started applying for disability the day after getting boxed (fired). His dad, Uncle Frank, had suggested him as a resource. During the application process, I spoke to other people who had applied for disability to find out what to expect during this process.

In June 2015, I wasn't up for going to my cousin Jessica's high school graduation. I had attended her convocation several months prior, so I got to see her in her cap and gown. I did make it to her graduation party. I remember sitting off to the side and not really talking to many people during the event. That was a bad day for me.

I've heard some people say cold or rainy weather affects them. Those problems are less common and I haven't noticed either of them affecting me. Let me clarify, I have noticed I move a little slower on rainy days, but I don't let the rain stop me. Nor do I stay in to avoid it. I don't mind driving in the rain. I am unable to tolerate heat. It absorbs all of my energy. It doesn't even have to be extreme heat. If I am just sitting on my porch reading or eating an Italian Ice and it is warm outside, by the time I come inside, I am ready to take a nap. This occurs even if I am only outside to make a couple of quick trips to my car. Sometimes the naps recharge me, but not always. Heat is like my Kryptonite. I have seen this visually expressed as legs start out as new spaghetti and the boiled spaghetti represents your legs after being exposed to the heat. I usually refer to my legs as feeling like Jell-O. During the Summer, I try to preserve my errand running for overcast days. For the days when I am out in the sun, I make sure to wear sunscreen and sunglasses. My vision has gotten so bad that even my sunglasses are prescription shades. My ideal situation would be Autumn temperatures with it staying light until late, like in the Summer. Unfortunately, Mother Nature does not ask for my opinion on the forecast. Sometimes I don't even realize how much the heat has affected me until I am away from it in the air conditioning.

I know you've heard the saying, knowledge is power. I consider myself a lifelong learner. I ask a lot of questions, but that may have more to do with my comprehension problems than anything else. I continuously try to absorb all types of knowledge, not just with things related to MS. I like to be in the know on many subjects, even if it seems like I'm learning random pieces of information at the time. I used to have a dictionary on my nightstand that I would use to look up a word I didn't know from a TV show. I no longer use the paper dictionary. There's an app for that.

I still see the same Neurologist that handed me the five color brochures. I am both happy and comfortable with my Neurologist. I have heard a lot of people that were diagnosed when there were only a few DMTs (Disease-Modifying Therapies/Treatments) were also given the task to select their own medication. More treatment options exist now than when I was diagnosed, so I have not heard of this process as of late. Now I am hearing of Neurologists working with their patients to select a DMT based on the medication's efficacy and side effects, as well as taking the MSers lifestyle, schedule, and risk tolerance into consideration. Different Neurologists' treatment philosophies vary. I feel it is an important piece of information to know and make sure that it meshes well with your own beliefs.

I attend most pharmaceutical company presentations, especially if my Neurologist is the featured speaker. He has never tried to put me on a medicine just because he speaks for them. I can appreciate his side hustle. Besides, he is not the only Neurologist that moonlights as a representative speaking for the pharmaceutical companies. During one such event, he suggested learning another language. Not to the point of becoming bilingual, just to keep the mind sharp. Since then, I have dabbled with the Duolingo language app.

I go to the pharmaceutical company sponsored lunches and dinners whether I am on the featured medication or not. There is always a doctor, nurse practitioner, or a nurse there than can answer MS related questions. One of the things they often ask is if the MSers have gotten their influenza vaccinations. I got my first and only flu shot in Fall of 2000. Shortly after the shot, my throat closed up and I had a fever of 103 degrees. I would have preferred to just have the flu. For that reason, I decline the flu shot each year. For programs I attend, the shot is suggested, rather than the nose spray, which is a live virus. I'm just sharing my personal experience. Many people get a flu vaccination and have no adverse effects. I have also learned that obesity has been known to affect MS. Good thing I have kept the weight off.

Not only are the events put on by the pharmaceutical companies informational, it is also my time to socialize. I try to learn all I can about this disease and if someone wants to give you a free meal while you learn, that's just a bonus. Actually, I call it an extra, added, bonus, but I know that is not grammatically correct. It is an opportunity for me to find out about available MS resources. I also try to be helpful and share resources I have learned along the way. I not only share and make suggestions, I also listen and try things that other people suggest. Also at these programs you usually get to hear from a MS Ambassador, someone that has MS, that is willing to share their story and their experience with the featured DMT (Disease-Modifying Therapy/Treatment). They have also been referred to as a Peer speaker or Patient/Peer Advocate. Some of them introduce themselves to the audience ahead of time. Not all. Some of them are great orators providing either funny or emotional stories. My cousin, Jennifer, has told me that is her favorite part of the program.

One ambassador's script includes a story about how he has heard from many people with MS have had spouses or partners leave them once they are diagnosed. He prompts you to tell those people "Thank you." He states that if the significant other left at the beginning, they certainly would not have been able to handle it once things got hard. They weren't in it for the long haul or the heavy lifting. Literally, in some instances. I had never thought of it in those terms.

One evening my former roommate, Keshia, was attending an event with me. The ambassador stated

he used a pill case attached to his keychain. I did not even know that was even a thing. I thought that would be a great idea for me and Keshia informed me that she had an extra one that I could have. That has been perfect for the days I forget to check the reminders in my smartphone. Since I usually drive myself everywhere, my keys are always on me. The pill case acts as a visual que to remind me to take my oral medication. Sometimes I still forget to take my medicine if my keys are in my pocket. I addition to forgetting my medicine in the car, I also usually forget a pen. I have tried to remember my pen by putting it in the seat of my car when I am on the way to an event. This strategy does not always work. Though I have several pens from pharmaceutical companies, I usually do not have one on me when it comes time to complete the survey after the meal or event. I refer to these evaluations as my homework, even though I am completing them at the event. Sometimes a pen is provided, not all the time. I purchased pens that I can also attach to my keychain.

I have learned that there is a correlation between EBV (Epstein-Barr Virus) and Multiple Sclerosis.

Mononucleosis or Mono is caused by this virus. People who have Mono as an adolescent are up to nine times more likely to get MS. I knew Mono as the kissing disease. I had Mono when I was 12 and I wasn't kissing anyone. I was shocked to learn that so many people are not compliant when it comes to taking their medicine. The thought of skipping doses or not adhering to my medication schedule never occurred to me. Medicine doesn't work if you don't take it as prescribed. I've learned that when I went blind in one eye before I was diagnosed, it may have been a case of Optic Neuritis. I have heard many people say that is their initial symptom. I did not have pain with mine. Most people do.

I attended the most informal, intimate pharmaceutical company dinner I had ever been to (only a couple of people showed up). I found that to be the perfect opportunity to ask the Pediatric Neurologist about me, Aunt Marian, and Uncle Wayne's theory about me having MS since my seizure at five years old. The doctor did not agree with that. I guess that's why none of us are doctors. The doctor did however think that I may have had it since I was 12 years old, even though symptoms did not present until several years later. That could explain why my disease was so aggressive when I was diagnosed. My MS had remained dormant until a stressor called life made it come to the forefront.

Though the exact cause of MS is unknown, it is not contagious. There is no algorithm for MS, however, there are some commonalities. The doctor seemed to think that the combination of my genetic predisposition; having a family history of MS, having Mono, and growing up in New York may have all been factors.

There is some evidence that suggests MS has an environmental component and may be tied to where people spent their childhood. There is a higher prevalence of MS the farther you are from the Equator. Due to the lack of sun in New York, I may have been Vitamin D deficient – which can also be a sign of MS. The doctor seemed to think I was part of the MS-trifecta. My word, not the doctor's. Women are more likely than men to have MS. So, I guess I am part of a MS-quadfecta. These components led the doctor to think I may have been more susceptible to MS. Of course, that was just their opinion, without actually examining me or knowing my complete medical history. Like with most professions, I'm sure if I had asked 10 different Neurologists that same question, I probably would have gotten 10 different answers. Different DMTs (Disease-Modifying Therapies/Treatments) have different mechanisms of action. Though it is unknown exactly how all the medicines work, the goal for all DMTs that treat MS is NEDA (no evidence of disease activity); specifically reduce relapses, slow the rate of physical disability progression, and slow the development of brain lesions visible on the MRI.

I used to think the disability progression that DMTs (Disease-Modifying Therapies/Treatments) try to halt was only physical. I thought disability just referred to mobility based on the EDSS (Expanded Disability Status Scale). It turns out it just means a loss of function or getting worse overall. I did not realize disability progression refers to, but not limited to, walking ability, cognition, vision, and sexual issues. Many MS symptoms are invisible so it is hard to explain what many MSers are battling daily. MS symptoms are often felt

89

and not seen. I have seen it visually expressed as an iceberg. The tip of the iceberg is things you can see like tremors and mobility issues. The much larger mass lurking beneath the water's surface includes a multitude of unseen symptoms like fatigue, numbness, bladder and cognitive issues to name a few. There is a lot more going on with us MSers than people can see. Sometimes I look like everything is fine and my body is wreaking havoc on itself.

I have heard MS described as a snowflake disease. That is a pretty accurate description, since each MSer is unique. MSers have several different symptoms of varying severity. I heard one person describe them as personality traits. That made me laugh. I have MS very different from my family members with MS and since no MS day is typical, each day brings new challenges. In addition to attending live events, I also read plenty of MS newsletters, magazines, any literature I receive in the mail, and participate in MS related webinars.

I try to get information at support group meetings as well. One such suggestion was the Squatty Potty and it turned out to be an invaluable suggestion. It is a stool that sits in front of your toilet and puts you in the correct position to easily "go" and is easily stored around the base of the toilet when not in use. I saw the Squatty Potty on an episode of the TV show *Shark Tank*, but never considered purchasing one. I finally purchased a Squatty Potty from Bed Bath & Beyond. I always keep coupons for that store in my car. They have plenty of tools for the differently abled. I was anxious to see if it would help me with my constipation issues. Fiber and stool softeners were not doing the job. Once I started using it, it was six weeks before I had to take my first BM cocktail. I have also gotten suggestions from the Webmaster of the Facebook page of one of my support groups.

I've never had any real arm strength. It's actually been a joke with me and Sandra for years. That explains my lack of success maneuvering a tennis racquet the one time I attempted to play tennis. I have learned that hand and arm weakness is an indication of inflammation in the spinal cord, which is something that I have. I've learned that the greatest amount of physical disability comes from spinal cord lesions.

Something else I have learned is to keep a positive mindset. That is certainly easier said than done. I heard that saying you're fine, even when you are not, puts you on the path to feeling better. It is the power of positive thinking. Besides, even though people ask you how you are out of politeness, they really don't necessarily want to know how us MSers really feel every day. My go-to response is "Wonderful." It is hard to be sullen after you say that. This idea is along the same lines of the concept "if you look good, you feel good."

Negativity will make you sick both mentally and physically. There have been several bouts of depression but I can say I have surpassed that hurdle. Though I do not do a lot of things until I am ready, I had no control over how long it took to beat the depression. It's funny how you don't realize the severity of the depression until you get out of it. Let me clarify. It's funny now. It wasn't funny when I was going through it. I've learned that MSers experience the highest rate of depression of all of the possible disabilities. I experienced high functioning depression. I took care of myself, my household, and went to work every day I was scheduled. I am envious of people who say they were healed from their depression in six months or less after diagnosis. The diagnosis of MS temporarily took my spunk away. I got it all back now, probably even more than before I was diagnosed.

In July 2015, R-Jay and I went to visit my friends, Tichanda, Vaughn and their family in New Jersey. There we go traveling together once again. While there I spoke to Vaughn, who was a school principal. I stressed the importance of making sure the school was handicap-accessible. I had heard folks complain about how they had to go through special entrances and made to feel like outcasts. I concluded they wanted accessibility with dignity. We also went to see a fireworks display. In fact, it was the best fireworks show I had ever seen. I remembered my VIP placard this time, so we were able to secure a close parking space for the outside festival. I usually do not remember to grab it if someone else is driving their vehicle.

While in New Jersey, R-Jay had my car, he got in a fender bender or someone hit it, something happened. All I know is he was alright. Since the car was in his custody, it was his responsibility to get it fixed. When we got back to Virginia, he had Uncle Frank knock out the dented fender. Uncle Frank is a jack of all trades. He removed the dent with a blow dryer. I was blown away, pun intended. While they were outside working on the car, I entertained myself by watching TV and talking to Uncle Frank's wife, Florine. She asked me some questions about MS and I shared with her how all my mom's sisters called me on diagnosis day. I also shared that I'm glad I have MS instead of R-Jay. Well maybe not glad, but if one of us has to have it I would rather it be me than him. I don't think I had ever said that out loud. That's not true, I told my friend, Regina.

I don't think it is necessary to go to church every Sunday to be spiritual. That's just my opinion. Though I do believe in signs from God. You just have to be paying attention. I often attend Bedside Baptist at Saint Mattress with Joel Osteen. You know, lying in the bed, watching church on television. Besides, he always starts off with a joke. I like a little humor along with my Christianity.

MS does not discriminate against race, gender, or age. Though you can be diagnosed at any age, most people are diagnosed when they begin to show symptoms between 20 and 40 (some sources report 50), in the prime of most people's lives. Like myself, many MSers feel they had MS long before they received an official diagnosis.

With MS, I don't have the luxury of being impulsive. I'm learning that the secret sauce for dealing with MS is strategic planning. I've always been a planner, but I am even more so now. Prioritizing is essential in the management of this disease. I have to pace myself. Some things get done later than I had hoped and some things get skipped all together. I have never been on a field trip with Kasharne's daughters, Kayden and McKenzie. I went on a bunch of field trips with my cousins, Jessica and Jennifer, when they were younger.

Chapter 7

When I am staying in a hotel ideally, I would request a room near the elevator. I usually forget, until I have already secured a room. When walking from point A to point B, I usually opt for the choice that has fewer steps, even if the fewer steps route happens to be a more challenging terrain or a route with stairs.

In November 2015, Aunt Marian's daughter, Shanta', coordinated a Thanksgiving holiday weekend trip for my entire family to North Carolina. This way family from different states could all meet in a central location. We normally have a family dinner somewhere in Virginia, but we were trying something different this year, so some out of town family members don't have to miss out. I made daily trips to go swim in the hotel swimming pool. Uncle Ralph first introduced me to swimming when I was a little girl. I have been a fan of swimming since my days of frequenting the IBM Country Club when I lived in Poughkeepsie, New York. There is a pool at Sheltering Arms, but the water temperature is too warm for me. I did not want a repeat of the hot tub incident. The great thing about the pool is even if you are walking and not swimming, it is like you don't have MS, while you are in the water. I was depressed then, even with all of my family there. Only one photograph was taken with my camera the entire weekend. I shared some laughs, but I stayed in the bed, in my hotel room a lot of the time. No, I did not remember to get a room near the elevator.

I went to several of my cousin Jennifer's high school basketball games, I may be biased, but she is really good. Our Special Times are taking selfies at her basketball games. Sometimes Aunt Elsie tries to photobomb our Special Times. During basketball game breaks, Aunt Elsie asks if I need to use the restroom. Even with help, navigating the bleachers is challenging. I found this to be a good reason to just wear a Depends and "go" at my seat. Though Aunt Elsie usually asks me if I need to go to the restroom during halftime or between games, I don't want my disease to be too much of an inconvenience to others, besides she is busy with concessions and speaking to other basketball parents and students. Also with my diaper on, I don't have to navigate the bleachers. All four of Aunt Elsie's sisters went to one of Jennifer's basketball games. She was receiving a special basketball accommodation that evening. The closeness of the sisters has trickled down to the closeness shared by the cousins.

I keep a towel in my car for any bladder or bowel accidents that may arise while driving. Sorry for the overshare. I apologize if you are squeamish. No one needs to be worried about riding in my car, I swap the towel out every time I have to use it. Sometimes making a trip to the restroom is too challenging or too far away if I'm by myself. If I am attending an event by myself and have to use the restroom at the end of the event, I usually will not go back to my table after using the restroom. I will usually head to my car if I do not pass my table again on the way back from the restroom. I guess I could wear a Depends every day but the episodes of urgency are intermittent. If I'm with someone else, I will tell them to remind me to use the restroom before I leave the establishment. R-Jay's girlfriend Christine is with me a lot, so she already knows to ask me if I have to use the restroom even without providing her with a friendly reminder. I also wear Depends undergarments on long car trips, on airplanes, and when I go to concerts.

I had won the lottery for four tickets to the Christmas Tree lighting at The White House. On December 3, 2015 R-Jay drove me, his girlfriend, Christine, and my friend, Paula to Washington, DC. We had to take a train, since there was no parking allowed near the event. The closest we could get was still a few blocks away. Paula and Christine were both taking me to the prom, each on either side of me. About 2 ½ blocks away, I told them I could not go any further. This was the second time I had been to this event and the last time the trip was not nearly as difficult. R-Jay put me on his back and we made it to the event just in time. When security saw me on his back, they directed me to the ADA (Americans with Disabilities Act) section of the audience. I was in the fourth row. I was sitting alone, but Paula was not far behind me. On the way home, an escalator was not working in the train station. R-Jay picked me up like I was a ragdoll and carried down the flight of stairs. Knowing Ma would love the way her son looked out for his big sister, we framed the picture of me riding on his back and gave it to her the following Mother's Day. I am giving a thumbs-up and the Washington Monument is in the background.

Also in December 2015, R-Jay, Ma, and I travelled to Doswell, Virginia to see the Illuminate Light Show. It was so neat. We drove through a Winter Wonderland of lights and tuned the radio to a particular station and it plays Christmas music along with the show. Every year before Christmas, the three of us would go shopping at the mall and out to eat. Due to my physical limitations, we had to take the mall out of the equation, but we still went out to eat.

By the time 2016 rolled in, a decision had been made that I was approved for disability and clearly it did not take 2 ½ years. I believe in follow-up. I am a big proponent in the concept of the squeaky wheel gets the oil. Ma never complained when she was paying my bills, but I am still sure she was happy that is was over so quickly. I don't care for the term Disability; I say I'm retired.

Once I had retired, I was looking for ways to fill my spare time. Based on my friend Tichanda's suggestion, I toyed with the idea of selling my gently used clothes online, but clothes are her thing, not mine. That was not my passion. I also toyed with the idea of couponing. It seemed like the perfect fit since I buy many things in bulk and like to save money. That was not my passion either. Now I purchase household items from other people who coupon.

Even though I spoke to my friend, Ta-Shima, at work every day, I never shared my diagnosis. I wasn't ready yet. I happened to run into her outside of Target one day after I was retired and told her everything. I let her know I was in a different, better place than when we worked together. We joked about the fact that she knew I never liked that job, even though we had never talked about that.

In the beginning of 2016, I had turned one of my journals from the pharmaceutical companies into a book of different sayings. Some of them are quotes from famous figures. Some are things I heard someone say, others are pulled from Facebook or TV. Most of them are inspirational or thought provoking; some are just funny.

The support group I attend with Sharon and Edith had a field trip to Sheltering Arms. The same Physical Therapy place that remedied me from falling down the stairs in my house all the time, just a different location. I had made up my mind. I was going to complete the 1 mile Walk MS later that year. On Monday, January 4, 2016, I started at Sheltering Arms with their PowerEx program. My Physical Therapist suggested walking poles. I had refused to get a cane even though I probably needed to be using one. She assured me the walking poles would allow me to maintain balance and steady me as I manipulated the walk. R-Jay had gotten me some new sneakers, Skechers – the ones without regular laces. Along with those, I was equipped with walking poles and a pedometer around the pseudo-laces, to keep track of my steps. I know most people use a Fitbit, but I am often late on acquiring modern technology.

Sheltering Arms is open six days a week and I was there most days working out in the gym and walking up and down the hall preparing for Walk MS. I was informed 24 laps in the hallway was equivalent to one mile. I know it's about the will, not the skill and my will was strong. I started with two laps, I had quite a long way to go. The first time I attempted three laps, I thought I was going to die. Okay, maybe not die, but it was hard, even with the walking poles. I would also listen to music I had purchased on iTunes on my smartphone. It was a welcomed distraction. As I slowly increased the number of laps, "Coach" began coming around. This is a former athlete and friend from VCU. He taught me breathing techniques, stretches, and other workout tips to complete Walk MS successfully. "Coach" is the name Ma used to describe him. That is one of the things that Ma started doing, coming up with a nickname for anyone I deal with. The individuals usually don't even know they have a nickname. She does not even have to meet the person in order to come up with their nickname.

It was in March 2016 I wish I could say that doing the laps at Sheltering Arms was all smooth sailing, but it wasn't. One day I fell in the gym, after completing laps in the hallway. Two physical therapists rushed to my side to make sure I was okay and to help me off of the ground. I was so embarrassed, even though no one else appeared to be paying me any attention. I guess if you have to fall somewhere, that is a pretty good place, surrounded by people who are trained to help with that particular situation. In my defense, I was just recovering from being sick with a cold and probably was doing way too much, way too soon.

Late March 2016 R-Jay and I had the following conversation.

"Are you going to keep going to Sheltering Arms?"

"No, I don't have money for that!"

"If I pay for it, will you keep going?"

I gave him a side eye (pursed lip, skeptical expression) before responding with a sarcastic "Yeah!"

In early April, 2016, R-Jay paid for me to continue to go to Sheltering Arms for another three months after my initial three-month PowerEx program was over. Realizing the benefit I was getting from Sheltering Arms, I added to R-Jay's gift and signed up for a whole year. People at Sheltering Arms are so inspirational. When I was struggling to do my laps in the hallway, people in wheelchairs would give me a thumbs-up. That would just make me do at least one more lap beyond what I felt I was capable of doing that day.

Mid-April 2016, I had conquered the 24 laps. Keep in mind I had mostly been practicing inside with no coat. I did go to the track at the recreation center near my house a few times. I figured that was good practice since the real walk was going to be outside.

My Arlington High School friend, George, posted a picture on Facebook of him and some mutual friends of ours skiing. I liked the picture, but then I thought I need to let him know what that picture meant to me. A "like" was just not good enough. That picture took me back. You see, I used to ski with him. I sent him a message on Facebook Messenger letting him know how happy that picture made me. Remembering the Special Times we had on the ski slopes put me in a certain place, especially since I was training for Walk MS. We had only talked one time since he came to my housewarming party in 2003. We talked that day.

Every pen I own is retractable. Something as basic as removing the top off a pen can create a challenge for someone with coordination issues. For comfort, in addition, they are either pens that already include a grip or I have attached one to it. R-Jay's girlfriend, Christine, got me some of those. Hand coordination also made it difficult to thread a needle. Christine also purchased me some needles with bigger eye holes. She was also the one who suggested that I put the pedometer on my sneakers, since I had lost a few that were in my waistband.

I volunteered to be a Political MS Activist at the Virginia General Assembly. It was my least favorite volunteer activity. I believe the work is important and I am grateful for other MSers that do it. I don't believe that assignment plays to my strengths. I believe that I can make a difference elsewhere. It was more walking than I expected, but I was happy to get that experience under my belt. Sitting next to me in the cafeteria was the CEO of the last company I worked for, along with the guy that boxed (fired) me. I approached them and was finally willing to tell them both why I was unable to handle my job duties. That day I felt vindicated. The CEO expressed he wished I had told them when I was still working. I let him know I just wasn't ready yet. He asked me what medication I was taking for my MS and told me to let him know if I needed anything. I hoped he was not making an empty gesture because I took people up on those kinds of offers.

My VCU friend, Keta, told me I need to do more than just attend MS events. When I was working, my only extracurricular activity was renting a Redbox movie. Don't get me wrong, she is completely supportive of me attending MS events, she just thinks I need to do more than that. She was right, I am now heeding her instructions and am now doing more non-MS activities. As usual, parking and going to the restroom can create a challenge but somehow, I figure it out. I still occasionally rent movies, just not nearly as often.

I saw a picture of my cousin, Jamila, with our Aunt Rachel on Facebook. Aunt Rachel and Uncle Oliver had moved to Virginia since I moved here. I have a few relatives that have moved from New York to Virginia. I thought Aunt Rachel was in New York, turns out Jamila was here in Virginia. I texted Aunt Rachel and she invited me to come over to her house. I also texted Jamila. Our cousin, Clyde, had given me her cell phone number a few years back. On February 26, 2016, I went to Aunt Rachel and Uncle Oliver's house to see my cousin, Jamila. I had not seen her since Uncle Vernis' birthday party in 2010. I also met her aunt, Michelle. I told her about the impending Walk MS. At the end of my visit, she said to let her know the next time I am in NY.

I walked into Aunt Ann's house and her daughter, LaVita, was there too. They both were so amazed by the progress I was making and how well I was walking. LaVita said "And you're not shaking!" Keep in mind, I didn't even know I used to shake. I wasn't sure if they really noticed a difference or just said it to make me feel better, knowing Walk MS was just around the corner. Either way, it made me happy and I think Sandra, who was there too, was also happy.

Some people I tell I have MS immediately say, "Oh, I'm sorry." Others assume I am in pain all the time. Thank goodness I have no pain, neither acute nor chronic. I have had plenty of episodes of the agonizing temporary discomfort of paresthesia (pins and needles), like a severe case of a body part falling asleep, but no real pain. I'm usually only telling them so they know why I'm walking unstable or holding on to furniture. I don't want anyone to think I've been drinking.

When I noticed the numbers on my mailbox looking worn and tattered, I looked up how to remove them. I tried a few techniques, with no luck. I had to get them off, I was going to have company soon. Finally, I called Uncle James and asked what he used to remove the numbers. He suggested I just cover the existing numbers with the new numbers. I'm getting a little sick of saying, why didn't I think of that? It is the same way I do the car registration month and year stickers on my license plates. I have never tried to remove those.

On April 20, 2016, I went 12 different places in one day. One of my 12 places was a support group meeting. One of my old support group leaders would say, "If you don't feel better when you leave the support group than before you got there, that is not the right support group for you." Again, another thing that seems so obvious. I am now adhering to this one. Edith gave me a shout-out that she had noticed a positive change in me since she met me crying at a MS lunch in 2013. That is just what I needed to hear before Walk MS. I'm sure that propelled me to get me to make those 12 stops also. Even though I was able to make multiple stops in one day, I don't make a habit out of doing that. My goal is always energy-conservation. Twelve places were quite a leap from the four places I went to in October 2014. 12 stops in one day was just me doing the most. I was just trying something, to see if I could do it. Basically, a personal challenge.

The weekend before my Walk MS event, Roy's youngest brother, Uncle Garry, did a MS Walk in his home state of Maryland in my honor. I did not even know he was doing that, until I saw the pictures on Facebook. It made me so happy.

It was April 29, 2016 the night before the big game. Play cousin, Tasia, was my first guest to arrive at my house. I have a mat that sits on my porch, it says "Welcome" on one side and "Goodbye" on the other side. Tasia noticed that the mat was backwards. I'm sure it had been backwards since I had the porch painted back in 2014. You would think I would have noticed it in all that time, but I hadn't. Regina was the next guest to arrive. She drove from NY, by herself this time. She had told me even before I started doing laps at Sheltering Arms, that if I did the walk she would come. She kept her word. When Regina arrived at my house that evening, she raved about audiobooks she had gotten that helped her make the long trip by herself. That sounded nice, but I did not know if my local library would have the type of books that I liked on CD.

Not only did Regina show up, but she also had a special t-shirt made for the walk. The front of the shirt read "On the team since 1987" and had a picture of us from the 2013 NKOTB concert in Philadelphia. The back of the shirt read "I walk for Danica Team MS

King." Get it, MS King, Ms. King? Regina also gave me my birthday t-shirt that evening, citing that she would not see me again before my 40th birthday. We had a slumber party that night. My friend, Keta, even made the trip from North Carolina, but I was already sleeping by the time she arrived. I took over-the-counter sleeping pills so I could get a good night's sleep. For me, it was more slumber than party.

The big day had arrived, April 30, 2016. I prayed it would not be hot or rainy on walk day. My prayers were answered! Not only was it not hot, but it was freezing that morning. That day I learned I needed to be specific with my future requests. I had a Made Strong sweatshirt over my MS t-shirt so I was ready, regardless of the weather. My friend, Ta-Shima, came to my house before the walk. Her along with my slumber party guests headed to the Walk MS location. At Walk MS, I gave my friend, Regina, the duty of collecting MS swag from the vendor booths. I wanted to save all my energy to complete the task at hand. She jokingly said I was famous, claiming people noticed me from her t-shirt. I quickly reassured her that people only know me in the MS community, not in any other aspects of life. She claims she got extra stuff when they noticed my picture was on her shirt. I don't know if they did or not, but her saying that made me feel good.

My Walk MS team consisted of family members from both sides of my family and friends from near and far. My friend, Tichanda, was even there in spirit. I had ordered cake pops from her and she shipped them from New Jersey. They were in the MS color of orange with black "MS" scrolled on some of them. My friend,

Kasharne, was there too with her husband, Jay, and their two daughters. I had been fundraising for the walk since February 1, 2016. Ma's friend Eileen, who was also in attendance, had done a very successful fundraising campaign at her job. My Aunt Cat, cousin Ta'Wana, former VCU roommate Keshia, and former coworker Lona all helped me with my gift certificate fundraiser for Walk MS. With everyone's help, I was able to exceed my fundraising goal. I knew some of the people that would be attending, but even more than I had hoped for were in attendance. I was overjoyed that so many people showed up to do Walk MS with me.

There were a bunch of my dad's side of the family there, I usually only see them once a year at Uncle Ralph's house around Christmas or at funerals. It was my first year as a team captain and my MS King team was turning out to be a huge success. Teamwork makes the dream work. I was so happy as my team began to congregate around me as I sat down, still preserving energy. I managed to keep my composure until my cousin, Jennifer, showed up. Ma had told me she wasn't coming, but I sure was glad she was able to make it. It was all over then. Once the water works started it was constant tears for a while. "Coach" called shortly before the start of the walk to tell me what stretches to do and wish me luck. I was admittedly disappointed that he did not show up for the walk. I mean how do you coach the season and not show up for the Super Bowl? Line dance warm ups with fellow MSer, Kemel began. It was time to head to the starting line.

I purchased a pair of walking poles from Dick's Sporting Goods and made sure to adjust the height to match the walking poles I had used at Sheltering Arms. Equipped with my walking poles, me and my team of 30 made our way to the starting balloon arch. Even if I wasn't preserving my energy, I would not have done the line dances. I barely got a decent 2-step, even before MS. We got there too early, time to sit down and cry some more. Characteristic of my style, all the tears were caught on film by my friends and family. The first ½ mile was fairly painless. The tears had temporarily subsided until I saw the ½ mile sign. I took a break to tie a ribbon around the wish stick. This is a Walk MS tradition where you are given a little piece of ribbon before the walk to tie around the wish stick during the walk course. Come to find out another person, Roy's youngest sister Aunt Audrey had joined us since we began walking. More tears filled my eyes. The entire team remained together until the ½ mile mark. During my ½ mile break I said, "I'm glad it didn't rain, because I'm sugar and I might melt." I shared with the team that my late grandfather, Buster, said that after my grandmother, Agnes', funeral. I figured it was an appropriate share, since so many relatives from my dad's side of the family had joined me on walk day. At the ½ mile mark, the National MS Society took group pictures that were later posted on their Facebook page. We had already been taking our own group pictures all day long.

Many of my team members continued on to the three-mile ending, but I turned around and headed back to start, at the half mile point. I was joined by Uncle Dwight, my friend, Regina, and play cousins Tasia and Lashi. Uncle Dwight was on my right and Lashi was on my left. Lashi was so attentive to me, it was evident that she had a friendship with someone else that has MS.

Regina was taking pictures and talking to people in a golf cart that had stopped several times offering to give me a ride to the finish line. I refused each time. I was determined to cross the finish line on my own two feet.

When I was at about 85 percent completion, I removed my sweatshirt. At the exact moment, a member of one of my support groups went by. She is the one that had given me the t-shirt I was wearing underneath my sweatshirt. The back of the shirt read, "One Day I Will Say I Used to Have MS." I can't wait for that day to arrive. As she went by, she gave me words of encouragement. That last part of the walk was a partial blur. I was concentrating on completing the mile – upright was all I could hope for at that point. With walking poles in tow and tears all across my face, I finally crossed the finish line. I was so happy as volunteers and other people cheered as I crossed. Play cousin, Tasia, had gotten me crossing the finish line on video. I wish I could say it was my idea. I never even saw her recording me, but I was glad she had done it. Apparently, I scared a few people that weren't at the walk with the Walk MS 2016 video. When I saw them, I got the impression that they thought the way I was walking after 1 mile, is how I was walking all the time.

Crossing the finish line was such a pivotal moment for me. I couldn't even grab the congratulatory MS keychain I got for completion. Uncle Dwight took that for me. My legs felt like complete Jell-O. I sat on the first piece of curb I saw. So much for meeting the rest of the team back at the pre-walk location as agreed. As I sat, I pulled out my smartphone and posted to Facebook "I have MS, MS doesn't have me." Then something about how I just finished Walk MS. I don't know what was going on with me but it was like my MS coming out party. I put it out for everyone to see that I have MS. That event changed me. It was the start of what I came to call my 40 Metamorphosis.

Come to find out, my cousin, Diane, had been posting Walk MS pics the whole time. So, my share was hardly breaking news. There is an option to post Walk MS fundraising on your Facebook page. I would imagine I could raise more money with a broader audience. I wasn't ready yet this year. I'm ready now, next year I will post team MS King to my Facebook page. Regina later told me Sheltering Arms was starting a MS Wellness pilot program. That's what she discussing with the people in the golf carts. Regina insisted I join this program and told me they were only taking 30 people. I just thought, 30 people and it's the 30th of the month, that's the same number of walkers I have on my team, is that a sign? All those 30s had to mean something.

After Walk MS when I thanked everyone for participating, Ta'Wana said, "We didn't have a choice, you've been recruiting for this walk for about a year." She said it as a joke but she was right, I had been talking about the walk since I got boxed (fired) in May 2015. Besides, I didn't mind her throwing a little bit of shade in my direction. After all, she did teach me how to spell my first word. It was tree. Yes, I remember that too.

The evening of the walk Regina and I had dinner with R-Jay and his girlfriend, Christine, at Bottoms Up Pizza. After dinner, R-Jay pulled the car over to the side for Regina and me to take pictures near the "Richmond" sign that sits at the entrance of Highway 64 East. The sign was put up before Richmond hosted the UCI Cycling event. Apparently even the city knows the concept of showing off for company.

I know I've mentioned my housewarming and Dirty 30 birthday party as some of my happiest days, but for real April 30, 2016 was my new favorite day. I was so lucky, all three of my best friends were there, Regina, Tichanda (in spirit), and Kasharne. I am so lucky to have these ladies in my life. I have two pictures of the four of us together displayed in my home. One from my housewarming party the other from my Dirty 30 birthday party. In both photographs I am standing to the far left and they are standing in the order in which I met each of them. I know having three people that you consider best is kind of oxymoronic, but they all mean different things to me and have all supported my MS journey in different ways. Okay, that is enough mushiness for one book.

Chapter 8

I signed up for the MS Wellness pilot program first thing Monday morning. In fact, I was the first of the 30 participants to sign up. Regina was so proud. I've been asked by an older gentleman why I am there working out with all of the old people, his phrasing, not mine. I share that I have MS. I am often wearing a MS t-shirt. I used to not ever wear MS shirts, not even in my own home alone. They used to be tucked away in the back of the drawer. I would wear every other kind of shirt from Breast Cancer and Alzheimer's to Arthritis, bringing awareness to every disease, except my own. That must have been another part of my denial. I am over that now. If I happen to be wearing a Walk MS shirt and someone asks me if I plan to do the walk, I proudly share that I already did it.

I put an orange MS ribbon applique' on my car rear, passenger side window. A VCU Alumni one is on the other side. I still continue to get mixed up with some things. I sent someone a text, when I meant to send them an email to their job. I was mortified when they replied asking who I was. They did not seem to be phased at all by my error. It was an employee of the National MS Society so I guess they are used to MSers doing these kinds of things. I appreciate that all employees of the National MS Society wear their nametags at every event, at least the ones I have attended. They know their audience and realize we probably won't remember their names.

111

I also turn the TV off when I merely intend to only change the channel or hit rewind on my TV remote when I want to fast forward. I will also grab the remote and turn the TV off when I get ready to leave the house and turns out I have already done that to the TV. Since my vision has gotten so poor, I am happy that I have the kind of remote control that lights up when I pick it up and it is dark. It is all about finding the silver lining. I have come home to a fully lit up living room or left on various lights throughout the house. If it is light when I leave, sometimes I just forget to hit the light switch. I've even left the upstairs lights on from when I first came downstairs earlier in the day.

I've been retired for a year and it's going swimmingly, even better than I could have ever imagined. Bored? Not hardly. If I'm home two days in a row, that is a rarity. Granted I take a nap most days and a portion of many of those days away from home is spent at Sheltering Arms. Edith from my support group has said she does not have time to work. My friend, Regina, has said the same thing about me with all of my MS activities. In 2016, I finally looked at my own MRIs with my MS Specialist. Previously I just wasn't ready yet.

I used to be devastated, well maybe not devastated, but I would get so upset if I would drop a fork at a restaurant or struggle trying to put the clasp on my watch. Don't get me wrong, those things still happen. Now I try not to get too bent out of shape when those mishaps occur and I see it as a minor inconvenience. I just use another fork and either keep trying the watch until I get it on or choose not to wear a watch that day.

Either way, I'm good. It's not like I need it, like so many others, I check the time on my cell phone. I often forget to put on any jewelry all together. Now, I will still occasionally put my leftovers in a Tupperware bowl and somehow it never makes it to the refrigerator or I forget to put food away altogether. Sometimes when I stand up off the couch, a chair or the toilet, I immediately fall back down. I just try again. Now I turn the oven timer on, even if I am preparing something quick on top of the stove. That is when I remember to do so.

On May 22, 2016, my cousin, Jessica, and I were hanging out. It was a few days before Red Nose Day, so I went to Walgreens to purchase my red nose. It is a fundraiser to ensure children are healthy, safe, and educated. I agreed to purchase Jessica one too, if she agreed to take a picture and post it on social media. She agreed to my terms. From what I understand, her dad, Uncle James, also purchased one for her little sister, Jennifer. On May 26, 2016, Jessica not only posted a picture, but her and Jennifer posted a dance video wearing their red noses. I saw the video first thing in the morning and it completely made my day. I play fair, I didn't post a video, but I did post a picture of myself wearing my red nose on Facebook. I wore my red nose to Sheltering Arms and left it on the entire time I was there working out. I even wore it to the bank afterwards. I did not do this as a book stunt, I didn't even know I was writing a book yet. Ma also wore her red nose to work.

On Saturday, June 4, 2016 (R-Jay's birthday) I volunteered for the Bike MS fundraising event. I was one of the members of the registration team. It was my second year doing registration and my third year volunteering for that event overall. I registered Bill Fitzgerald, a local news anchor on CBS. He looked slightly familiar, but I didn't know who he was immediately. I usually watch ABC local news. On Sunday, I worked the merchandising table, selling shirts and other things. We were under a tent, blocked from the sun's violent rays. The tent started swaying viciously from the wind, so they unassembled it. By then I was so tired I stayed under the tent while they collapsed it above my head. I was considered brave for not moving, but I really could not muster up the strength to move. I wanted to enjoy protection from the sun as long as possible. After the tent was removed, I ended up retrieving a cooling towel and sunscreen from my car.

June 8, 2016 was the MS On the Move Luncheon sponsored by the National MS Society. The "Women" has been removed from the title. Bill Fitzgerald from CBS news was the emcee for the luncheon. I approached him before he started his duties and told him I registered him for Bike MS on the previous Saturday. He claimed to remembered me. That evening I watched the CBS evening news for the first time. There was Bill, still wearing his orange tie from the luncheon. They showed clips from the luncheon. I never even saw television cameras at the event, but they were present.

The speaker for the event was Ronda Giangreco. She talked about the project she did after being diagnosed. She also wrote a book, *The Gathering Table*. Her story was so good, as had been the case for all of the previous luncheons I attended. After the luncheon, I purchased a copy of her book and she signed it for me.

Christine often got prescreening tickets for movies. She always invited me to join her and R-Jay. I thought that was the case again for seeing *Central Intelligence*. She had two tickets for me, so I asked 14 people if they wanted to join me. I mean who doesn't like a free movie? I had no takers. The day of the movie I found out her and R-Jay weren't even going this time. If I knew that, I would have asked more people. Well I wanted to see that movie, so I'll somehow figure it out. I got to the theater super early so I could get the closest VIP parking space. That worked. I left everything in the car, except my MS bracelet – just in case. I find it necessary to take additional precautions when I am by myself. I know previously we have not been able to take cell phones into prescreenings and I certainly would not be able to make an extra trip to the car if that were the case this time.

I walked in the theater and there were about 15 people in line in front of me. I did a lot of leg stretches and moving from my left foot to my right foot. A theater employee told us to move closer to the wall, I ended up becoming really good friends with a gumball machine. That is what I used to help me remain standing. Now I have to use the restroom but I'm alone and I don't trust anyone to save my spot. This would have been a good day to wear a Depends. Soon the lady comes to scan our tickets and I'm relieved that I'm getting closer. The restroom is right next to our theater but if I stop to use the restroom, all the seats might be taken by the time I finish. I made it into the theater alone and grabbed a good seat. I still knew there was no way I could sit there for another couple of more hours without using the restroom. After I had people on both sides of me, I excused myself and told them I would be right back. I was hopeful they would save my seat in the row. At this point, I had no choice. After my trip to the restroom, my seat was still available and I was ready to watch the movie. A DJ from the radio station was there to get the audience hype, so the movie did not start right away. I was feeling so good after the movie. Now I have to make it back to my car by myself. Things like that used to be so easy, now pretty much everything has to be planned out ahead of time. I noticed there was a slight hill on the outside of the theater to get to my car. I hadn't noticed that before I entered. I walked to the car, holding my hands together in front of me, as not to throw off my equilibrium. I was so excited when I made it safely to the car. I immediately called Christine on FaceTime. I was so excited; I had figured it out.

On June 18, 2016, the Saturday before Father's Day, I posted pictures of my cousin, LaVita, and me both with our deceased father's, with the caption, "Daddy's Girls." In that same photo album, I stumbled upon a photo of me and Beverly, an old friend from Arlington Elementary School at one of my elementary school slumber parties. I thought, won't it be funny to friend her on Facebook and post this picture for Throwback Thursday. On Wednesday night, June 22, 2016 I went to take the picture of Beverly and me so I could post it Thursday morning. As I perused the photo album I saw baby pictures of my cousins, Ta'Wane, Leticia, and LaVita. Even Aunt Cat was present in a couple of the photographs. My only thought was, my family will get a kick out of these pictures, so I will post these also. I posted the snapshot of Beverly and I with the caption "slumber party #tbt." I added the other pictures with only a #tbt label. I told you I don't sleep through the night so I posted the pictures about 5 a.m. Thursday morning. By the time I woke up for good I grabbed my cell phone and I had a big smile on my face when I saw how many notifications I had already received. The cell phone ringer was not on, so the notifications did not interrupt my sleep. I knew immediately it was from my Throwback Thursday posts.

After I return home from Sheltering Arms, I usually spend most of the day watching television. I could not turn the TV channel. The television would come on, but I was unable to turn to my desired channel. I was bewildered because the Internet and the house phone, that are on the same bill, were both working just fine. I called the cable company and discovered it was slightly pass due by $81 and change. I didn't think things got cut off for such a minuscule amount, but whatever. Maybe that was my sign that I need to be doing something else. Something more substantial than watching TV. I could always be working on my Lamborghini puzzle. I'll get back to it later. I promise.

I went back to reading *The Gathering Table*, besides I'm almost done. I finished reading it on Thursday, June 23, 2016. I'm inspired to do something but what could I do? Though an intriguing idea, I don't have the money, skill, nor desire to do what Ronda did in her book. What I do have is an absolutely insane collection of photographs. I read that photographs are the best cure for a bad memory. Hopefully my huge collection of photographs will help me maintain mine. I just love pictures, I have them all over the house. No landscapes or anything just friends and family living our regular lives over the years. As the likes continued to flow, I exclaimed "Eureka!" along with a celebratory hand gesture. Yes, I actually said that out loud. I got it. I had one of those "aha" moments I have heard other people speak of.

I will do Throwback Thursday posts. This will be my new thing. In addition, I will write a book about me and my personal experience with MS. I am by no means a wordsmith. My last piece of original writing, that I did not have to do research for, was a haiku in first grade. No, I don't know anything about how to get a book published, but using my existing skill set and the entrepreneurial spirit I inherited from my dad's side of the family, I will figure it out. I believe I can figure it out eventually, so the way I see it, I'm already halfway there. Knowing my cousin, Tracie, was an avid reader, I immediately called her to share the new project I was about to start. I was so excited when I called her. Ronda Giangrego's book inspired me to share my own MS story. I know it sounds so cliché, but I really believe reading *The Gathering Table* changed my life. I had read other books related to MS, but none of the others affected me like this one had done. If I could inspire or motivate someone else the way she inspired me, that would just be divine.

Ronda had pasta, wine, and friends. I have family, friends, and photographs. Sounds so simple but these comments are really making me happy. I by no means am trying to take credit for the concept of Throwback Thursday, trust me, I'm not that creative. Throwback Thursday is a trend on social media where people post older photographs. I just feel that with my vast collection of photographs I can do it consistently.

Hindsight being 20/20, another source of Throwback Thursday inspiration was a picture of my cousin, Diane. I wasn't even born when the picture was taken. I never knew her daughter looks exactly like her when she was younger.

My cousin, Leticia, called her brother Ta'Wane, "Winky" from my first post of him. He did make a really cute winking face in his baby picture with Aunt Cat. My cousin, LaVita, referred to him as the "first real emoji." That was a funny day. Aunt Cat said we were not going to "make game" of her son. That's a term that was often used by my grandfather, us older Grandkids called him Grandaddy James. I think the younger grandkids called him Pop Pop or something like that.

After I texted Leticia that this was going to be my new thing, she actually sent me a text request for a specific photograph that included her holding R-Jay's hand. I knew exactly what snapshot she was referring to. I let her know that my photos are in chronological order and that I am not even close to R-Jay even being born yet. I told her to stay tuned, it's coming. I have finally found my passion, photographs and MS. Leticia will be so proud.

I won't be including any fancy PhotoGrid app borders or titles. My pictures are all in chronological order, but my posts won't all be. It will be pretty close though. I am going to want to switch up between family and friends. The positive remarks I have received so far today are enough to get me to continue. As I post pictures, I am not asking anything of the people in the photos. The likes and comments are the goal. I like taking my family and friends down memory lane.

Once I committed to writing a book, I took out a pen and paper. I only wrote one sentence toward my manuscript and then took out the laptop. As I began typing, I recalled an episode of the sitcom *Mike & Molly* where Molly was an aspiring author. Susan Sarandon, playing the guest starring role as an experienced writer told Molly to "Write what you don't want people to know." I know it is just a sitcom, but that is just what I am going to do. I am putting it all out there. This is the best day I have had since Walk MS on April 30, 2016. No, it's not my new favorite day. That night my mind was racing with so many book ideas, I took over-the-counter sleeping pills to be able to get a good night's sleep.

On June 24, 2016, I reflected on the previous day. Day One had been such a success; I am looking forward to next Throwback Thursday. I have already started to make Facebook friend requests for people if I know I have pictures of them. Since my long-term memory is pretty good, I remember most of the first and last names of my classmates all the way back to Arlington Elementary School. Most of my middle school and high school photographs are labeled on the back with the person's name. I'm glad I had the foresight to do that. Hopefully, even the few new friends that may not be tagged will enjoy seeing their old classmates. Some people I have pictures of I did not meet until later in my teenage years or until adulthood. They just have to be patient until I get to their snapshots. Little do my new Facebook friends know they are about to go on this journey with me. I realize, not everyone will accept my friend request by the time I get to their picture, if ever. People may have various reasons for not accepting me as a friend on Facebook, but I can't concern myself with their issues. I'm certain many of my new friends don't even know I have MS. Maybe some of my old friends don't even know, if they missed my April 30, 2016, Walk MS post.

I considered asking my childhood friends if they minded me posting old photos of them, but after careful consideration I remembered, it is a lot easier to ask for forgiveness than permission. If people object, they can always unfriend me. I think all of my friends will be good sports about it. I told you I play fair so I will also be including pictures of myself, even the embarrassing ones. My horoscope for June 24, 2016 mentioned something about a project I am working on is about to pay off, I may get a lot of attention suddenly and social networking could be an important part of future business. The horoscope was from a free app so I don't plan my life based on it, but maybe it's another sign that this project is a good idea. At least I hope that's what it means.

I was so hype, I typed several pages, over several hours on Day One. Good thing I had dinner plans with my friend, Lona, or who knows how long I would have kept going on that first day. My right hand was pretty much useless on Day Two. Most of my texts were sent verbally. I didn't even play Candy Crush as much, admittedly I didn't stop completely, as I probably should have. For the next few days I used a stress ball shaped like a brain to get some function back to my right hand.

That was another piece of swag, complements of one of the MS pharmaceutical companies. I really over did it on Day One. I won't make that mistake again. I will try to limit myself to no more than two hours of typing per day.

I talked to my friend, Keta, and told her I had been distracted yesterday by my Facebook likes and comments. She said, "You always get so carried away." She's right. I have an all or nothing personality. The real distraction was me writing this book, but I did not share that with her.

On that same day, when I shared my Throwback Thursday plans with my friend, Regina, she said, "It's just like you to make a project out of Throwback Thursday." Around the same time, I matter-of-factly tested out the book writing idea to my friend, Tichanda, asking if she thought the idea was ridiculous or not. She thought it was a great idea and she thinks Throwback Thursday is a good project for me. Little did she know I had already started writing a book and had already committed myself to the Throwback Thursday project. I only told a few people about Throwback Thursday ahead of time. Everyone else will experience it as it is happening.

I am a fairly new "active" member of Facebook. Before my smartphone, I might have made five postings since I created my page, and that's probably being generous. One year I posted a message thanking everyone for their birthday wishes and my cousin, Frank, Jr., texted me saying he thought my Facebook page had been hacked. He was only kidding. To put things into perspective, I didn't even get my first smartphone until October 2015. Before that, I was taking all my pictures with an actual camera. I am so old-school, I still use a paper Rolodex. I even put my coins in paper coin wrappers that I get free from the bank, rather than use a Coinstar machine. As much as I love counting change, it is becoming increasingly more difficult to do with a numb hand and I also have a limited amount of time I can tolerate sitting on the floor at one time.

I was so excited to have the kind of phone that could recognize the artist and name of a song that is currently playing. I was so impressed by this parlor trick when my former roommate, Keshia, did that when we went out to lunch earlier that year. Since my smartphone had the selfie feature, I no longer had to say, "Excuse me kind sir..." to request someone to take a picture. Okay, I still do it sometimes, but not as often. For years, friends have told me to get a smartphone and my family joked me for not having one. I just wasn't ready yet. I took classes at the Verizon store on how to use my smartphone. Truth be told, I learned more from Christine's teachings. Taking the classes are pretty much indicative of the nerd I am.

I am still in the process of learning how to use my smartphone. R-Jay had to show me how to use the flash when taking pictures with my smartphone. My cousin, Jessica, set up my smartphone to blink with an LED light whenever I receive a call or text. Uncle Ralph is the one that showed me that was even an option. This is a useful feature since my ringer is never on. I am such a Facebook novice. I recently learned you could not tag someone unless you were already friends with them on

Facebook. I thought you could tag anyone, just as long as they had their own Facebook page. During a cookout at Aunt Cat's house, play cousin, RonShai' showed me how to post birthday messages on someone's Facebook timeline. Prior to that, I would send someone a birthday greeting on Facebook Messenger or send them a text if I had their cell phone number. I have started posting fairly recent random picture of the birthday person and me on their timeline, if I am not going to be celebrating the person's birthday with them. So far, I have not used throwback pictures for birthday posts.

My friend, Kasharne, taught me that you can change your emoji selection. I never considered that I had the capability to make such a change if I accidentally selected the wrong emoji. I had a hand spasm right after I had liked something. To my surprise, the thumbs up was deleted. Sometimes I figure it out, by accident. It should have been obvious that I could leave an item deselected since I had recently learned I could change emojis, but it wasn't. My friend, Regina, told me how to tag someone on an existing post. I only knew how to tag people if they were included in a picture that I posted. The first time I shared a picture on Facebook, I did not realize it went to all of your friends. I thought it was going to allow me to select a certain person that I wanted to share it with. It was just a joke about how candy is 50 percent off the day after a holiday. That is when I buy my M&M's. No harm done. My friend, Aloma, liked it.

I realize you don't need a smartphone to use Facebook, but it sure makes it a lot easier. Though I've had a Facebook profile since 2008, I have only updated my profile picture three times. My current one is from

2014, I need to get on updating that. I only created a Facebook page because my friends Tichanda and Kasharne insisted. Aside from not having a smartphone with virtual constant Facebook access, my excuse was I didn't care enough to want to know every move a person made all day. I've since learned Facebook is so much more than that. On a daily basis, it provides a source of comic relief. For instance, when people post two pictures, the first being something they saw and wanted to try, the second being their tragic attempt at the first picture, and they caption it with, "Nailed it" or when people ask a question, claiming they are asking for a friend. Both of those things make me laugh. I also read inspirational quotes and see the "Goin' longs" of others from my past and present. That is another term coined by Grandaddy James. You know, see what everybody is up to.

Facebook provides me with all sorts of things. The "Do You remember?" feature allows me to recollect times from my childhood. I smile when I see things like the Snoopy Sno-Cone machine I had or the stationary horse toy just like the one I had in my room as a little kid. My cousin, LaVita, shared a necklace charm photo frame from this feature. I let her know I used to wear one containing her baby picture. I gave her the charm. Yes, I still had it and I knew where it was over 30 years later. I have also gotten some pretty good one pot recipes and cleaning tips from Facebook.

Chapter 9

One person was not included in my 2014, visit to New York, collection of photos. Not due to lack of a picture, of course I have an old picture of her. I just didn't know I was going to see her that day. I will make sure she is included in a future Throwback Thursday post.

On June 26, 2016, I went to my friend Janene's graduation party when she got her MBA. I already knew her sister and her mother but the rest of the crowd felt so warm. It was like being with my own mother's family. At Janene's MBA party, a few of her family members and close friends did tribute speeches. It was so touching. I thought, there I go, it's time to go talk to someone again. As I listened to people give speeches and share kind words about Janene, I had to look away as I started to get teary-eyed. Funny that is was three years later to the exact date that I was crying at work when someone retired.

In late June 2016, I told Ma I was going through a 40 Metamorphosis. I made up that name. I'm surprised I did not make up something that rhymed. I'll be 40 in a month and a half and I just feel different. I feel good, really good. I think she is going through it with me. She went to her 40-year high school class reunion. She had never been to a class reunion. Sandra really enjoyed her class reunion. I was not aware of this ahead of time, but

Ma graduated with Uncle Garry, so he attended one of the reunion events she was at as well.

I received an invitation in the mail for a 3-day MS event. It listed a flat rate for couples. I have no problem going by myself, however I do have a problem being charged the same price whether I am by myself or I have a companion. I called Ma to tell her of my dilemma. She said she would think about who could go with me. She finally said, if I don't find anyone else to go, she would go with me. That seemed like a begrudging acceptance, but I'll take it. See with the exception of my most recent Walk MS event, she has never been to a MS function since I have been diagnosed. Other family members have attended MS dinners with me, Aunt Ann, Aunt Elsie, my brother, R-Jay, and my cousins, Jennifer, Jessica, and Frank, Jr. On more than one occasion, I heard through the grapevine that Sandra is in denial. I'm certain I was in denial for a while too. Well it's time to get over that. I guess her going to this event is a part of our joint 40 Metamorphosis.

June 30, 2016 my first "real" #tbt post. Of course, I had to go backwards. It was a picture of me and Ma from when I was only 2 years old. She used to cut the bottoms off of her old jeans and then put them on our heads like a bandana. It was so fun and yes, I remember that too. That's one of my favorite pictures because it was my first Special Times activity. The picture is displayed in a frame in my living room right now. That day I put a short description of exactly what was going on in the photograph. Future posts will simply only have a #tbt label, no description of the event. My plan is to let the pictures speak for themselves.

I always keep a pen and paper in my car. At first, those items were getting utilized more than ever. Before long, I started saving book notes in the calendar section of my smartphone whenever I was away from my laptop. I would usually add them to my calendar using my smartphone recorder. Since I remember dates so well, I started listing all of my book notes in my smartphone under one particular date. Mysteriously, all of my notes were deleted from my smartphone on that particular day. To no avail, I tried to remember some of my anecdotes. My resolution was to start saving notes in my smartphone calendar under a different date. Weeks later, all of those notes somehow were deleted too. I'm sure both instances were a case of user error. You would think I would have begun typing items right away, instead of saving them under a different date. Again, it takes me some time to come up with some things that should be so obvious. After brainstorming, I had another "aha" moment as I remembered this cloud thing. I had R-Jay's girlfriend Christine, helped me retrieve items from the iCloud and I was back in business. Thank you Apple. How can I write a book titled Figure It Out and me not be able to figure this one out? This issue has taught me to transfer ideas from my smartphone to my laptop frequently, rather than fill up a particular calendar date and risk the items disappearing once again. If they do disappear, at least I know how to retrieve them now. Aside from asking people if I could use their name, "if" I wrote a book about my MS journey, I had not shared my book writing idea. So, if Christine knew what she had retrieved, she never let on.

Once I think I have finally woken up for the last time, I check my smartphone. I keep the phone in the

128

bed with me as a precaution. I hope this never happens, but if I can't move one morning I may need to call someone, probably R-Jay, for assistance. Before I attempt to get out of the bed, I interlock my fingers and stretch them way above my head towards the ceiling. That is when I remember. I do this because many times when I wake up I have twitching muscles and my body is having all kinds of spasms. On some days when I get out of bed I look like a newborn animal trying to walk for the first time.

I learned from a nurse that visited one of my support groups to schedule a "sit-down" as part of my morning ritual. You know, sit on the toilet and try to "go." That is easy to remember now that my Squatty Potty is in the bathroom to remind me. After completing my morning grooming routine, which includes applying sunscreen on sunny days, I go to Sheltering Arms. Once I return home, I have lunch, which is usually something I can microwave or put in the oven or toaster oven. Since I am unable to easily stand for extended periods of time, that limits the amount of cooking I do. After lunch, I usually fall asleep on the couch to some TV show. I usually don't go back upstairs until I am ready to retreat for the evening. If I know I have to go somewhere, even if it is later in the day, I will get dressed before I head downstairs for the first time. The exception being days I go to Sheltering Arms. Depending on where I have to go, I may even just wear my gym attire in order to avoid going back upstairs to change.

When I told my brother, R-Jay, that I don't even go back upstairs to brush my teeth after my nap, he suggested I keep a toothbrush downstairs. Again, why didn't I think I that? I now have an over the door caddy in the laundry room with an extra toothbrush and other hygiene products. After the umpteenth time of trying to fit the toothpaste tube squeezer in the over the door caddy in the laundry room, I finally realized I had to put it in upside-down, with the tube facing out. I also keep an extra scarf and other hair supplies downstairs. That way I can freshen up my do before leaving the house, if I happened to take a nap that day. I keep these items in the salon in my house. Okay, not a salon. It is just one section of the dining room table that used to be in Grandma's house.

On July 1, 2016, I started driving up North. Prior to my trip, I let my cousin, Jamila, know I would be coming to New York soon. I hoped she was not kidding when she told me to reach out to her the next time I was in her area. My first stop was to visit my friend, Tichanda and her two boys in New Jersey. I also stopped by her mother's place. They were all in the process of packing up preparing to make a move to Tennessee. After New Jersey, I drove to New York and stayed with my friend, Regina and her husband, Charles' family again. This time there was a heart-shaped cut out, with a picture of a foot on it, and the letters MS were written. That picture is posted on the cork board in my home office. The least I could do was visit her for her 40th birthday weekend after she drove to Virginia alone, just to do Walk MS with me. I went equipped with audiobooks from my local library. I enjoy reading, so I never even considered listening to audiobooks. Turns out my local library did carry the genre of books I liked in audiobook format. The last time I went to the library was when I was doing research for my MBA Thesis.

Charles, who is very handy, installed an air conditioner unit and moved a futon into what became my temporary room in preparation for my 2014 visit. Keeping with tradition, he installed stair railings at the front door in anticipation of my 2016 visit. Regina even purchased my favorite snacks of Sprite, M&M's, and Doritos just for me. During this visit, Regina informed me that when she saw me in Philadelphia in 2013, she thought I would be in a wheelchair in six months. Now she does not see me wheelchair bound anytime in the near future. She is famous for telling me stuff way after the fact. After I had lost a lot of weight and maintained the loss for a while, she said one time she flew from New York to Virginia and did not recognize me at the airport because I had gained so much weight. I just laughed when she told me that one. During this visit, we went to Waryas Park or down the river in Poughkeepsie to see the 4th of July fireworks. I just love fireworks and I was the only person making the "Ooh" and "Aah" noises, including the kids that were near us. Eventually I kept myself quiet as I wore my red, white, and blue, star-shaped headband. On this trip, I also met my friend, Aloma, at a diner for breakfast. When she walked up to my car window, she nearly scared me to death. I told you I have become jumpy.

During the same trip, I went to Jamila's house for what I thought was a simple dinner with her family. She always posts pictures of all of the great food she prepares on a regular basis. So, when she asked me what I wanted for dinner my answer of fried fish was easy to come up with. I've seen that picture on Facebook several times. Apparently, she has found her passion and it is cooking. Jamila had planned a surprise party for me. We did not grow up together, how did she possibly know I love a surprise party? Before I was aware of the party, I sat on the porch talking to her husband, Eddy. I later found out, she had left us alone to go pick up the cake she had ordered from a neighbor. The party was a MS celebration for those that were not able to attend Walk MS in April. I later found out our Aunt Rachel helped her with what to have displayed on the cake. It was decorated in the signature MS color of orange.

Friends from Jamila's church were even in attendance. She had invited one of my uncles, Clyde's sister Gloria, and her husband, Hugh. Clyde was not there. We had our Special Times lunch the previous day. I sat at the head of the table. After dinner, we sat outside enjoying fried dough (funnel cake) prepared by her aunt's business, Michelle's Traveling Treats. The same aunt I had met in Virginia in February. While we enjoyed our fried dough, our uncle entertained us, as he always had. My father came from a family of 13 kids and in my opinion this particular uncle is the funniest. He even made me do a walk test to the mailbox. He had heard that I wasn't walking very well at all. He was happy to see me walking so well. He even made me call Sandra in Virginia. He made her laugh as well and told her he was happy to see me walking so well. We went back inside the house. It was now time for cake. Jamila and Gloria even serenaded me before we cut the cake. I cried like a baby during that whole time. My uncle comforted me as I cried. Who knew he had a soft side too? He later told me I didn't walk far enough for him during my walk to the mailbox test. There that amusing behavior I had grown accustomed to.

July 2016 is when I really started to notice an improvement in my walking. Maybe I was shaking before, but I am certainly not shaking now. I used to walk in a store and immediately gravitate toward a shopping cart, to use as a walker, in order to navigate through the store. Preferably the smaller carts, if they are available. This is what I had been doing for the last several years. Now if I am only going to the grocery store for one thing and I already know exactly where it is located, I do not always even need a shopping cart. I often take a trip to Kroger grocery store just for the grapes. I have a knack when it comes to making a good grape selection. My friend, Kasharne, calls me the Grape Whisperer. Though I am definitely walking better, often when walking down a hallway, I usually touch the wall along the length of the hallway, as a way to steady myself. The exception to me using the wall as a guide is when I am walking through the hall of Sheltering Arms with walking poles. I have even gone so far as to sit on the floor in a store. So far, I have only done it if the store is carpeted.

My brother, R-Jay, calls me a corn ball. I think it is so cute. I say I am whimsical, quirky, and eccentric and wear those titles like a badge of honor. When I used to see ISO or HMU on Facebook I would have to look it up to know what was being referenced. I learned there's an app for that too and July 2016 I installed the free app on my smartphone. I now know they mean In Search Of and Hit Me Up. My friend, Aloma, used HMU when we were making breakfast plans earlier this month. Apparently, she thought I was as cool as she is. She's known me since third grade, she should know better by now. I am such a square.

On many occasions, I used to go to family events out of obligation but I wasn't really feeling it. I would go to a cookout, show my face, eat of course, and then leave early even if I didn't have anywhere to be the following day. Another thing I do to try to keep my mind sharp is to pay in cash and try to figure out my change before it is displayed on the cash register. In addition, this whole swipe or chip nonsense is quite a quandary. Another issue at the cash register is that my hand coordination issues won't allow me to easily and accurately type my email address so that I can receive an emailed receipt, rather than a printed one.

On July 17, 2016, we had a family roller skating birthday party for Shanta's son, Jordan. During the party, Xavier, Jr. asks me, "Why aren't you skating?" Knowing I skated at the last family roller skating party we had in 2007. In fact, I used to enjoy both roller skating and ice skating.

I was certain he knew I had MS, but I replied, "Because I have MS and I can barely walk, I'm certainly not going to put skates on."

He said, "We can help you." How nice was that, especially coming from a teenager?

I said, "Nah I'm good, but thank you." I was so touched, I told several people about that conversation we had. His parents were so proud of him. I don't know why I was reluctant to tell people I had MS, everyone, even non-family members, have been so nice and helpful. My family often has a gathering after the main event. This time the after-party was at Aunt Marian's house.

I'll admit, getting used to a minimal, fixed income and only getting paid once a month has been quite an adjustment. It is frustrating not being able to pay every single bill down to $0 every month like I used to do. I never thought I could be so happy with this little amount of money. But I am. I try not to blame MS for all of my issues, but it attributes to a lot of them.

Years ago, Aunt Ann suggested I wear a MedicAlert bracelet. "I'm not doin that," was my response. I called to tell her I sometimes wear an orange MS bracelet, my version of a MedicAlert bracelet. I texted her a picture of one of those bracelets. She approved. I do a lot of stretching, especially after I have been sitting for a couple of minutes. I often have to get up and stretch my legs. I also do hand exercises while I am sitting down. Some things I just don't do anymore because it takes too much energy and I want to preserve energy at all cost. I haven't gotten my eyebrows arched since March 2015 when R-Jay and I visited our cousin, Leticia, in Alabama. In fact, I tried eyebrow threading for the first time that day. I usually got my eyebrows waxed. Anyway, I pride myself on being on time. Now I have to arrive extra early, especially if I'm alone, in order to secure a decent parking space. VIP parking spots tend to be at a premium at some places. I have not been able to attend every event or attend every party I have been invited to, either because of parking struggles or seating restrictions, but I try to attend most things.

The Throwback Thursday photographs are taken at least six weeks in advance. I also enter in my smartphone calendar which snapshots to post on each upcoming week. As I search through my photo albums to make Throwback Thursday selections, I relive moments and experiences that I did not remember. I saw a few pictures with people that I did not recall taking. Perhaps my long-term memory is not as on point as I once thought. I make my Throwback Thursday post any time after 12 a.m., since I am up usually several times through the night.

On July 23, 2016, I went to a birthday party cookout with Ma. Uncle Ralph and Uncle Dwight were there too. When I look back on pictures from that day, I notice I am sitting down in the first few pictures when it was really hot outside. I had a cooling towel around my neck, but it was no match for the harsh Summer heat. I am standing up in the pictures taken later in the day once the temperature had cooled down a bit. Ma was at the beverage cooler and asked me what color Gatorade I wanted to drink. I told her orange because it's the MS color. I guess I was loud because someone came over to me asking if I had MS. Turns out they had MS as well. We ended up talking for a long while.

On July 26, 2016, I woke up about 6:00 a.m. having to use the bathroom. When I went to step out of bed, I immediately hit the floor. As I think back, it was like a scene from a cartoon, but it certainly wasn't funny at the time. Turns out my left leg had gone completely numb. I reached to the bed and grabbed the phone, just in case. No, I didn't call R-Jay, but I was glad my phone was within reach if I needed to call someone. Once I confirmed that I wasn't really hurt and only had a skinned knee, I realized I still had to use the bathroom. I was still unable to stand. That had never happened to me. I've had numb or tingling appendages, but never the entire leg. I crawled to the bathroom, like a baby, careful not to further injure my skinned knee. While holding onto the toilet, I used my good right leg to climb up on the toilet. By the time I finished using the bathroom, feeling was restored in my left leg. I got up, washed and dried my hands, and returned to my bedroom. This episode was not at all like my December 2012 fall. The old me would have sat on the floor crying her eyes out. The new me was just mad I had skinned my left knee. No time for woe is me!

I had a Tai Chi exercise class at Sheltering Arms in a few hours. That is a good exercise to help with range of motion and balance. Anyway, I turned to Married...With Children reruns on the TV and reset the sleep timer. Eventually, I fell back to sleep. I always try to make sure I get my bearings before trying to climb out of bed even in the middle of the night. I tend to run into walls on the way to the bathroom if I start to head there before I get my bearings, but sometimes the urgency to get to the destination supersedes my desire to make sure I don't run into anything.

On July 30, 2016, I went to a National MS Society fundraising event. Fellow MSer, Kemel was line dancing at his job. When I was about to leave, he shared with the dancers my diagnosis year and told them we dance for people like her that can't dance. The other dancers didn't need to know I couldn't keep up with Kemel before I was diagnosed. After the event, I called Uncle James to tell him how much fun the event was. You see, Uncle James and Kemel were former coworkers. It is such a small world.

On July 31, 2016 R-Jay and I attended one of our Special Times concerts. It was an old-school artist along with a new school artist. We both enjoyed both of the performers. It was my gift to R-Jay for his June birthday.

I decided I wanted to try to get out of an escape room as my 40th birthday event. Once I told R-Jay's girlfriend, Christine, what I wanted to do for my birthday, she emailed me a Groupon for it. The escape room is something I saw on an episode of the TV show *Impractical Jokers*. You are locked in a room and you have to work as a team to solve clues to get out of the room. I asked R-Jay if he would join me, of course he agreed. Later R-Jay asked if I was aware there would probably be a lot of standing. He sure does love his big sister. I told him I figured there would be a lot of standing. The truth is I had to do something outside of my comfort zone for my 40th and I would figure it out.

Unlike Ronda, I don't have a set time limit for my coping with MS Throwback Thursday project. I am starting out with my own personal supply of photographs, not going into Ma's stash, at least not yet. I haven't decided yet but I may post pictures from Ma's photograph collection after I have gone through my own collection.

When I told Christine I was possibly going to continue to do Throwback Thursday until I ran out of photographs she sarcastically said, "So eight years?" She was totally joking but she might actually have been more right than she ever imagined. I am not even posting every photo I have and I am only posting one snapshot per week. Maybe only posting one picture a week will have folks looking forward to the next week. At least I hope so. I may be putting too much thought into this, but that's what I do. I overthink most things. I have always been like that. Since I am going to continue to post current pictures along with my throwbacks, people may not even notice I'm doing a thing.

My oldest photo albums have been kept in a hope chest that sits on one of my closet floors. The hope chest is white and was purchased to match my first set of childhood furniture, including my canopy bed. I only wanted a hope chest because my cousin, Ta'Wana, got one. My first 20 or so photo albums are numbered so that will help with my project. The first few were labeled by my friend, Regina. She has great handwriting. I labeled the remainder, those labels are not so nice. The photo albums are sprawled out in chronological order, on the bed in my spare bedroom. There are currently over 30 photo albums and I constantly take pictures. With the exception of a couple of elementary school class pictures and one of R-Jay and me with Santa Claus, I'm not going to post any professional pictures. Some people will probably be happy about that. I have quite a collection of other people's old, school pictures and family photographs. The 8 X10 photo albums containing those pictures are not in chronological order like my regular snapshots. Throwback Thursday will be all of my own snapshots, taken with my own camera, mostly taken by me, except the ones that include me. We didn't do selfies back in the day.

I created a vision board. This is a collage of what you want your life to be or what you want to do or have. Visualization is a powerful mind exercise so I put it in a place I can look at it often. It started out small using a 12 X 12 scrapbook page. Once things started coming to fruition, I upgraded to a very large piece of poster board. I included both words and pictures. Some things are items I had on my bucket list. I use adhesive runners (glue sticks) to affix items to the large poster board. I try to remember to look at it every day as a source of inspiration for goals I want to accomplish. Since MS related magazines are the only ones I receive in the mail, I used free magazines and newspapers from Kroger and my local library to complete my board. I could not find everything in those magazines. I cheated a little bit and ended up having to print a couple of pictures from the Internet. I used large Command strips to attach the vision board to the wall in my home office upstairs. I understand some people do a vision board for things they want to complete in a particular year. I chose to do a more long-term board. My plan is to change the words or pictures on the board once I have achieved a particular goal or completed a task.

Chapter 10

On August 6, 2016, the Saturday before my 40th birthday, I went out to dinner with my friend, Kasharne, as I had done every year since we met. As a birthday gift, she gave me a framed picture of us from her 40th birthday party a couple of months prior. The frame had inspirational sayings all around it. I did not realize until that dinner that we both had on animal print shirts at her birthday gathering. That picture is hanging on the wall in my home office. Anyway, I ordered dessert and posted our party on Facebook.

After dinner, she said her husband, Jay, was bartending a party and we were getting in free because it was my birthday. When we got to the party location, Jay came outside and we looped arms and went to the prom together. When I walked upstairs, everyone yelled, "Surprise!" I thought how nice that Jay had his friends give me a shout-out for my birthday. I saw Aunt Ann, then started seeing other people that should not be at this party. It was all for me. Turns out Jay was bartending a party, my party. Then Regina walked out. My knees buckled, good thing Ma was there to catch me. R-Jay had thrown me a surprise 40th birthday party. Not only had he coordinated the party, he was also the DJ. Regina informed me she would be spending the night at my house.

As I'm in shock looking around the room. I don't know how he did it, but I sure was happy he had done it.

Of course, the tears flowed and Janene and Lona were both there, we had to once again joke about me having to go talk to someone. I had seen some of the attendees the previous day. In fact, I had sat next to my friend, Tonya, at the place we were the previous day. She mentioned that I told her five times I was turning 40 on Sunday. I even talked to some of my guests earlier that day. Regina even texted me when I was having dinner with Kasharne.

At the party, Uncle Ralph reminded me that I had said I love surprises, referring to the party my cousin, Jamila, had thrown for me in New York the prior month. Sandra's friend, Eileen, once again graced us with her decorating talents. Everything was decorated in my favorite color, purple. She even filled up candy dishes with items and signs related to being 40. I had a gum bowl with a sign 40 & Poppin. Another dish filled with lollipops read, Turning 40 Sucks. I didn't think it would, but that was very clever. They were even better than the candy bars R-Jay had at his VCU graduation party.

One of the parts that made me very happy was the cake. The picture on the cake was my Throwback Thursday photograph from two days prior. It was a picture of me from when I was 10 years old at Walt Disney World. My cousin, Diane, had commented I look like our grandmother, Agnes, in that photograph. My cousin, LaVita, had posted some of the party on Facebook Live, so people that were unable to make it to the party, could watch the event unfold. True to form, months later, Regina told me my leg buckling reaction to seeing her was worth the 16-hour commute, 8 hours each way. The party of the year is what I call it now. All facets of my life were represented, friends from NY, Surry, VCU, previous employers, and a couple from the Richmond MS Community. The party was everything. That was a phenomenal day for me. Hands down, my new favorite day. For real, for real this time.

At 12:14 a.m., my birth time, on August 7, 2016 while still at my surprise party, I posted a picture of me in a bikini. Talk about a 40 Metamorphosis. I had never worn a bikini outside of the house. I used to temporarily lose weight to fit into an outfit that I bought on sale to wear to a particular event. As competitive as I am, you would really think I would have played a sport. Me not playing sports must have been due to that overweight thing I used to have. The post of me in a bikini on my 40th birthday had nothing to do with me being lewd or sexy. It had everything to do with me celebrating my over 70-pound weight loss and the fact that I have been able to keep it off for a few years. I keep an old badge picture of me, at my largest, with long hair, in my car.

Now I have no choice but to keep the weight off since I do not have the income to buy all new clothes. Good thing I like going to Sheltering Arms. When Regina and I got to my house she had to move the massive collection of photo albums before she could get into bed. I was up watching Facebook Live videos and other videos from my party, like I hadn't just left there. I just kept saying, "Stop Playing!" and "I can't take this!" on the videos. R-Jay's girlfriend, Christine, even got a video of my stunned, deer caught in the headlights, expression after hearing "Surprise!" and my legs buckling when I saw Regina. I felt so bad when I saw video of myself walking right by people and not acknowledging them. People had traveled a long way to come to my party. I was so overwhelmed at the party. I only got two hours of sleep that night.

Regina left my house first thing Sunday morning; it was her wedding anniversary weekend after all. I was wearing my Made in 1976 t-shirt. You know, the one Regina gave me for my birthday when she came for Walk MS back in April. She really knew how to play off a surprise; she had been in cahoots with R-Jay the whole time. My first stop was to pick up Aunt Elsie and my cousin, Jennifer. Next, we went to the local church so I could donate school supplies. Regina even brought me additional school supplies to put on the donation bus. I had told her of my donation plans the prior week. My cousin, Jennifer took pictures of me on the donation bus and the person in charge of collecting the donations took pictures of me approaching the bus. I even made the church's Facebook page. Ma's friend, Eileen, told me I probably would. R-Jay ended up not coming to the escape room. Two SUV loads of Christine's family from Brooklyn, New York had come to the party, so he was entertaining. Plus, he was tired from the party. Aunt Elsie, Jennifer, and Kasharne accompanied me to the escape room adventure. We managed to get out of the escape room with over four minutes remaining. Aunt Elsie was glad R-Jay didn't make it. She was his replacement and she had a ball.

Next, I went by myself to take advantage of some of the birthday freebies I had been emailed. Then I went to Ma's house. I ate some of the delicious food she had made for my party, as well as a piece of my Throwback Thursday inspired birthday cake. I was too stuffed for dinner or dessert at the party the previous night. People were telling Kasharne not to feed me, but she knew I would think something was up if dinner was not part of our birthday plans. It was then time to retire to my house. Eileen even came over that night to bring me some of the party decorations as keepsakes. Being Ma's friend did not give her project immunity. Upon my request, she was kind enough to change the battery in my carbon monoxide detector.

The smoke detectors I have are the ones that last for 10 years without having to change the battery. I can't tolerate the noise they make when the battery needs to be changed. I have gone as far as wear ear plugs to stifle the sound made when it is time to change the batteries, if it is time to go to sleep and I don't want to risk a trip up the stepstool. I was still so hype about the party, I talked a hole in Eileen's head that night.

Sometimes I joke that someone is going to give me low self-esteem by something they may have said. It has yet to happen. I have high self-esteem and plenty of confidence. I often tell people, "You don't know me!" The truth is I'm pretty predictable and I've been okay with that. Time to change things up a bit. My friend, Kasharne, was totally surprised that I posted a picture of me in a bikini on Facebook. I already had that idea before the party. I guess this unpredictable side is all part of my 40 Metamorphosis.

On August 11, 2016, Regina made her Throwback Thursday debut. I posted our first picture together. The one from my scrapbook of us wearing matching outfits on a school field trip. The timing of that snapshot had

145

nothing to do with the fact that she came to my birthday party. The decision to post that photograph on that particular day had been made several weeks before. I'm going to see if I can use that snapshot on the cover of this book.

On August 14, 2016 R-Jay and I went to go see Uncle Vernis in New Jersey. The trip to see Uncle Vernis was planned weeks before my 40th birthday party. Uncle Dwight called Uncle Vernis while R-Jay and I were there. Uncle Vernis made the telephone conversation brief and got back to his company. Uncle Vernis also told us Aunt Rachel calls him every Monday. On the way home I was going to text Aunt Rachel that we visited Uncle Vernis. R-Jay told me not to so he would have something else to share during their Monday conversation. Uncle Vernis is not the average 86-year old, he has a Facebook page. After our visit, he put a post on Facebook that R-Jay and I had made him one of the happiest men in the world. That made me feel so good.

The last week in August 2016 I babysat Kasharne and Jay's daughters Kayden and McKenzie. Kayden knew I was going to camp soon. I'm sure she thought it was real camping in the woods. She asked if I packed an emergency medical kit. "How insightful for an 8-year-old," is what I thought at the time. I knew I had a few of those from pharmaceutical company events. After our conversation, I packed one with Band-Aids and such. Luckily, I did not need it but it was a good idea to have one all the same.

On September 4, 2016 Sandra and I attended a painting birthday party for her friend, Eileen. Some of Sandra's other coworkers were there as well. Me and Sandra's paintings were both a hot mess, mine more than hers. Neither of us has any artistic talent. It was the second time I had attended a paint party. The first time was when I took my friend, Kasharne, for her birthday and my skills had not improved. We even got a swag bag and gifts at her party. The swag bag contained a colorful, jeweled selfie stick. I already had one, but it wasn't nearly this fancy. The venue was decorated very well. I guess her daughter got some decorating skills from her mother.

One day I went to visit Aunt Rachel and Uncle Oliver. Aunt Rachel shared with me pictures she had colored from adult coloring books. I had seen this advertised as a new big thing, but I hadn't tried it. My immediate thought was that maybe that is something I will try. I attended an adult coloring class at my local library. The same library I go to for my audiobooks. For someone with no artistic talent, I sure do attend a lot of artistic things. The class was an hour long. Maybe "class" is not the right word. A bunch of adults were in a room together, everyone selects a picture, and you color it using the colored pencils provided. It was very relaxing and I even think it helped to get my creative juices flowing for this book. The program monitor was playing Stevie Wonder songs over the speakers in the classroom. The hour time frame was perfect. That is just about how long my right hand had before it was about to give up having the ability to grip the colored pencils. After class I texted Aunt Rachel my completed picture and told her she inspired me. She replied that she liked the colors and told me to keep up the good work. At that same library, I later volunteered to do voter registration with my friend, Paula.

On September 9, 2016, I traveled to the 4-H Center at Smith Mountain Lake in Wirtz, Virginia for a MS Weekend Escape. It was the Brian Mason Respite Camp, hosted by this fellow MSer in partnership with the National MS Society. The camp started with about 40 people as a way to provide respite to caregivers and has now morphed into an event for over 200 people including MSers, their families, caregivers, and friends giving them an opportunity to enjoy a weekend that emphasizes fun and relaxation. It was about a four-hour drive that I made by myself. All of the attendees received a t-shirt marking the year of the event.

This was my first year attending. I just heard about the camp for the first time in 2015, but I was unable to attend that year. 2016 was the 20th year of the event. I told Sharon from my support group about camp. She stated based on the pictures from previous years, she was under the impression that camp was primarily for people with mobility devices. The pictures did not dissuade me, but I hoped that was not the only audience that camp would appeal to since I did not have a device of my own. I did not want to be wrongly taking someone's spot. When I told an employee of the National MS Society of Sharon's concerns they said that the pictures show a lot of people in wheelchairs so that people requiring those devices knew it was accessible to them. Of course, the flip side is that those pictures act as a deterrent for other's not needing a device. It didn't discourage me from wanting to attend. I had heard camp was a lot of fun from members of the Richmond MS Community.

Prior to the start of camp, they had emailed a schedule of available activities and I selected events for every hour of the day. I liked the fact you could do as little or as much as you wanted to do. With that being said, I will make sure to incorporate naps or rest breaks the next time I attend. Since it was my first year, I tried to attend everything. Now that I am not working, I take great comfort in the fact that now everything I do is optional.

Respite Camp really gave me a chance to be off the grid. Well not totally, but semi-off the grid. I did talk to Ma Friday night and I sent a few text messages during the weekend. I did not watch any television, go on Facebook, or go online at all. It really was a chance to relax for the most part.

I met a lot of new people at camp and most were positive and happy to be there. I saw a guy that I used to work with years ago. It turns out he had already been diagnosed before we met and I never knew. He tried to show me how to text with my thumbs. I did fine during the lesson, but was unable to continue. Based on the fact that I was speaking to so many people, he said I was like the Mayor of MS Ville. That made me laugh. The truth is, there were several people at camp from the Richmond MS Community.

Camp included a great event called Cinderella's Closet. This event is put on by MSAV (Multiple Sclerosis Alliance of Virginia). You get to pick out formal wear. They have items for men and women in every size. You also get to pick out shoes, jewelry, purses, all of your accessories. I selected a strapless number, since I had never purchased anything like that. They even alter the dress to fit you. They have people there to do your hair, nails, and makeup. I decided against hair, nails, and makeup and chose to wear my own New Balance sneakers with my formal gown. Even with the sneakers, I looked quite snazzy if you ask me. MS camp is the only place I would ever wear sneakers with a ball gown and feel completely comfortable. I was with "my people." Cinderella's Closet can be a life changing event for some that would normally not ever dress up.

I was elated to find out that I got to keep my new dress and jewelry. I thought they were just items on loan. The camp party included makeovers. The most drastic makeover was a guy I had seen all weekend. He had long hair that was tied in a bandana and wore jeans and a t-shirt. During the reveal, he sported a fresh, new haircut and dress clothes. You guessed it, I cried. I had never met or even seen this man before this weekend. MS Respite Camp lead to an increase in Facebook friends and they did not even know about Throwback Thursday.

MS Respite Camp had numerous fun activities. One such activity was bingo the first night. Prior to attending, I was informed there would be a bingo marker competition. With my friend Regina's suggestion of Girl Scout swaps, my cousin, Jennifer being able to see and reach items on the top shelf in the craft store, and R-Jay's girlfriend Christine's artistic skills, I presented fake smores with smiley faces as my bingo markers. I won the competition and received a charm bracelet as my prize. I often have to join forces to figure things out.

Camp also included relaxation activities like massages, but it was also informative. I learned that a MS assistance device is a tool to help with your mobility and allows participation to occur and not a deterrent item that should be seen as a weakness. Maybe my theme park days aren't over after all. Though I learned it is just a tool, I know myself and I know that if I got one of those tools to use on a daily basis, I would begin to rely on it and not work so hard to walk better on my own. For this reason, I will continue to work on getting stronger.

When I was packing up my car to leave camp, a kid I didn't know asked if I needed help. I accepted and he lifted the suitcase into my trunk. I know they had separate sessions for the kids that weekend. Perhaps they had been instructed to assist people with our particular physical limitations. Maybe he was just a nice kid that was raised right, either way I was grateful for the help. My car broke down at Wendy's on the way back from camp on Sunday. A couple from the Richmond MS Community came and checked on me when they left MS Respite Camp. It was a huge ordeal. I was supposed to get home at 2 p.m. and I did not get home until 8 p.m. My brother, R-Jay, came and picked me up. This still did not break my spirit. I went to Sheltering Arms on Tuesday telling everyone about how great MS Respite Camp had been.

A care/support partner (family and friends of people with MS) from the Richmond MS Community offered to take me to go pick up my car once the repairs were completed. By Wednesday evening, the stress of the car situation finally had me upset. I am only human. After venting to my friends, Kasharne and Regina, I took a few deep breaths and realized I am too blessed to be stressed. R-Jay let me borrow his spare car while mine was in the shop.

For years, I have had long, permed hair. I used to say "Long hair, don't care." I am now sporting a natural hair style or no maintenance braids. Now it's "Big hair, don't care." If it is raining before I leave home, I will grab my windbreaker or rain slicker with the hood. Holding an umbrella usually throws off my equilibrium. If it starts raining while I am already out, I have ponchos, compliments of a pharmaceutical company, in my car. There is also a rain coat and a couple of umbrellas in my car. The lady that does my hair is like my counselor and she doesn't even know it. She is unaware of my crying episodes and me having to talk to someone. She has become that someone. On the occasions when I do my hair myself, I use flexi rods, the soft, flexible rollers. Even my rollers are MS orange, okay orange and purple.

On September 5, 2016, I went to Lewis Ginter Botanical Garden for their LEGO exhibit. I talked to a parking attendant and was able to secure a parking space right outside of the garden door. I just love the creative things made with LEGO bricks. I was only able to see the first couple of giant LEGO brick structures closest to the entrance.

During a rare breakfast-time pharmaceutical company meeting, I heard the phrase "Paying a MS tax" being used. These breakfast events are where I first started eating yogurt. I normally don't like that consistency of food. I like to add granola to mine. Anyway, the way MS tax was previously explained to me is that MSers only have a certain amount of energy dollars to use each day. You have to try and make sure you do not go over your daily allotment of energy dollars. People also explain this concept using the term spoon theory. Basically, on days you overexert yourself, you may experience a slow recovery the next couple of days.

September 24, 2016 was an unseasonably warm day for this time of the year and I had run a couple of errands. I lost my footing and hit my nose on the wall separating two rooms in my house. It was like someone had grabbed me by my hair and slammed me against the wall. I was grateful that R-Jay's girlfriend, Christine, was there to retrieve an ice pack from the freezer and clean up the blood. There was so much blood. Knowing I respond well to humor, Christine said it looked like a CSI crime scene. A few weeks after the nose incident, I was exiting the storage closet beneath my stairs and I hit my head real hard. Another day I could not take a nap, fearing a concussion.

At the end of September 2016, Ma and I attended the Take Charge Program sponsored by Can Do Multiple Sclerosis. Even with a printed MapQuest and my smartphone I got us lost on the way to Norfolk, Virginia. Ma was driving, but I was supposed to be navigating. Once we finally arrived, I saw people from other events I have attended. I even met a couple that lived down the street from where my car was getting repaired in Lynchburg, Virginia. One couple at the event from

Roanoke, Virginia recognized me from MS Respite Camp. They asked me if I would link my Kroger Community Rewards card to MSAV (Multiple Sclerosis Alliance of Virginia). I agreed. The only thing I knew about the organization was Cinderella's Closet, but it had MS in the name and my card was not linked to any other organization. I figured my purchases of grapes could go towards supporting this non-profit MS organization.

When I shared my positive results about the Squatty Potty, a nurse suggested limiting the use of the Squatty Potty, citing it could lead to hemorrhoid issues. That was not an issue I had, but I feel it is my responsibility to share all possible outcomes, even the negative ones. I didn't really pay attention, since that was not a problem for me. Unfortunately, several months later, I developed hemorrhoids for the first time. It was probably a result of my daily Squatty Potty usage. I should have paid more attention to the nurse's warning. It was still better than the severe constipation I had been experiencing. I had heard hemorrhoids were painful. Luckily, I had no pain with mine. The nurse also suggested double voiding (completely emptying bladder). I was proud to admit I was already doing that.

One particular thing that I learned was Acceptance vs. Adaptation. Now that I have accepted that I have MS, I now look at it as MS affords me the opportunity to be creative and figure out another way to do things. I try to look at challenges and obstacles as an opportunity to try something new. Even with decreased cognitive abilities, I really have to use my noggin. I also learned about self-efficacy. If you think you can do it, you can. I think I can write a book, so here we go.

Ma seemed to enjoy the event, and said she learned some things, especially when the MS care/support partners were separated from the MSers. I did not cry until the last session of the final day. Ma said, "You almost made it." At Take Charge, I wasn't the only one crying this time.

After the Can Do MS Take Charge Program, I invested in some additional tools. I purchased foam tubing to put on my toothbrush for better gripping. Aunt Elsie had told me this kind of contraption existed, but I didn't know the name of what to search for on Amazon until now. I get so tired of brushing my left cheek. I remember one of the speakers from the MS On the Move Luncheon expressed having the same problem. I have tried electric toothbrushes, but I prefer the manual ones. After I cut my desired length of foam tubing, R-Jay's project was to put it on my toothbrush. It did not totally eliminate the brushing of my left cheek, but it greatly decreased that from happening. I also purchased some Crockpot (slow cooker) bags. Earlier this year, Regina had suggested I use my crockpot to make meals. I ordered a crockpot cook book from a fundraiser Kasharne's daughter Kayden had for her school. I hadn't used it yet, but I will now that I have these bags. When I finally got around to making one of the crockpot meals, I set the oven timer while I was using the crockpot. The slow cooker bags really sped up the cleanup process. I also learned that regular ski resorts offer adaptive skiing. I need to look into that.

Chapter 11

I tried grocery pickup. You select your groceries online, pay for them, and schedule a time to pick them up. People from the store even load the groceries in your car for you. It is great for people with physical limitations, like myself. The only energy I have to exert is taking the groceries out of the car and putting them away inside of my house.

When I get home, I would try to put an equal amount of groceries in each hand, cognizant of my equilibrium issues. Now I use Grocery Gripps. They are hands-free straps that allow you to grab several bags at once. I had never seen them before, one of Regina's sisters-in-law shared the video on Facebook and I thought they were a great idea. After I have removed the bags, I put the Grocery Gripps near the front door, so I will remember to put them back in my car. I still go into the grocery store if I am not doing a major shopping trip. Following my cousin Leticia's lead, I tried one of those delivery food services that mail you detailed recipe instructions and all of the ingredients, but I was struggling just to lift the heavy box off of the front porch. Needless to say, I left that idea alone once my Groupon ran out.

A while back, I learned that I should do a big shopping trip early, using my morning legs. Something else I learned the hard way after work one evening. I am able to go to the store in the evening, if I am only picking up a few things. I also try to workout at Sheltering Arms earlier in the day. I guess I have morning brain too. Sometimes I have to sleep on things to be able to make a more clearheaded decision the following day.

I was featured in the volunteer spotlight section of the Fall 2016 *MS Connection Newsletter* published by the National MS Society. They highlighted my volunteer efforts. The picture they used was from the day I went to the Virginia General Assembly. I was wearing a blue business pantsuit. I had bought the suit for a job interview a while ago. I also had on a sheer, orange, scarf inside of my suit jacket.

One Friday morning I went to visit my friend, Keta, in Greensboro, North Carolina. I went to see her oldest son, who was a Senior, play high school football. All weekend I joked that I came to visit her son and not her. She knew better. When I drove back home Sunday, I quickly went to sleep. Monday morning, I fell partially down my flight of stairs. I had been doing too much. I was definitely paying the MS tax for the next couple of days. I was back to my typical self by Wednesday.

On October 27, 2016, I added a Facebook cover photo. Prior to this day, I had never had a cover photo. I used the picture I had taken at MS Respite Camp. Yes, the one where I am in a ball gown wearing sneakers. Though you cannot see the sneakers on Facebook. Other than my Facebook friends that attended MS Respite Camp, no one will know I'm wearing sneakers with my gown. I still have not updated my main profile picture yet.

Late October 2016, Sandra, R-Jay, and I attended a 70s-theme party with several members from our dad's side of the family. Aunt Ann was also in attendance. On October 31, 2016, I went to Sheltering Arms wearing a Halloween costume. I was dressed like a baby. I had on a purple onesie, wore two ponytails and was carrying an oversized rattle and an oversized bottle. I did my normal gym workout that day. I even made it onto Sheltering Arms' Facebook page. After my workout, I ran other errands, as if I was wearing jeans. I arrived at my hairdresser's house and even said "Trick or treat!" I don't know if she thought it was funny or not, but I did. I can't even mislead you and say I purchased the onesie especially for the costume. I actually own three of them and I wear them on those cold Winter nights. Again, not a book stunt. I have worn this exact Halloween costume to work. After work that day, I went to my friend Paula's house wearing my costume and saying "Trick or treat!"

November 2016 started with a friend of mine from Arlington High School, posting a video of a bunch of pictures of us together. Our good old days skiing were amid some of the memories. The next night Sandra and I attended a Sheltering Arms event for people with disabilities. It was a celebration of The Power to Overcome, which is their motto. During that event, I discovered that if I hear a touching story that includes humor, I do not cry. Though the speaker's story was not related to MS, it is the kind of story that would normally have me crying. Maybe that's why Joel Osteen's sermons don't make me cry, because he starts with a joke. Anyway, Ma stayed at my house that night and the next morning she discovered I had left my interior car light on. The following evening, I attended the National MS Society's annual meeting. I was elated both times I saw myself appear on the slideshow displaying the various MS activities I had attended. That evening I found out there would be no MS On the Move Luncheon in Richmond in 2017. I learned that CBS news anchor, Bill Fitzgerald, was one of the top fundraisers for Bike MS. I really appreciate that he has been willing to lend his celebrity to the cause. The next night R-Jay and I attended another Special Times concert. This time the concert was R-Jay's Christmas gift. It was an old-school '90s concert, so I had seen some of the artists already.

The week ended with my friend, Kasharne, her husband Jay, and me attending a masquerade soiree hosted by her sorority. Kasharne and I even wore our Mardi Gras masks. It was a fundraiser and the proceeds were to benefit scholarships and be used for other public service initiatives. Kasharne met me at my car and we walked inside together. Luckily, I left the party early. I had left my lights on again, the exterior ones this time. I was just happy the battery was not dead after leaving lights on two different times. That was a good week for me.

Even though last week was jam-packed, I did not have any days of paying the MS tax. I am learning to budget my MS energy dollars more wisely. I interposed a couple of naps in, had a few lunches with friends, and I even continued to work out at Sheltering Arms a couple of those days.

November 8, 2016 was election day. In 2014, I had purchased a seat with a cane attached, specifically to wait in line during the next presidential election, anticipating waiting in line to vote. I say it was one of those just in case purchases, but I believe I had almost given up on trying to retain mobility at that time. I am in a different, much better, head space now. A MS nurse suggested I at least put the cane in the car before I drove to the polls. I didn't do that. I listen to all suggestions, even if I don't always do what has been suggested. Leaving my house, I was confident I would not need it. I guess I could have done early voting, but with no job I am free to go to the polls anytime of the day.

On November 10, 2016, I finally posted the picture that Leticia requested on the first Throwback Thursday. I can see why that's her favorite. I am slumped over Grandma in that picture. Leticia is sweetly holding onto R-Jay's baby hand. Our cousins, Shanta' and LaVita, are in the picture as well. She even shared it with her Facebook friends and added a whole write up about how it is her favorite picture and she even gave me a shout-out for making it my Throwback Thursday post.

The following Saturday, I started the day attending a church health fair with play cousin, Sharna'. I then went to Uncle Ralph's house for a visit. I left there and went to Sandra's house. We attended her company picnic. It was so cold, but I'll take cold over hot any day. Later that evening Sandra, Aunt Ann, and I went to the movies. That was a good day for me. Once I got home to Richmond, I stayed in the house all day Sunday and Monday. I did not want to pay that darn MS tax.

On November 14, 2016, I heard there was going to be a supermoon. This in experience that occurs about every 18 years where the full moon appears extra bright because it is closest to Earth. This is certainly not something I would have checked out in 1998. The first

160

time I went outside to check for the supermoon, it was raining. I waited a few hours, checking every window in my house and saw nothing. It looked brighter than normal outside, but I could not see the moon. After 11 p.m., I drove to the gas station near my house and still could not see the moon. I was really looking forward to it. I guess I will try again in 2034.

It's wild how being diagnosed with a chronic disease changes your whole outlook on life. I remember complaining to my Neurologist that I felt like I was losing my hair. Yes, my edges are thinning, but that seems so insignificant now in the grand scheme of things. Now I will wear my hair up giving no thought to the fact that I have no edges. Well maybe I give it some thought since I am talking about it now. But in general, things that used to seem so important are not now. It puts life in perspective and makes you appreciate the little things even more. If you don't have your health, nothing else matters. I just love that Sheltering Arms has a hand lotion dispenser in their restrooms. There is a bunny rabbit that shows up at my house every Spring. I call it Peter Cottontail. I have no way to know if it is actually the same rabbit, but it makes me smile every year. I also get so excited when I can remember the definition to a word that I seldom use. It's the little things. It is unfortunate that it takes something as drastic as MS to make you gain perspective.

During one of my Bedside Baptist sessions with Joel Osteen I learned he would be in Norfolk, Virginia. I even had someone lined up to go with me and help me navigate through the venue. I would have loved to see that. The only problem is the program was scheduled for

Friday, May 5, 2017, the evening before Walk MS. So much for that. I can't miss Walk MS. I am in competition with myself to have an easier time with the walk in 2017. The person who was going to accompany me mailed me a copy of a Joel Osteen book. I just love unsolicited gifts and was grateful that someone had thought of me. I've added that to the collection of books to read after I publish my own.

On November 24, 2016, Thanksgiving dinner was at Aunt Marian's house. We were about 40 people deep, mostly family, but friends as well. That is usually how Ma's side of the family rolls on the holidays. I hope I never develop sensory overload like some MSers have or I will never be able to attend a family function. Even with that many people, having enough food has never been an issue. We went around and everyone said what they were thankful for. I was crying almost immediately. Clearly, they did not start with a joke. I went last. I was thankful for my 40 Metamorphosis and Throwback Thursday. That day's Throwback Thursday post was a picture of Aunt Elsie and Uncle James when they were dating. Usually I do not preplan Throwback Thursday posts, but I must admit I selected that picture for that particular day. It still was within the general timeframe of nearby Throwback Thursday posts. I felt a picture of family was an appropriate share for that day. I think I'm going to post a family picture every Thanksgiving, since it is always on a Thursday.

I saw a Salvation Army Angel Tree commercial on TV. I remembered being instructed to pay it forward. This was the perfect opportunity for that. I soon realized I wanted to get an Angel. It had been over 10 years since the one time I had participated in Angel Tree. A former coworker of mine was doing it, so I followed her lead. Other than seeing trees in the lobby of former employers, I only recalled seeing them at the mall. Even the TV commercial only listed mall locations. Making the trip to the middle of the mall was not going to happen, so I had to go to Plan B. Some would argue that having a Plan B means you are giving up on Plan A. The Girl Scout in me completely disagrees. I find a Plan B necessary because something unexpected could come up and disrupt everything. No matter how well you think you are preparing, you can't anticipate every possibility.

I remembered my friend, Kasharne, telling me there was an Angel Tree at her job. I had her reserve an Angel for me. I waited until the last minute, so I got whatever was left on the tree. I did not even know what the toys were that were on this eight-year-old boy's gift wish list. Another thing I would have to figure out. Kasharne even offered to come pick up the items and drop them off at her job. I offered to bring them to her, but I think she felt bad because I told her I had a BM accident when I was Angel Tree shopping. I had a BM accident standing up, right in the boys clothing section of Target. It happens. I am usually constipated, but sometimes I have loose stool. Again, sorry if you are squeamish. Not having a gallbladder in addition to the MS may be a cause for this issue. I certainly was thankful I keep a towel in the car that day. I also have a bottle of Febreze in the car. I went home and cleaned up and went back out to finish my shopping. I felt good after my Angel Tree purchases, much better than I have ever felt purchasing gifts for friends or family.

Since I began at Sheltering Arms in January 2016, I have taken every chronic disease or MS class I am eligible for. During these classes, I continue to learn strategies to help me cope with my MS. One of those such strategies to help with sleep was to put Vicks VapoRub on my feet, under a pair of socks. I thought it sounded peculiar, but it actually helped me sleep. My feet are always cold, so I'm usually wearing socks to bed anyway. Another thing I heard about was a MS related bumper sticker. It had a very witty saying that I had never heard. This is the first bumper sticker I have ever had on my car. I have heard of people with MS getting comments, looks, or even receiving notes on their car being asked to leave VIP spots for those in need. I have never had that issue, at least I haven't noticed the looks if ones were sent my way. My friend, Kasharne, said that people have bumper stickers to really emphasize the personality of the individual displaying them. I just thought it was funny, so I guess she was right. From a Sheltering Arms member, I have also learned about magnetic clasps that help you more easily secure your necklaces. I ordered them from Amazon, even though I do not wear a lot of necklaces. I even got some paperback books from a member of one of my Sheltering Arms MS exercise classes. I read these when I am on my recumbent bike.

I have done circuit training, taken Tai Chi, Pilates, and Yoga, including seated therapeutic and laughter Yoga as part of Sheltering Arms classes. I took my first Yoga class at another gym with my friend, Kasharne. It was long before my MS diagnosis and I did not like it back then, but now I see the balance and coordination benefits it offers. Many of these activities can be done in a chair or wheelchair. One instructor urged us to visualize doing the movements, even if you are not physically able to do them. It allows you to do short visualization exercises throughout the day. During one of my MS exercise classes, I learned an exercise that has decreased the instances of me having to lift my left leg in the car before I start driving. I've also learned other exercises that assist with ADLs (Activities of daily living). Regardless of what kind of class I take, it is amazing that I always have to be reminded to breathe. I could always go to another gym where everything is on the bottom floor, it is less expensive, and closer to my house, but I continue to go to Sheltering Arms because I like it and people have told me I inspire them and that makes me feel good. There are also people there that inspire me, that's another reason I keep going.

I ended up taking The Chronic Disease Self-Management Program put on by Senior Connections, The Capital Area Agency on Aging twice. Both classes were held at Sheltering Arms. The first time I took it I was the only person in the class with MS. The second time, all of the participants had MS. I learned valuable information during both classes, but I like being with "my people." I learned about trying to create a more colorful plate and also learned about creating an Action Plan. I purchased a dry erase board that I keep on the side of my refrigerator to record my weekly Action Plan. I read somewhere that a person is 42 percent more likely to complete a task if they write it down. It is even higher if you tell someone. I guess it's all about the accountability factor. All attendees received a Certificate of Completion at the end of both classes.

I have started to appreciate the significance of a good night's sleep. I was so ignorant to think sleep was only important if you have somewhere to be early in the morning. I have found I am less irritable with a good night's sleep. I no longer wear my glasses all night, every night. I do leave my glasses on Wednesday night, in preparation for Throwback Thursday. I leave them on until I have made my Throwback Thursday post, whether it is 12:01 a.m. or 3:00a.m. Sometimes I take Melatonin after I have made my Throwback Thursday post. Most nights I remove them and put them in my bedside caddy along with the box of tissues. I turn the TV volume down real low. I can barely make out any of the characters without wearing my glasses. I set the sleep timer, then I do the VapoRub trick. The only thing I had ever put on my feet under socks was lotion and the occasional Vaseline to extend the time between pedicures. I had a couple of bottles of the VapoRub greaseless cream, not the thick grease Sandra used to put on my chest when I was a sick kid. I was chagrinned to learn that the VapoRub greaseless cream had been discontinued. Good thing I had purchased a few bottles when I did. See buying in bulk saved the day. The vitamin Melatonin has also been successful in helping with my sleep. I still sometimes take over-the-counter sleeping pills if I have any early morning plans because the VapoRub does not always work as fast as the sleeping pills.

I have a spastic gait. Getting up in the middle of the night to use the bathroom or the first few steps I take after waking up from a nap are when I notice it the most. I have heard a Neurologist describe spastic gait as walking like the Tin Man from *The Wizard of Oz*. When I wake up in the middle of the night to go to the bathroom, I still

166

sometimes turn the TV back on, and set the sleep timer for a short amount of time. I guess I have just become accustomed to falling asleep with the TV on. I do not put my glasses back on, so I am back to sleep in no time. I had forgotten how refreshing a good night's sleep could be. I'm still tired a lot during the daytime. Sometimes when I yawn, people will make comments like "It's the weather." I just nod, all the while thinking, "No, it's the MS."

MS fatigue is no joke and affects most MSers. I am no exception. And let's not forget lassitude, a kind of extreme fatigue that has a sudden onset. It takes fatigue to a whole other level. I refer to lassitude as fatigue 2.0. Everything makes me exhausted. Even doing nothing makes me tired, so I figure I might as well do stuff. Fatigue is having no energy and encompasses mental, physical, and emotional exhaustion. It is not about being lazy. Sometimes I feel like I am running on fumes, physically unable to function at all. It gives a whole new meaning to being tired and it is not necessarily related to how active you have been. It seems a nap is not at all refreshing and no amount of sleep will fix the amount of tiredness I feel constantly. One afternoon after my MS exercise class at Sheltering Arms, I went to a support group meeting. After the meeting, Sharon said I looked different and asked me what was going on with me. I said life was good, but nothing was going on with me. She looked me in the eyes, and asked, are you sure? We laughed after I reassured her there was no new man in my life. Clearly, the two of us don't only talk about things related to MS. Then I remembered, I look different because of all of the good sleep I had recently been getting. I had not even realized it was noticeable to the outside world.

I tried acupuncture even though I had heard the real benefit is for people that are in pain and luckily, I don't have any pain. People had told me it didn't hurt, well it hurt me. I should have known better based on pictures I have seen of the procedure. I felt like a human pin cushion. I have no threshold for pain, Sandra calls me a punk and jokes that I am a delicate flower. After I felt I had been there long enough, I started counting the minutes, literally. I was slowly counting to 60, because I was not wearing a watch and my phone was not near me. The acupuncturist showed up before my mental buzzer went off. I'm almost certain I won't try that again.

I tried a mat that you lay on that is thought to improve microcirculation (blood flow). After the initial session, I felt I had improved mobility. It may have just been a case of the placebo affect and me noticing improvement because I believed it was working. In either case I tried the mat a few more times. I also tried a float suggested to me by Sharon from one of my support groups. It was a very relaxing experience where you float effortlessly in a tub of water. Sharon also told me of the great results she experienced after receiving chiropractic adjustments. I yelled the first time the Chiropractor cracked my neck. Not because it hurt, because I was having flashbacks of so many movies where people met their demise like that. I tried a few visits with a Chiropractor, but I was not noticing a difference, so I stopped going. I get the occasional massage. I wish it could be more often, but my shoestring budget won't allow that.

I tried a salt massage. It was a new feature, so it was offered at a discount. I try to keep an open mind, but it turned out to be quite a peculiar experience. I don't know why the word "massage" is used, since no one touches you. I was prepared to get undressed when the employee told me I remain fully dressed. I was then handed a pair of booties. You know, that kind that are on the cable TV commercial showing that is what their technicians wear over their shoes, even though they rarely ever really wear them. Anyway, they gave me the option to select one or two blankets, stating that it could be cool in the room. As the employee opened the door I saw a floor made of large salt granules and four beach-style chairs decorating the dimly lit room. As I entered the room I thought, "This is different." As the door to the room was closed I sat in one of the chairs, covered myself with the blanket, closed my eyes, sat back, and relaxed. Then I heard a loud machine start running. The noise didn't bother me too much, since I am used to the loud sound that accompanies a MRI. During the "massage" I noticed the faintest taste of salt as I licked my lips. Once the loud noise stopped 45 minutes later, I opened my eyes and remained in the room listening to soft music until someone opened the door to retrieve me. I could barely hear the music above the roar of the loud machine. Once I was out of the room, I had to admit it was quite relaxing. The salt massage is specifically for people with dermatological and/or respiratory issues. My interest was piqued when I saw that it reduces inflammation. Even though it is only reducing

inflammation in the airways. As you can see, I will try
pretty much try anything once.

Chapter 12

Back when Janene and I were office-mates on the second floor, I never told her I had MS. One evening I invited her to a pharmaceutical company dinner and let her hear for herself. I don't even recall how I approached the topic. I probably just told her we were going out for dinner. Now that I am retired, Janene still attends pharmaceutical company dinners with me. We joke that the meals are payment for the IT Specialist services that she provides. In actuality, it is our Special Times for us to catch up and she absorbs the material. At one of those events I forgot to tag her on Facebook when we took a selfie before the event began. I don't know how I forgot that, she was sitting right next to me and I attempted to post to Facebook immediately after taking the picture. I noticed the error immediately, deleted the post, and made the correction. Good thing, my friend, Regina, showed me how to delete a Facebook post when I was in New York in July 2016.

During one of those events she gave me a Christmas present of a custom Christmas Tree ornament. She has a business making different craft items. "Made to Survive" was on the front of the ornament. I told her I had recently ordered a shirt with that same slogan on it. My name was on the back of the ornament. She knows that I just adore things with my name on them. My friend, Kasharne, gave me a plastic mug with my name on it when we were freshmen at VCU. I still have it. It is on one of the bookshelves in my home office. I even like those noncredit courses where you get a certificate with your name at the end of the course. Anyway, both the slogan and my name were in the MS color of orange on the ornament. No, I did not cry, but I was close to tears. I have not put up my artificial Christmas Tree since about 2012, it just takes too much effort now. My Lamborghini puzzle is now in the place that used to hold my Christmas Tree. Since all of my Christmas decorations are in my attic, Aunt Elsie suggested I use a paperclip to make an ornament hook. I did so and the ornament is now hanging from one of the fake floral arrangements in my house. Aunt Elsie suggested I get a tabletop Christmas tree. I just may do that in the future.

I visited another library, a new one my friend, Kasharne, had told me was real nice. This library was a little further away, but I don't mind venturing out. I attended a free computer class to learn a new skill. Who cares if I am going to forget what I learned immediately, it's free? I received a Certificate of Completion at the end of the class. This library even has a drive-through book drop. That will come in handy when returning my audiobooks. I am all about conserving steps whenever possible.

I attended an all-day MS event. Okay, about three hours. I consider that all day in my MS world. Sometimes just doing something for a couple of hours feels like working a double shift. The event had a camera and you were able to choose your back drop. No MS event I have ever attended had a camera like that. I chose the New York City landscape as my background. You got to love green screen technology.

On December 18, 2016, I finally completed my Lamborghini puzzle! In 1991, I had a Lamborghini calendar hanging on the wall in my bedroom. No, I didn't remember having that calendar that specific year. I discovered this as I searched my photo albums for Throwback Thursday photographs. Completing this puzzle was quite the arduous task, but I am happy to report no pieces were missing after all the time that had passed. I told you I would get back to it. It was taking up a valuable piece of real estate in my living room for far too long. I was starting to think it was going to be a permanent fixture on my living room floor. Another item from my vision board completed. My first attempt to flip the puzzle over and keep it in tact was an epic fail. Of course, I could have waited for someone to come over and help me flip it over, but I wanted to figure it out on my own. I had to come up with Plan B. After putting the 100 or so pieces back together, I slid the puzzle off of the table onto a few large pieces of poster board. I cut a piece of landscape fabric and put it on the now empty table. I slid the puzzle from the poster board onto the fabric. I repurposed Glad Press 'n Seal to secure the puzzle to the fabric. Of course, that is not one of the suggested uses pictured on the side of the packaging. After successfully flipping the puzzle over, using a paint brush I put Mod Podge on the back of the puzzle to keep the pieces secure through transport. My cousin, Ta'Wane, put me on to this product for puzzle preservation.

One reason it took me so long to complete it was I had it on the floor and I can't sit on the floor too long and didn't want to risk losing pieces by moving it to a higher elevation. This puzzle had the smallest pieces of any puzzle I had ever seen. Another reason is that my elbow was hurting after a few minutes of leaning on the textured table. I figured out I needed to put a washcloth down on the surface of the textured table to cushion my elbow. I put a small bottle of water on a coaster on the floor and I was able to resume working on the puzzle. I could not do a lot of the puzzle at one time. My knees lock up after a few minutes. In between attaching puzzle pieces, I did floor stretches. The sun peering through my back door had faded the picture on the puzzle box from what was once a vibrant bright yellow Lamborghini to a dull, pale yellow color. Most of the yellow puzzle pieces were away from the sun, in Ziploc bags, so they did not fade. The Lamborghini puzzle is hanging up on the wall in my home office. After I moved the puzzle upstairs, I returned the folding table back to its home behind the couch in the living room.

Not only do I make up additional uses for Press 'n Seal, I use all kinds of things, in a way other than their intended use. The landscape fabric was left over from when the mulch was put down in my front yard. I have used wooden skewers, zip ties, and Command strips to jerry-rig all kinds of things around my house. Pretty much any modifications I can do that can help me make life easier.

I had a fall on the concrete, that lead to a bloody hand and another skinned knee. After that fall, I started keeping one of those emergency medical kits that Kasharne's daughter, Kayden, had suggested for camp. This way I will always have a Band-Aid on hand. I sure do keep a lot of supplies in my little car. I have an organizer that hangs behind my driver's seat to hold many of my items. I also started keeping an emergency medical kit downstairs, in the kitchen. Now when I get those mystery scars, burns or have another fall, I can put some antibiotic ointment on it, cover it with a Band-Aid, and keep it moving.

On December 23, 2016, I went skiing! It was a great Christmas present to myself. Sandra drove us, no she doesn't ski. I figured I would probably need help navigating the ski lodge. I had not been since I was a teenager living in Poughkeepsie, New York. Certainly, I could have gone since I have lived in Virginia, before my MS diagnosis, but I never did. I did not miss skiing this much until I was not able to easily do it anymore. I filled out a rather extensive, online application for Wintergreen Resorts adaptive skiing program. Even though the application was long, I believe anything worth having is worth working for. Part of the application asked me to describe any incentives or rewards that would promote my learning or behavior. I informed them that I just wanted a picture of myself on the ski slopes.

I had printed out directions from the resort, a MapQuest print out, I also had my GPS, and Waze app going. We took the scenic route up the Blue Ridge Mountains. This time the scenic route was intentional. After a quick tutorial to Ma on how to use my camera phone, we headed to check-in. I wish I had thought to wear my snow boots or at least my Timberlands to trek through the slushy snow between VIP parking and what they described as a charming wooden building. Sandra was wearing hers. I had my own ski coat and ski gloves. I used to have my own Rossignol Skis, but not anymore.

175

They equipped me with bibbed ski pants, ski boots, and a helmet. Virtually every skier on the slopes was sporting a helmet. No one ever wore a helmet for skiing back in the day.

They even had an official adaptive ski dog, but I did not need the dog's services. I warned my two trainers that I would probably start crying, but surprisingly I didn't. I did not get on a ski lift, like I used to do. We made our way to the designated learning area. I used to sometimes ski without poles, I was holding onto my ski poles for dear life that day. I did not ski moguls like I used to do. I stayed on one portion of one small hill, okay it was barely an incline. I was just happy I was standing up since I thought I was going to be lying down like in a sled. That is the only kind of adaptive skiing I had seen people do. Sandra took a bunch of pics and I was smiling extra cheesy in most, if not all of them. I'm even smiling in the photo of me on the ground after my fall. I was happy I only fell once. They even moved a chair onto the slope, so that I could sit down and take rest breaks often. My training session was scheduled to be 2 ½ hours long. I knew I was not going to last that long, but I was out there longer than I expected. It was the least coldest day that I have ever been skiing. I guess that's what happens when you ski in Virginia, rather than Vermont. Another item from my vision board had been completed. After skiing, I was drained and starving to death. Okay, maybe not to death, but I was quite famished. On the ride home, I learned I needed to keep a grippie on the passenger side of my car as well.

On Christmas Eve 2016, I was not hurting as much as I had expected from skiing the previous day. It was the annual Christmas dinner at Uncle Ralph's house. The main difference for me this time was I had seen members of that side of my family since last year's dinner. I told you I was going to do better. R-Jay and I spent the night at Ma's house. Christmas 2016 dinner was spent at Aunt Cat's house. Again, we rolled about 40 deep. Though we had plenty of room, the decision on where to spend the holiday has never been based on who has the most space. We don't need a lot of room, it is all about the comradery.

The following day Sandra, R-Jay, and I went to see the movie *Fences*. My parents and I had seen the play in New York when I was about 10. It was my first Broadway play. Since R-Jay is a junior, I thought we had come full circle. The symbolism again was completely lost on Sandra. She did not even remember we had seen the play. She just thought we were catching the new Denzel Washington flick. I keep forgetting that not everyone's long-term memory is as good as mine.

On January 3, 2017, I started back doing laps down the hallway of Sheltering Arms to train for Walk MS 2017. I was equipped with walking poles and a pair of hand-me-down Nike sneakers from my cousin, Jennifer. These sneakers had cushioned insoles, something I thought would be of great benefit. I also had my smartphone and earbuds to either listen to audiobooks I had downloaded or '90s music on the Pandora app. I had not done any laps since before the April 2016 Walk MS event. It was a slow start, since I was just recovering from a cold. I had been experiencing a pseudo-relapse (worsening of MS symptoms) a few days prior. I did not want to risk falling, by overdoing it after an illness, like

I had done last year. My plan was to stop taking the MS exercise class when I started doing my laps. I had told everyone I was stopping at the end of December. A class member suggested I continue with exercise class and just do the seated alternative to all of the exercises. The instructor always gave a chair option as well as a standing up or floor option to most exercises. My brother, R-Jay, paid for me to attend exercise class in January.

I started my Walk MS team member recruiting and fundraising about a month earlier than last year. Aunt Rachel has suggested that I ask people to "save the date" as soon as I learn the date for Walk MS 2018. The photo I used for my recruitment page was a picture of the back of Regina's shirt from Walk MS 2016. Starting the process went a lot smoother than last year. In 2016, even after R-Jay's girlfriend Christine helped me set up my Walk MS page, I still had to have an in-person meeting with the National MS Society to help me figure out the team captain dynamic. Just like last year, my cousin, Clyde, was the first person to make a donation after my initial contribution. This time I even put my fundraising goals on my Facebook timeline. I let my fundraising efforts scroll on my Facebook timeline every few weeks bringing awareness to MS. A couple of people even voluntarily shared my request for donations on Facebook.

In January 2017, we had a pretty big snowstorm. It was not Snowmageddon or anything, but big for Richmond. In the past I have either paid a local teenager to shovel or R-Jay has come over to do it. I have even shoveled it myself a time or two. Okay, I shoveled once.

I've even had a neighbor help me clear snow from my car before going to work. Now that I am not working and have nowhere that I have to be, my plan was to just save my money and wait for the snow to melt on its own. That plan changed when a man decided to make some money by shoveling the snow. I stayed home for three days in a row, that never happens. By day four I was suffering from cabin fever. I was mad I had forgotten to back the car up the hill in the driveway to ensure easy travels if I decided to leave before all of the snow had melted.

On January 11, 2017, I was featured in the #WellnessWednesday campaign on the National MS Society's Facebook page. Like with my Fall 2016 National MS Society newsletter article, I was happy to be featured. In both instances, employees from the National MS Society reached out to me for a submission. My brother's girlfriend, Christine, helped me edit both articles. For #WellnessWednesday I shared when I was diagnosed and what I do to stay active. You already know, I mentioned Sheltering Arms. I included a photograph of Ma, R-Jay, and me from Walk MS 2016.

As I was working on my laps up and down the hallway at Sheltering Arms, I noticed I was having trouble keeping track of what lap number I was on. I had to figure out a way to keep track of my lap numbers. I had the same problem last year, but I would not lose track until I was at about lap number 15. My remedy was to get to 24 laps in two sets of 12. That seemed to work in 2016. This year I am losing track around lap number four. I came up with the idea to use a Post-it note to keep track of my laps. Though Sheltering Arms front desk had pens and Post-it notes, I brought my own from home. I always had a pocket either in a workout jacket or in my sweatpants. This way I had somewhere to put my smartphone, so taking something else inside would not be too hard. I put the Post-it on the door found at the end of each lap. I only recalled seeing someone use that particular door once when I was doing laps last year. Each time I made it back to that location, I would use my pen to put a tick mark on the Post-it indicating the completion of another lap. This new activity gave me a break and allowed me to focus more on my laps, not having to keep track of every lap or ½ lap once I reached the other end of the hallway. Having the Post-it on the door became a visual cue for me to remember to add the tick mark. Even though I workout several times a week, come lunchtime, I had noticed that I was hungrier on lap days. I started keeping Nutri-Grain bars in the car. I prefer Apple Cinnamon. I also found that I took naps on most days I did laps.

After I noticed success with tick marked Post-it notes, I also put a more brightly colored Post-it on the wall near my bed with the word "Stretch" written on it with a Sharpie. The Post-it on the door is perfect because it is only temporary. I used a small Command strip for the one on my bedroom wall, since I want that one to stay there for a while. This exercise is necessary because sometimes I wake up with my hands trembling or legs twitching. Sometimes both. Turns out I did not even have to read the word "Stretch," because without my glasses on I could not see the word anyway. Just seeing the colored Post-it was enough of a visual cue to remind me to stretch.

One day when my cousin, Ta'Wane, was visiting I asked him about my shaking, citing that to my surprise other people have told me I was shaking. He also agreed I used to shake, but he attributed it to me trying to maintain my equilibrium, which is probably what I was doing. He checked the mail, as always, but I came up with a few more projects for him. He didn't mind, he knows that is par for the course.

I attended a Casino Night at another Sheltering Arms location. That was just the title, the event was in the middle of the day. It was at a location I had never visited. I paid a minimal fee to participate ahead of time. Each participant was given a drawstring backpack. The bag contained gambling chips and snacks, including M&M's. How did they know those were my favorite? I got to meet some new people. I'm not a big gambler, but I already knew I enjoyed playing Blackjack from my visits to Atlantic City and Dover Downs. I tried Roulette and a few dice games as well. The room housing the table games was even dark like a real casino. They even had a slot machine room. I also played bingo, which I have always enjoyed. They had these bingo cards with red, plastic windows that you slide the plastic tab over the number once it is called. This kind of board was not familiar to me, but it eliminated the need for bingo chips or markers. After about two hours of playing games, raffle tickets were put in a drawing giving participants a chance to win various gift cards and other prizes. Whether you won a prize or not, everyone got a cupcake as they exited the event. "Winner, winner chicken dinner!" That was a good day for me.

The morning of February 7, 2017, I had an appointment. I noticed the walk down the stairs was not as smooth as it had been lately. When I got to my appointment, I let the nurse know I was not moving too well. She said, "Maybe you're just having a bad day." That's probably what it was. It was a perfect 72 degree day, 30 degrees warmer than the previous day. I had a class at Sheltering Arms, so I went to take the class, but did not do any laps that day. It was the chronic disease self-management program and one of the techniques we learned was sometimes we need to say, "No." Regretfully I had to do that on this day. My cousin, Jennifer, had Senior night, she was playing her final basketball game ever at her high school. I let Aunt Elsie know I wasn't going to be able to make it. She offered to pick me up when I told her I wasn't going to make it. As poorly as I was walking, I needed more than just a ride to the school. It sickened me not to be there. I also had to let my friend, Tonya, know I wasn't going to make it either. I had invited her to the game, since she had attended several of Jennifer's home and away basketball games with me over Jennifer's high school career. My cousin, LaVita, went Facebook Live from the game so I was kind of there. I was glad to see so many people, but morose that I was not one of them. I got in the bed very early that night and did the Vick's VapoRub trick and took some Melatonin. A good night's sleep would certainly be the cure-all. That was a bad day for me.

The following morning, I stayed in bed longer than usual, scared I might not be moving too well again. I went down the stairs better than the previous day. I stepped outside to head to my car, it was another day of great weather. The temperature was slightly warmer than the previous day. I stumbled as I was making my way to the car, but I was going to push through. I went to Sheltering Arms. I was only able to complete five laps down the hallway, and I was struggling after lap number three. I had recently gotten up to 10 laps with the walking polls. I got to talk to some people that I had previously been in MS exercise class with. Even being around "my people" was not working this time. That evening I called my cousin, Dennis, to see if he was having trouble with his MS. He wasn't, but he gave me a pep talk and shared some encouraging words. I seriously considered not putting this paragraph in the book. I am supposed to be writing a story of inspiration and I am not feeling all that inspiring right now. Doesn't my body know it's in the middle of a 40 Metamorphosis, how come it's not cooperating?

The following day I skipped Sheltering Arms altogether. Even though I did not leave my house, I knew it was cold because the temperature had gone back down about 30 degrees. That evening I had a pharmaceutical company dinner. The only reason I went was because my Neurologist was the scheduled speaker and I needed to see him immediately. Unfortunately, no one was able to accompany me, so I arrived more than an hour early to ensure I got a good VIP parking space. My plan worked and after I laboriously made it into the restaurant my Neurologist and I devised a treatment plan. I even left before dessert was served. I must have been feeling bad, that had never happened. I was feeling bad that evening. The next day I avoided Sheltering Arms once again. I will use this time to tackle items on my action plan.

I'm back! Well back to baseline at least. I'm going to be honest, it took me a minute to figure that one out. I was in my feelings over this situation. It's almost like MS did not want me to forget its presence. It's not like that could ever happen. On February 10, 2017, I saw a story on the news about a lady that did seven marathons, on seven continents, in seven days. Granted she doesn't have MS, but if she can do that, surely, I can walk up and down a hall a few times. You never know where you may experience a source of inspiration. I didn't like being off my game. I had to get back to being positive and focus on all the things I am grateful for and there are a lot of them. I still was not moving great, but I had to put my strong will into overdrive.

On February 11, 2017, I completed 10 laps. Yes, it was a struggle, but I completed them. It was a case of mind over matter. Minor setback, now we move forward. I did some additional research and learned that MS symptoms are triggered with sudden temperature changes. Even though it wasn't hot, apparently, the sudden, drastic temperature increase presented itself as a relapse (also known as an exacerbation, attack, episode or flare-up). This ordeal taught me I need to be more cognizant of temperature changes as they can trigger MS symptoms.

On February 15, 2017, my friend, Tonya and I traveled to Surry County High School, Home of the Mighty Cougars! in Surry, Virginia to see a girls' basketball game. We are from different graduating classes, but we have the same alma mater. Our mutual friend, Brayon, who also was at my surprise birthday party, was the basketball coach. I saw Uncle Ralph and other people there. Some of which I had not seen since I was a student there.

The next day my friend, Janene, and I went to see the Broadway Musical NEWSIES. It was a true story set in 1899. We just saw it at the movie theater. It is called being a baller on a budget. They even had an intermission like an actual play. During the play, a female was trying to write a news story. Her pep talk or pep song to herself inspired me with my own writing. Again, you never know where inspiration is going to originate. Janene and I were prom dates as we exited the movie theater.

Chapter 13

On February 17, 2017, I drove to Roanoke, Virginia, for the first time, to participate in an event called the Snow Ball. My friend, Tonya, was gracious enough to put my suitcase in the car the other night before we drove to Surry. This event was put on by the Roanoke Valley MS Support Group in partnership with MSAV (Multiple Sclerosis Alliance of Virginia). I had learned the MSAV is an organization totally run by volunteers and not only supports people with MS, but anyone affected by MS including friends and family by providing programs that educate and empower. I forgot to get audiobooks for my ride to Roanoke. The view of the Shenandoah Valley was stunning, but I could not get clear reception on any radio stations. It's times like that I am grateful I always keep a Beyonce' CD in the car.

This time I remembered to request a room near the elevator. Once I was in my room I got in the bed, thinking it was nap time. I did not nap, just rested. Why not take advantage of all of these premium channels I don't have at my house? I ended up watching the movie *The Nice Guys*. It was a fairly recent movie set in 1977. In the movie, I saw a latch hook item hanging. Sandra and I used to do those when I was a little kid. I need to get one of those. I think it will help with my hand dexterity. I know I've said it a couple of times, but you never know what will be the source of inspiration.

Later that night I had dinner in the hotel restaurant with other members of the Roanoke Valley MS Support Group. I apologized after saying "Oh!" when I went to tell a story. Suzanne Oconnell, a fellow MSer and President and Founder of MSAV (Multiple Sclerosis Alliance of Virginia) told me it was a MS thing to interrupt people and get excited when you remember something. I do it all the time, it was nice to hear that I was not the only one. While in the restaurant, I tried to participated in karaoke in the hotel restaurant. I was apprehensive about trying something I had never done before, but I was once again with "my people." Karaoke was an item on my vision board, so I was going to give it a try. I selected a Bobby Brown song, inspired by the recent New Edition biopic. I would have thought if I ever participated in karaoke, I would sing Montell Jordan's "This is how we do it." Sometimes I surprise myself. They did not have my song, so I sat down. A new MS friend along with the DJ came up with a Plan B. Since they didn't have my song on karaoke, the DJ just played the song. After some coaxing, I bravely made my way to the DJ. No, I can't sing at all if you were wondering. I'm certain I have not been the center of attention like that since a childhood piano recital. I did not face the audience as I sang along with the track from memory. I'm counting that as participating in karaoke. Another item completed from my vision board.

The next day I participated in several activities. One of them was adult coloring books. Since I colored at my local library, I have learned there is something called adult coloring therapy. It is actually used as a tool to help adults relieve stress. I partially colored a sign that read "Dream Out Loud." Another activity was a mini version of Cinderella's Closet. When I spoke to one of the people coordinating the event, she wanted me to go to a mall and select an outfit to wear. I let her know I don't do malls due to my physical limitations. In order to make life easier, she suggested I wear the same dress from Cinderella's Closet at MS Respite Camp. I had dry cleaned my strapless dress so I was good with that plan. The dry cleaners is a place I used to frequent when I worked, not so much now.

This time I made sure to bring my own flat shoes, so I did not wear my sneakers with my ball gown. I got some new jewelry to accessorize my outfit. I don't know what happened to the old earrings. This time my jewelry was on loan. A lady removed the flat twists from my hair. My hairdresser had put them in before my trip to Roanoke, Virginia. I normally would have taken them out on my own, but hair and makeup assistance was offered, so I took advantage of both. My makeup regimen usually consists of ChapStick, or the occasional lip gloss. I had a different hairstyle so even wearing the same dress I looked a little different. I was in a fashion show. Not something I would normally do, but I was with "my people." I was about eight years old the last and only time I had ever been in a fashion show. It was a church event I participated in with my father.

The emcee for the fashion show was someone from one of Roanoke's local TV stations. Having such a bad week last week made me really appreciate the mobility that I have. I tried to make the most of it this week. After the fashion show I updated my Facebook cover photo. I used the picture that I modeled my outfit in from the mini Cinderella's Closet. My new cover photo is me wearing the same dress sans the sneakers and the diaper. I am so over being embarrassed. I was wearing a diaper under my ball gown at last year's Cinderella's Closet. Since it was my first year attending MS camp, I did not know how accessible restrooms would be. This time I was in a hotel and confident restrooms would be easily accessible. I mentioned the New Balance sneakers when I referenced my October 27, 2016 post, but not the diaper. I just wasn't ready yet. I'm ready now.

The original image is in a frame which decorates my living room, showing the sneakers. Knowing that is not something I would normally do, my cousin, Ta'Wane, asked me why I was wearing sneakers and hadn't asked the photographer to not include them in the photograph. I told him that being with MSers AKA "my people" was the only place I would feel comfortable doing something like that. Anyway, that picture was taken by a professional photographer, so I am standing with my hands clasped in front of me. My new Facebook cover photo was taken with my smartphone by the lady that took the twists out of my hair. I am standing much more naturally. I am not wearing glasses in the picture, but I put them back on immediately. I don't ever remember taking my glasses off for pictures. Another picture that decorates my living room is one of me the first time I wore a diaper when I was dressed up at a public event. It was in 2014.

In addition to all of the planned activities, the Snow Ball also had plenty of vendors selling their goods in the hotel. I purchased a handmade version of The Roanoke Star from the couple I had met at the Can Do MS Take Charge Program in Norfolk, Virginia. The star was made from yarn on a plastic canvas. It is also known as the Mill Mountain Star, which is the world's largest freestanding illuminated man-made star. I did not get to see the real thing that was created in 1949. I did not even know the star's historical significance when I made the purchase. I just thought it was a neat, little box. I will have to check it out the next time I make it to Roanoke, Virginia. I slept really well that night from all of the day's activities. The next morning I went to Bedside Baptist.

Fresh back from the Snow Ball I removed the "Karaoke" sign from my vision board. I haven't decided what I am going to replace it with yet. I took a few days off from doing laps at Sheltering Arms. I continued with all of my other duties like attending support group meetings, classes, pharmaceutical company lunches and dinners, as well as other meetings.

My friend, Tonya, and I were even able to attend one of my cousin Jennifer's basketball games. It was not a replacement of Senior night I had to miss, but I was still glad to be able to attend. My friend, Paula, was also at the game that evening. I had purchased a stadium seat to use at basketball games. I used it last basketball season. Now it is just too much trouble to ensure I get me and the seat inside safely. Now I just sit in the bleachers with a sore rear end.

Later in the week, I had a pain in the right side of my chest. It bothered me so much, had it been on the left side I would have thought I was having a heart attack. No, I've never had a heart attack, but that was the best way I could come up with to describe the episode. When

I told Ma, she thought I was kidding. It wasn't causing me any breathing disturbance so I just took some pain medicine. It turns out I was having a MS hug. Since it is a neurological condition, the pain medicine was ineffective. The pain was uncomfortable, but tolerable. At least that was my experience. I realize the nickname comes from the way it wraps around your body like a hug, and that sounds nice, but it felt like anything but what the name implies. It felt more like a death grip. I had heard of them, but I had never experience one. The pain didn't last all day long, but I did notice it two days in a row.

I was doing some of my own MS research and found out that some people with MS have sleep paralysis. During it you briefly experience the inability to speak, react, or move. You have the desire, but not the ability. I distinctly remember experiencing this twice once I had moved to Virginia. Both times I was at Grandma's house. I had awakened from a nap. I could not open my eyes or move, but I could hear everything that was going on around me. I don't know exactly how long it lasted, but it was more than a couple of minutes. Not that I am looking forward to it happening again, but I would be interested to know if I would have been able to feel it if someone had touched me during one of those episodes. Even once I was diagnosed with MS, I did not tell my Neurologist about it. I was having no pain and afterwards everything went back to normal. The thought never crossed my mind that I was experiencing anything medical.

On March 1, 2017, I woke to the bottom of my big toe on my right foot being numb. I previously had a transient case of numbness around my knee and that went away. I looked at it as my body's way of ushering in MS awareness month. Even though it didn't hurt or affect my walking, I chose to stay home that entire day.

My friend Aloma's youngest sister performed at the legendary Apollo Theater in Harlem, New York. She is a singer. Unfortunately, I was unable to make it to the performance. I posted a Throwback Thursday picture of her and I from when she was about three-years-old. So far, that has been the only picture posted that I thought the person might be upset. Though it was a cute picture, I didn't know if she perhaps did not want her Facebook fan base to see the picture. I was so happy to see that she loved the post.

On March 4, 2017, I traveled to Norfolk, Virginia for a program called Resilience: Addressing the Challenges of MS. Resilience deals with the ability to bounce back from adversity. This event was sponsored by the National MS Society. This time I traveled to Norfolk by myself. The speaker said her MS patients do more than her colleagues. I get that. I'm sure some of that has to do with not working a full time job and being available to do more things. No one from the Richmond MS Community attended the event, but I did see some people I knew from other events and I met some new people. Just like every event I attend, I love to pick up something other than MS information. One of the snacks provided that day was trail mix with real M&M's. What could be better? I duplicated the mix with my own homemade version, slightly different from the ones sold in stores. It is a healthier alternative to eating a whole, large bag of Starburst minis in one sitting.

In celebration of MS Awareness week, which began on March 5, 2017, I temporarily updated my Facebook profile picture with the frame, "We Are Stronger than MS." I used the photo from yesterday's event, where I am standing next to a National MS Society banner that read "Join The Movement." I selected the option to display the new picture for seven days. I wish I could say the picture update was my idea, but my friend, Regina, and other Facebook friends made this update first. My friend, Kasharne, followed suit and temporarily framed her Facebook profile picture as well.

On March 8, 2017, I went to see a free screening of the Shirley MacClain movie, *The Last Word*. This time I arrived super early anticipating a long line and since there was no line I just sat on the carpeted floor outside of the theater until my movie started. A couple of people spoke. Some just stared inquisitively. One theater employee asked me if I was okay. I let me know I was fine and had him help me off of the floor. I also did something grandiose earlier today. Okay, maybe not grandiose, but it was kind of a big deal to me. You will have to keep reading to find out what else I did that day. Even though the movie was at my most frequently visited movie theater, I missed my turn when I left to go home. It was definitely because I was doing too much that day.

R-Jay's girlfriend, Christine, suggested I pack downstairs when I shared with her that I had managed to carry my small, packed suitcase downstairs by myself. Why didn't I think of that? Now I just leave my empty suitcase and the Mary Kay travel roll-up bag my cousin, Leticia, gave me for Christmas in 2016 in my living room. This bag holds all of my toiletries and medicine for nights spent away from home. What's even better is the bag displays my name in purple script. Like my friend, Janene, Leticia knows I love things with my name of them.

On March 10, 2017 R-Jay and I flew to Alabama to visit our cousin, Leticia. Even though R-Jay was traveling with me, I know it is my job to keep track of the flight details so I put the arrival and departure information in a folder in one of my pharmaceutical company drawstring backpacks. I was just trying to play my position. I used to never pay the additional fee to check my luggage. I pay the fee now, it is just too much of a struggle to navigate through the airport with a bag, even a small one. I attached an orange ribbon to my suitcase, in order to easily identify it on the luggage carousel. I also pay to park now, waiting for a ride creates too much of a challenge. The extra pocket in my car vent organizer comes in handy, as a place to leave my parking pass, when I leave my car at the airport parking garage.

My friend, Kasharne, has urged me to let the airline know I need assistance. Each time I fly, I tell her that's what R-Jay is for. I just walk through the airport holding onto his hand. His hand is so much bigger than mine that I can only hold onto two or three fingers at a time. R-Jay and I were in the last row of the airplane. Along with having the longest walk of any other travelers, they were out of Sprite by the time they got to me. I also should have researched where to park in the airline parking lot to limit the amount of walking I had to do. I will have to try and plan out the next flight better. The last couple of times I have flown, R-Jay and I have boarded just in time. Because of this, I have agreed to get assistance in the airport the next time I fly.

Several hours after Leticia picked us up from the airport, we finally made it to see the new home Leticia had purchased. I was happy to see the MS magnet that I had sent her being displayed on her refrigerator. There were even items in her home with words I was able to put into my sayings journal. She had a few pineapples displayed as part of her decor and told me they were a symbol of welcome and generosity. I decided I wanted to have one of those displayed at my house. She took me to the Pineapple Emporium to get an item. Okay, I made up that name. I told you I do that sometimes. Leticia had me thinking we were going to some exclusive pineapple store. It was Hobby Lobby, which we have in Richmond, Virginia, but I found something that suited my style perfectly. I even saw some things to add to my sayings journal at that store. While in Alabama, I learned about a drive-through oil change spot. I did not even know that kind of thing existed. R-Jay told me about a location that provides that service in Richmond. I will definitely be visiting them.

The morning after arriving in Alabama, my cousin, Leticia, put a chair near the stove in the kitchen, to allow me to watch our breakfast cooking, while her and R-Jay got dressed. Leticia later drove us to Tennessee. It was my third visit to the state. We went to see my friends, Tichanda, Vaughn and their boys, including welcoming the arrival of their third son. He was born about two months prior to our visit. When we went out to dinner we even played several rounds of Heads Up at the dinner table. This is a game made famous by Ellen DeGeneres. We had so much fun that night with all of their hilarious antics, which started when we first arrived at the front door. Their family is funnier than any show I have seen at the FunnyBone Comedy Club. It was snowing in Tennessee and I joked that we left Virginia to get away from the snow that we were expecting. That weekend, I laughed until my chest hurt. It was so good to have chest pain from laughter, rather than a MS hug. Laughter is good for the soul.

I did not remember to pack any jewelry for the entire weekend, but I was okay with that. I did not even remember my orange MS bracelet and I had placed that right next to my keys. My visual cues do not always work. I managed to work daily naps into my travel schedule, so I did not have to pay the MS tax when I returned to Richmond. I can take a nap anywhere; in the backseat of a car or sitting up in a chair. I prefer to have a blanket or throw, but one is not required.

March 17, 2017, Saint Patrick's Day, I wore my green MS t-shirt to Sheltering Arms. I also wore a green sweater that evening when I took my friend, Kasharne, out for her birthday. That was one of the rare days that I went upstairs and changed clothes before bedtime. No, I'm not Irish. That is just something I have done since my days at Arlington Elementary School. I did not want the Pinch Police to get a hold of me.

On March 19, 2017, I completed a latch hook kit. The void left by the skiing picture on my vision board was replaced by a picture of a latch hook photograph. I had purchased a colorful Treble Clef design from

Amazon. There was no real significance to picking that design. I just liked the picture. The latch hook tool was slightly different than the ones I remember as a kid. I was just happy I remembered how to use the tool without having to read the instructions. The latch hook kits we used to work had color coded gridded canvases. This one contained a legend on the instruction paper to determine which colors went in what place. This set suggested sorting the precut yarn in a muffin tray, which I did. That was a great suggestion and it allowed me to stay more organized. I don't know if that suggestion was made back in the day, but Sandra and I never did that step.

Several times I lost track of where I was on the canvas compared to where I was on the legend. I would fully complete one color at a time, rather than follow the suggested row method. The jagged edges on the canvas left scratches on my hand. Silver lining – it was my right hand so I did not feel it, so I just kept working. It was not easy, but I attached 1600 short pieces of yarn to the gridded canvas. It was indeed a great hand exercise for me. I put the leftover yarn in Ziploc snack bags, separated by color, just in case I decide to do another one of these. Another item completed from my vision board.

I recently saw a picture from my cousin Jessica's 2014 high school convocation. I knew I was not up for attending the actual 2015 graduation, but I did not realize I was unhappy at the convocation. The picture was of Jessica, our cousin, Frank Jr., and me. I was present, but I was the saddest person ever. I did not even manage a fake smile for the picture. Later that day I had a job interview for the last job that I worked. I guess I pepped up and was able to pull off a successful job interview. Sometimes you got to "Fake it 'til you make it," and I guess I did just that. I'm glad I can laugh about it now.

Other things I can laugh about now: I have forgotten my mother's address and she has lived in the same place over 20 years. I once found a bag of Christmas Tree ornament hooks in the glove compartment of my car. At no point was there any reason they should have been in my car. I often joke about someone coming in my house when I'm not home and taking things or moving things around. No one is doing that, but the humor of it all helps me cope.

On March 24, 2017, I started attending another pilot program, at Sheltering Arms, with the National MS Society. This program was called Live Fully, Live Well and was put on in conjunction with Can Do MS. This program was held at the Sheltering Arms location I visit most days. This six-week program was about wellness behaviors and promoting overall health. We were given weekly assignments the instructor referred to as at home work, rather than homework. I like homework, so I was good with that. A book that was advertised at the Can Do MS Take Charge Program was part of this class curriculum. The book was very informative. Now that I've read it, I wish I had read it before I figured out so many things on my own. I just wasn't ready yet.

In this book, I learned in addition to memory issues regarding recent events, some MSers have difficulty learning new information. This explains the issues I was having when I started a new job in January 2015. If I knew then what I know now, I may have handled that situation differently. This also would explain why redundancy is necessary when it comes to pharmaceutical company events with the same ambassadors and medical personnel. With short-term memory issues, I have to keep learning the same stuff over and over again in order to retain the information. I have started taking notes at the events, even repeat events, but unfortunately, sometimes I leave the notes at the table.

I stepped up my sleep game even more. I first take Melatonin most nights. I reduce the volume on the TV. I put my TV remote control in the bedside caddy along with my glasses, at bedtime. I still set the sleep timer for a short amount of time, even though I am not watching. I guess I need the noise to help me get to sleep. I then put on a sleep mask. I have to use the ones with the cotton interior. The ones with the polyester interior were making my night sweats worse. That is another symptom common to MSers and I am no exception. My masks are all colorful with different sayings. By wearing the sleep mask, I no longer sleep with the cover over my head. I still sleep with my smartphone in the bed next to me. When I go to bed now I have a pair of earbuds attached. When I wake up in the middle of the night, the veil of darkness hides the light from the alarm clock or any other lights that may have normally disrupted my sleep. If I don't have to go to the bathroom, I can usually go right back to sleep. When I wake up in the middle of the night and do have to use the bathroom, I lift the sleep mask for the trek to the bathroom. When I get back in bed, rather than turn the TV back on, I listen to relaxation sounds from a free app I downloaded onto my smartphone. This is another strategy that was suggested during the chronic disease self-management program I took at Sheltering Arms. I slip the sleep mask back down and fall back to sleep to the relaxing sounds of wind or white noise. The app allows you to listen to multiple sounds at once, providing a virtually unlimited number of sound combinations. Sounds of rain and other water sounds make me have to go use the bathroom again, so I skip those ones. You may be thinking, why don't I just play the sounds when I first go to bed, rather than turn the TV on? I tried that and was unsuccessful. This is what works for me. I tend to be laxer on the weekends. On Saturday night, my intention is to stay up to watch Saturday Night Live. I usually don't make it.

Chapter 14

On March 29, 2017, I reached my goal of 24 laps or one mile down the hallway at Sheltering Arms. That morning I was wearing a t-shirt that my cousin, Leticia, had given me while I was in Alabama. I had just eaten a free breakfast from Chick-fil-A, something I learned about compliments of Facebook. I mean breakfast is the most important meal of the day. I also received a Walk MS donation from another fellow Sheltering Arms member. A new DMT (Disease-Modifying Therapy/Treatment) had been approved the previous day. I had heard this one was a game changer. It was the first DMT to treat PPMS (Primary-Progressive MS). Also, I had forgotten my earbuds in the car and I certainly wasn't going back to get them, so I heard numerous words of encouragement as I did my laps. It was a perfect storm, if you will. When I got home I received a telephone call that I won a drawing of four free tickets to FunnyBone and my friend, Tonya, attended a pharmaceutical company dinner with me for the first time. She also made a donation to Walk MS that night. As you might imagine, I slept very well after I made my Throwback Thursday post. That was a good day for me.

I am happy to report I did not have any falls this year while completing my laps at Sheltering Arms. Since my fall last year, I have noticed that whenever I hear a loud noise in the gym, the physical therapists reflexively turn toward the sound. It is usually no more than someone accidentally knocking into something. I feel safe knowing the physical therapists are always on high alert. Keeping track of my laps using tick marks on Post-it notes had been successful. Employees that needed to gain entry to the door containing my Post-it did not seem to mind sharing their door with me. On the occasions when I would leave my Post-it in the car, I would ask the Administrative Assistant at Sheltering Arms to share one from their supply. I was not going to go back to the car for a Post-it. I sometimes had to remove my jacket or sweatshirt in order to regulate my internal body temperature. I would always take a deep breath when I got to either end of the hallway. There was sometimes a chair in the hallway at the opposite end of where I made my tick marks. I don't remember a chair ever being there last year. If there happened to be a commercial on Pandora when I was at that end of the hallway, I would sit down and rest. When the commercials were over, my break was over.

On April 4, 2017, I went to the Cultural Arts Center to check out the Vibrance LEGO exhibit. The exhibit put the LEGO windmill I often made with my LEGO bricks as a kid to shame. After I heard about the exhibit on the news in March, I called to find out the best place to park and what day to go to avoid foot traffic.

On April 8, 2017, I drove R-Jay and his girlfriend, Christine, to the airport in Raleigh, North Carolina. Okay, R-Jay drove, but I dropped them off. I spent the night with my friend, Keta, in Greensboro, North Carolina. Keta yelled at me for climbing her stairs a couple of times that evening, knowing I don't do that at home. I guess I not only show off for company, but as company also. I drove back to Virginia the next day.

My friend, Randi, was in Virginia and we made plans for her to visit my house. As we were hashing out our plans she said LMK (let me know) in Facebook Messenger. Good thing I downloaded that app back in July, so I knew what LMK meant. We had not seen each other since we had breakfast in New York in August 2014. She had been very busy since then. She left New York and rode her motorcycle to Canada. She then traveled to California via the historic Route 66. She stopped in several states along the way. I watched as she chronicled her cross-country trip on Facebook. It was such an inspiring three-month adventure. Rather than go back to New York, she chose to settle in North Carolina when she returned to the East Coast.

We reminisced as we looked through a few photo albums and talked about our times on the ski slopes. After another slumber party, the following morning Randi took pictures of me sitting on her Harley Davidson. I was not in full biker garb like she was. The engine was not even turned on this time. I had not sat on a motorcycle in 35 years since I burnt my leg on Uncle Ralph's motorcycle when I was five years old. Apparently, I had been traumatized. I did not pay the MS tax after this busy weekend. After resting, I even went to Sheltering Arms after Randi left my house. I didn't complete the whole mile, but I managed to get a few laps in.

April 11, 2017, started out like most other days. I heard it was going to be hot and sunny so I applied sunscreen before heading out to Sheltering Arms. You can't forget those ears. After completing some laps, not 24, I decided to try out a new nail salon. I keep a pair of purple flip-flops in my car specifically for last minute pedicure decisions. That is the only time I wear flip-flops. This salon gave you a glass of water and a plate of fruit while you get a pedicure in their massage chair. My friend, Janene, didn't tell me about the snacks when she referred me to this place. My regular salon does not offer snacks. Even though I don't usually eat melon, I am trying to create more colorful meal plates as part of my nutrition plan, so I ate the melon. Besides I had just finished working out, so I was hungry. I got a pedicure with orange polish, not because orange is the MS color, but because my Easter dress was orange and white. I have noticed I have quite a bit of orange in my wardrobe. That increase was an unconscious decision, but I like the orange. I left the salon, went home and took a nap.

Thanks to Facebook, I had seen there would be a Full Pink Moon that evening. This special moon represents new beginnings and gratitude for the new things coming into your life. I missed the supermoon in November 2016, so I made sure to try and catch this one. Reaching 86 degrees, it turned out to be the hottest day of the year so far. Since it was still hot, I wore a cooling item, filled with ice packs, around my torso. I also had a Chilly Pad around my neck. That is a cooling towel you just have to wet and it keeps you cool for hours. I applied a fresh coat of sunscreen and sprayed on some insect repellant. Armed with my Kindle, a bottle of water, and a cold, half sleeve of Girl Scout Cookies, Thin Mints, I headed out the door. I went to Three Lakes Park.

I decided to post up in a shaded location near VIP parking. I grabbed my prescription sunglasses, which stay in my car. I also took a folding chair, which is always in my car trunk. The folding chair I use has straps like a backpack for easy transport and a canopy so I was protected from the sun. The Thin Mints I was eating cancelled out the melon I ate earlier, but that's okay. I ended up not needing the cooling items. I attached my regular glasses to my t-shirt, so I would not have to walk back to the car once it got dark. I even tucked my smartphone away in my pocket. I had selected such a nice place to sit, relax, and collect my thoughts. I initially recall being told to identify a MS-free zone at the Can Do MS Take Charge Program. When I traveled to Norfolk, Virginia learning about resilience and how to cope with the challenges of MS back in March, it was also suggested we do this kind of thing. The concept of finding a MS-free zone was revisited in my Live Fully, Live Well program, so I figured it was time to put this into action. I just previously had not been ready yet. After taking some time to decompress, I enjoyed a good read on my Kindle.

The night air was cool and I regretted not bringing a windbreaker to cover my short sleeve t-shirt or changing from my nylon capris, into long pants. I was parked close to where I was sitting and I borrowed light from the lamppost to make it back to the car safely. Though I could not see the moon from where I was in the park I did not regret going there, if only to read. Even though I am always aware that I have MS, for a short time I was in a territory free of MS. I was able to catch a glimpse of the moon on my ride back home. It was beautiful and positioned lower than normal. From my vantage point, the Full Pink Moon was full, but not pink. I later found out the moon was named after pink flowers, called phlox, that bloom this time of year, not the color of the moon. Next time I will be sure to do my research ahead of time.

On my Kindle I have always read books using a white background. Due to me becoming increasingly more light sensitive, I had to change to have a sepia (reddish-brown color) background on my book text. This color makes the words appear less bright. I took someone's suggestion and tried to watch TV using the closed caption feature. I thought this was a great idea, since my hearing ability has decreased. I soon learned this was not a good idea for me. I don't read nearly as fast as I used to be able to do. Even without closed caption, TV shows periodically show dialogue or text messages. The words are displayed and usually disappear before I finish reading the thought. I sometimes find myself rewinding a TV show.

In late April 2017, I began to notice difficulty with swallowing. You guessed it, that is another possible MS symptom called dysphagia. I have been seeing it as a possible symptom, but never had any issues with it. I first noticed it when I had dinner at Mexico Restaurant with my biker friend, Randi, earlier in the month. I had a severe coughing spell. At the time, I thought it was just something going down wrong. I soon began to notice swallowing issues almost daily. I just try to make sure that I chew my food very well before I attempt to swallow. I thought I was already doing that, but I chew even more now. I asked a Neurologist about it at pharmaceutical company lunch. In addition to chewing thoroughly and drinking something while eating, I was instructed to put my head down with my chin toward my chest to swallow. If problems persisted it was suggested I see a Speech Therapist. I no longer have the same angst about having to add another member to my healthcare team.

On April 28, 2017, I completed a windmill LEGO structure. You should have seen something like this coming. The void left from karaoke was replaced with LEGO. It was not like the yellow windmill that I used to build, but it did have rotating blades like that one. When I first opened the package, I did not remember LEGO pieces being so small. The last time I created a LEGO structure I was small too, so I guess it makes sense. I did notice several new piece options that did not exist the last time I put a LEGO structure together. Similar to when I was putting together my latch hook, I had trouble following the instruction booklet. Even though it showed step-by-step instructions with pictures, on a few occasions I selected the wrong piece to attach. I worked in the same area where I had put together my Lamborghini puzzle on the floor in the living room. This time I just used a piece of poster board, rather than the textured table. This was a 3 In 1 set so I put the extra LEGO pieces in a Ziploc bag and the instruction booklets aside. A few times I heard parents talk about stepping on a LEGO is the worst thing ever, so I made sure all of the pieces were out of my walking area. I put the completed structure on a bookshelf in my home office.

Later that day was my final Live Fully, Live Well class. I had a paradigm shift during this program. I learned that a community is considered a relationship. This led me to increase my presence in the community, not just the MS community. The participants of this pilot program received a very nice Certificate of Completion with our names on it. The certificate contained words in both orange and purple letters. You know, how I just love those. It's the little things.

On May 1, 2017, I attended Richmond Times-Dispatch's All-Metro Basketball Banquet with Aunt Elsie, my cousin, Jennifer, and a few other family friends. One of the speakers was Virginia Union University's Head Women's Basketball Couch, AnnMarie Gilbert. She posed the question, "What's your why?" She stated the athletes need to know their purpose. In reference to staying the course and taking your medicine as scheduled, one of the pharmaceutical companies has also asked "What's your why?" My "why" is so that I can continue to achieve my goal of living safely and independently. I hope to continue to be able to handle ADL (Activities of daily living) like maintaining my house, preparing meals, and grocery shopping. I would love to have MS cured in my lifetime, but for now I want to continue to ensure I have a good quality of life. She also spoke about having an impact. I hope I am able to have one with this book and my very active MS life. The speaker that followed her said AnnMarie Gilbert "Spit fire." That's exactly what she did. She was such a dynamic speaker and her speech was phenomenal. I approached her after the program. I tried to tell her that I had MS and compliment her on how inspiring her speech was, even for a non-athlete like myself. At least that was my intention, but all I had for her were a bunch of tears.

On the morning of May 5, 2017, I went to Aunt Rachel's house for breakfast. To my surprise, my cousin, Jamila, her aunt, Michelle, and two friends that attended the party Jamila had for me in New York in July 2016 were there. Also present, was one of Jamila's cousins from her mother's side of the family. She jokingly commented that she was not given a choice. Even if she was there begrudgingly, I was still glad she came. Several months prior, Jamila had told me she was 85 percent sure she was coming. This crew of five had driven from New York to participate in Walk MS alongside me. I was definitely feeling the love. After breakfast, I went home and took a nap. After my nap, I went and talked to someone (got my hair done) and did several "Wooosahhhs." A word said to calm and relax yourself. After getting my hair done, I met the breakfast crew in Petersburg. After taking some photos in front of a mural in downtown Petersburg, we had dinner at Croaker's Spot.

After a good night's sleep, it was May 6, 2017, game day. Time for what I referred to as MS Super Bowl 2017. I wore both a MS t-shirt and a hoodie. The combination of wearing two tops served me well last year. The t-shirt said "Made to Survive" and the hoodie read "Please find a cure before MS gets on my last nerve." It was a double entendre. MS is a disease that damages or eats away at the myelin sheath (protective covering) of your nerves. Anyway, I also wore some canvas black sneakers with flat orange shoestrings. I decorated each shoe with "MS" using self-adhesive gems. The small gems were a challenge for my hand dexterity issues. The shoes looked bedazzled by the time I finished decorating them. I wish I could say it was my idea, but again, I am not that creative. I saw something similar on Facebook. I could have gotten someone craftier to make a better version, but I wanted to try to do them myself.

I had a Nutri-Grain bar for breakfast. Sandra came to my house to drive me to the walk. It was cold, but not nearly as cold as I remember it being in 2016. Uncle Frank's wife Florine and his daughter, Tracie, were my first team members to arrive. R-Jay soon followed. Once again preserving my energy, I enlisted Sandra to collect swag from the vendor booths. I took several pictures with my team and Uncle James held my jeweled selfie stick for a few group photos. I had a doughnut from the Sheltering Arms table right before the walk. Isn't that what athletes do, carb load? Anyway, my cousin, Diane, went Facebook Live as my team of 30 headed to the "Start" arch with my walking poles. It was not all the same 30 from last year, some repeats, some newbies. I was grateful for all of them. As I began Walk MS 2017, my only goal was to have an easier trip across the finish line than last year.

Some of the team had walked ahead. I sat down when I reached the ½ mile mark. I did not sit down at all during Walk MS 2016. We took pictures at this milestone, then I turned around and headed back. Some of the team continued on to complete the entire course. Throughout the course, I switched from hoodie to no hoodie, had several swigs of Gatorade, and sat down several times.

When I was 80 percent finished with the walk I saw Uncle Ralph for the first time that day. Ma said that was just the inspiration I needed to continue. I'm sure it helped, but the truth was I was determined to cross the finish line standing up even if I had been the only one left out there. Feeling something wasn't right, Aunt Elsie and Aunt Ann came back to the walk after they had already reached the finish line. A couple of MSers I knew from Sheltering Arms urged me to keep going. I was not going to give up.

I was wearing an orange lei I had received earlier that day from a Sheltering Arms MSer. With the finish line a stone's throw away, another MSer that I knew from Sheltering Arms abandoned her motorized assistance vehicle, grabbed her hand crutches, and said we would walk across the finish line together. I struggled, but continued to give it everything I had. With the pageantry of so many people cheering us on, we made it across the finish line. I high fived the lady that crossed the finish line with me and the words that followed were neither deep nor profound. As I jubilantly crossed the finish line, I said, "That was hard!" Knowing I would see the pictures, Ma told me she cried at the finish line. She was not with me at the finish line last year, so she did not cry in 2016. While reviewing the pictures after the walk, I saw a lady from another team carrying a sign that read "Walking By Faith." She was standing right next to me and I was so focused on completing the walk, I never saw that sign.

Another MSer that I didn't know, wearing a clown costume, handed me a MS keychain. Similar to last year, I grabbed the first piece of curb to sit down. The sister of the lady that walked across the finish line with me gave me a very special coin to signify the accomplishment. She told me she had traveled from Texas for the event. That coin in on a bookshelf in my home office. Even though I cried a lot less than in 2016, it was much harder physically in 2017 and the finish line was much more emotional. I moved from the curb into a chair. The chair was brought to me by one of my team members whose family had traveled from Northern Virginia for the walk. My cousin, Diane, massaged my achy legs as I sat in the chair.

Reaching 24 laps at Sheltering Arms earlier in the training process did not give me the desired outcome. That just means I will have to work even harder next year. I had set that as a goal in my Live Fully, Live Well class. Good thing I set two goals, just in case. In 2016, I split up my trips to Sheltering Arms between laps and working out in the gym. In 2017, I only did laps since February. I will go back to regular gym workouts in conjunction with laps when I start training for Walk MS 2018. I also did not take any trips to the outside track this year. I will make sure to incorporate a few of those next year as well.

They had food at the walk, but after the walk Ma, R-Jay, and I went to eat at Kickback Jack's. After we ate, I got a flat tire when Ma went to get her car from my house. She let me use her car and she waited for Roadside Assistance with my car. I went to a program at Aunt Rachel's church with the breakfast crew and Aunt Audrey, a repeat Walk MS team member. I was still using my walking poles at the church program. After church, all of us traveled to Uncle Ralph's house for a fish fry. That night I learned that I get my tendency to overexaggerate numbers from Uncle Ralph. He said 199 million referring to something. I may say 864 billion when it is only like 10, okay five. Ma and R-Jay came to the fish fry as well. I decided to go to Ma's house for an impromptu slumber, no party. Even if I had driven to my house, I am certain I would not have been able to make it to the bedroom or showers that are all upstairs. Everything is on one floor at Ma's house. I slept so hard that night that Ma had to help me find my cell phone the following morning. It was under my bed. I only had underclothes and jeans in my bag in the car. I normally would not wear jeans to church, but they say, "Come as you are," and that's what I planned to do.

The following day as I was pulling out of Sandra's driveway about to go to church, I received a text message containing a 21 second video of me crossing the finish line. It was from that couple that I met at the very first Richmond, Virginia MS event I had ever attended. As I watched the video with tears in my eyes, all I could think is "You may see me struggle, but you'll never see me quit." That has become another one of my mottos. Though the video does not tell the entire story, I decided to share it on Facebook. Following my play cousin Tasia's lead from Walk MS 2016, I had asked people to record me crossing the finish line. I had not planned to share that on Facebook. I had been featured in videos, but this was the first one I ever posted. My friend, Kasharne, was the loudest person on the video. Over the sounds of cheers and noisemakers I could hear her say, "Go Neek!" (what she usually calls me) and "You did that!" I received a tremendous number of comments on the video and an outpouring of love and support. People commented that I had inspired people with my video. I had not expected that at all, my main objective was to finish, so that I could sit down. My cousin, Clyde, was the first person I shared the video with, even before I put it on Facebook.

I had retired my walking poles by now. Sandra also wore jeans to church, so I wouldn't be alone. She didn't have to do that. Using my bootleg version of sign language, I admired the orange tie worn by the pastor. I'm sure that was just happenstance. After church, I went home to relax on the couch and watch a Redbox movie I had gotten from R-Jay. After the movie, the breakfast crew, plus one more cousin, had dinner at Mama J's. I told you, I have a lot of cousins. When I told Jamila it was ridiculous we just started hanging out in 2016, she said, "It's not how it starts, it's how it ends." All weekend I referred to Jamila's aunt Michelle as the team lead, since she alone drove the whole way from New York. That was a great three days, even with the struggles at Walk MS.

I can't put my finger on it, nor have I come up with a clever name for it, but that video did something to me. That experience transformed me again. If I keep doing Walk MS, I'm going to turn into a whole different person.

As of May 8, 2017, I have been retired for two years now. Retirement is good. I felt hapless when I first got boxed (fired). I'm good now and don't miss the daily grind at all. Granted I don't have much discretionary or residual income, but I am extremely happy. I am slightly amused when I hear people say they can't or won't stop working. I remember when I was like that, but my brain had another plan entirely. Now when people ask me what I take for energy, my response is "A nap." When I was working, I would usually go upstairs and get in the bed around 7 p.m. Now that I am not working, if I am home, I still go upstairs and get in the bed fairly early. I get so tired of running into things and if I am still up and downstairs, I will continue to keep moving around and trying to do things.

Chapter 15

May 10, 2017 was my first day back to Sheltering Arms after Walk MS. Time to get back to working out, minus the laps. I planned to show the 21 second video to a couple of people, but I ended up showing it to several people that I knew had seen me training up and down the hallway. The man that had given me an orange lei at the walk was there. We had on matching shirts we received on walk day. That was unplanned. I was there a couple of hours, much longer than my usual workout time. People asked me how long the mile took me. I had no idea. One Sheltering Arms employee suggested I try to make the video go viral. I was happy to share the video, but I was not going to post it to YouTube or anything like that. Another employee told me to share it with the National MS Society. I let her know someone from there had already seen it. I later took her suggestion and sent it to a few more people with the National MS Society. I even shared it with my plumber and my hair dresser. After a couple of errands, I went home and took a nap.

After my nap, it was time to go to a pharmaceutical company dinner. I got there early and drove around several times looking for a parking space. I ended up parking very far away. I looked over to the passenger seat, grabbed my walking poles, and headed to the restaurant. They are always in the car, but they were still in the front seat from the weekend. It was my first time using walking poles, not in relation to Walk MS. I'm sure the fact that I was going to be with "my people" played a large role in my willingness to carry the walking poles. My friend, Janene, was attending the dinner with me. By the time she showed up to pick me up, I had almost made it all the way to the restaurant on foot. Similar to the anxiety I face driving across a bridge, I was feeling uneasy as I walked across the third-floor breezeway at the Boathouse at Rockett's Landing restaurant. Also like the bridge anxiety, it didn't stop me from attending the event. I had Janene take a picture of me on the breezeway, holding my walking poles, so that I could send it to my friend, Kasharne. I knew she would love it, she had been urging me to use an assistance device for years. After dinner, Janeen drove me to my car. She did not park near me and was surprised I had walked so far.

I had previously missed some events because I did not want to use my walking poles. The old me would have gone home if I was unable to find a close parking spot. I was just not ready yet. I'm ready now. I realized I don't need a new name for my most recent change. I am still in my 40 Metamorphosis, it is just evolving.

On May 12, 2017, I once again temporarily updated my Facebook profile picture. Again, I selected the option to display the new picture for seven days. This time the frame read "Be strong to fight...One day you'll be MS free just wait and see..." I was posing in my "Made to Survive" t-shirt. This one was not my idea either. Someone I met from the Resilience program in Norfolk, Virginia used that border.

Shortly after Walk MS 2017, I started noticing another new symptom. I noticed my feet were swelling, regardless of whether I was wearing socks or not. I ignored it the first few times and it eventually went back down to normal size. I called my Neurologist and did some research as soon as pain was included with the swelling. Okay, I called Aunt Elsie first. I figured she may be able to assist me since she works with the senior population. My research revealed swollen feet were common in MS and often the result of being sedentary. The lack of mobility allows lymphatic fluid to accumulate. The remedy was aerobic activity and moisturizing. After applying lotion to my feet, I was good to go. As I thought back, I had been frequenting Sheltering Arms less since Walk MS. This was a clear sign that I needed to increase my Sheltering Arms visits.

May 25, 2017 was Red Nose Day. While sitting in a chair on my front porch, I took a selfie and posted a picture of me wearing the red nose on Facebook. I purchased my red nose the very first time I saw them in Walgreens even before I ever saw a TV commercial or an ad on Facebook advertising them. My first stop was the gas station. My gas light came on shortly after leaving home and my car felt like it was pulling. Anyway, again I wore my red nose to Sheltering Arms.

A lady there unfamiliar with Red Nose Day said, "What's up with you?"

As if I didn't know what she was referring to I said, "Nothing." I was just having a little fun with her.

"You have something clipped onto your nose," I then explained to her the concept of Red Nose Day.

After my Sheltering Arms workout, I headed to a pharmaceutical company lunch. I had worn a t-shirt to Sheltering Arms advertising the drug company represented at lunch, so I did not feel obligated to change my clothes. Without warning, the pharmaceutical company representative asked me to explain my red nose to the other lunch guests. That was okay, I prefer to do things off the cuff. It reminded me of when my friend, Regina, asked me to give an impromptu wedding speech while at the wedding reception. I feel it is too much pressure if you know ahead of time. Anyway, because of my recent swallowing issues, I removed my red nose to eat lunch.

I put the nose back on after lunch, okay after dessert. My friend, Regina, thinks it's funny that I am not at all embarrassed about wearing the red nose or some of my other outlandish gear or accessories in public. In fact, I think it is kind of fun. I am certainly willing to spend $1 to help the indigent population. It started raining as soon as I got inside of my house. My belly was full, it was the perfect time to take a nap.

I have graduated from sitting on only a carpeted floor to sitting down on a tile floor in public places. Maybe graduate is not the right word. Graduations are good things. I changed my ways when my friend, Lona, and I were watching a prescreening of the movie *Wonder Woman*. No, I am not a superhero enthusiast, but I did like the TV show as a kid. It was a 3D movie and it had been a while since I had seen one of them. It was a first come, first serve viewing so I got there early to reserve our spot in line. Once Lona arrived a few minutes after me, I told her I needed to sit. She asked me if I would be better leaning on the nearby wall. I let her know my knees were still going to lock up. When that happens, it renders me virtually immobile. I don't know if she was embarrassed by me sitting on the floor or not, but we kept talking like I was standing right next to her.

May 31, 2017 was World MS Day. I started the day at Sheltering Arms, wearing one of my Walk MS 2017 t-shirts. Then I continued to celebrate by going to Baskin-Robbins for an ice cream cone. No, that had nothing to do with MS, but anytime is a good time for ice cream. Besides the workout cancels out the ice cream, right? After I changed clothes, I traveled to Smithfield, Virginia for a pharmaceutical company dinner about Navigating MS.

Taking suggestions from other MSers, I tried a few other incontinence tools. While I was wearing Depends, fellow MSers have told me they do not like them, claiming they are too bulky. Either that was their slick way of telling me they noticed my diaper or they felt able to speak freely because they did not notice the diaper. I choose to believe the latter. My occasional Depends usage used to be such a secret. Now if I am wearing one when someone asks me if I need to go to the restroom, I nonchalantly say, "I just went." The response I usually receive from non-MSers is, "TMI" (too much information).

I did try the female travel urinal. I tried it at home before I took it on the road. The directions were easy enough, hold against your body and "go." It made me envious of how men can stand up and "go." I did not have to pull my pants all the way down my legs. Okay,

220

that's enough details. They are described as washable and reusable and one suggested use is for camping. I plan to use them in a port-a-potty and dispose of them after one use. It will eliminate the need to line the toilet with toilet paper, squat, or hover over the toilet seat. They are made of 100% TPR (Thermoplastic Rubber), so I can fold it up and put it in my pocket. Another thing I purchased was disposable urinals for women. This is another item I plan to use to make my trip to the port-a-potty as pleasant as plausible. It is reusable until full, but I plan to discard them after one use as well. I keep one of each of these in a Ziploc bag in the glove compartment of my car.

On June 3, 2017, I visited Three Lakes Park again. This time I participated in Picnic at the Parks. I left home with a premoistened Chilly Pad around my neck to avoid an unbearable heat situation. I had registered and ordered my lunch prior to the event date. When I initially registered for this event, I had made a note in my smartphone of where to pick up my lunch. Wearing a drawstring backpack, me and my walking poles headed to the Nature Center to pick up the lunch I had preordered. Participants were handed our lunch in a nylon bag with a handle. I headed back to the car to retrieve a blanket from my trunk, another item that is always in my car. This back and forth was a lot easier with the walking poles. Who knew? I put the blanket in a shaded spot under a tree. Though it was 83 degrees, it was cool under the tree and I was able to remove my Chilly Pad and put it in the plastic bag I had brought with me.

I pulled out the box lunch complete with fruit, snacks, condiments, and plastic ware. I had a grippie in my drawstring backpack to open the Gatorade. The kicker was the mini basketball included with lunch, not only was it orange, but I was wearing the t-shirt representing my cousin Jennifer's high school basketball team. So what high school basketball was over. When I decided on doing this activity, my plan was to read while I ate lunch. Unfortunately, I forgot to charge my Kindle before bringing it out there. No matter how good of a Girl Scout I try to be, I just can't always remember everything.

An employee of the park even came to take a picture of me enjoying my lunch. How did he know I love pictures? After the sun found me under the tree, I regretted my decision to wear black sweatpants. It was time for me to move anyway, I had forgotten to apply sunscreen, which is also always in my car. I took my blanket back to my car and after trading my sunglasses for my regular glasses I headed back to the Nature Center with my walking poles. That became my Plan B since reading wasn't going to happen. I did the abridged version of the trail and made my way back to my car before it got too crowded. I saw both land and water animals. I even saw a turtle that made me think of my cousin Jessica's turtle, Squirt. Anyway, as soon as I got home I looked into my *Program Guide*. This is a magazine I get from my local library and where I learned about this activity. I emailed the county how much I enjoyed the event and how I hoped it would continue.

On June 7, 2017, I started taking MS exercise class at Sheltering Arms again. That was not my plan. I had not been since January 2017. I went to Sheltering Arms planning to just workout in the gym. When I walked in class to speak to everyone, they asked if I was staying and I did. I had not even paid for the class, I joked that I hoped I wouldn't get written up for that. I was not walking all the way back to the car to get my money. I will just take care of the payment next time I am there. The instructor asked how my weekend was and I had to think long and hard to come up with the answer. This brain really frustrates me sometimes.

My second goal from the Live Fully, Live Well class was that I decided to expand my volunteer efforts from the National MS Society alone. On June 9, 2017, inspired by AnnMarie Gilbert's speech at the basketball banquet, I volunteered with the Special Olympics. I cheered at the opening ceremony for the track and field athletes. That part was inspired by my friend, Tichanda. I know how much hearing cheers means to me at Walk MS, so I thought this volunteer activity was a good fit. I wore a t-shirt that read "Odds were Meant to be Overcome." I purchased mine in purple. All of the proceeds from the t-shirt sales went directly toward medals for the Special Olympics Summer Games.

The event took place outside at the E. Claiborne Robins Stadium at the University of Richmond. I saw several people that appeared to be facing great developmental challenges. On the large video screen, the well-wishers were telling the athletes to do their best. That was different, the emphasis for all of the other sporting events I attended was to win. I sat in the bleachers and cheered. There was a cover band out there and everything. I forgot to wear one of my MS bracelets so Plan B was to put my Disabled Parking Placard Identification Card in the silicone wallet that is stuck on the back of my smartphone.

I left before everything ended. I wanted to make sure I was able to safely make it back to my car before dark. On the walk to my car, a group of women asked if I was okay because I was holding my stomach. I told them I was okay and I have MS and they told me I did not need to explain. Until they said that, I had never realized I looked like I was having some stomach distress as I hold my hands in front of me to maintain my equilibrium. I believe it is my calling to educate people on MS and that seemed to be the perfect opportunity for a teaching moment. After I asked one of the ladies to take a picture of me, I asked if we could go to the prom. It turned out to be a very funny trip to the parking lot with a stranger. She told all the passersby we were prom dates. I had to let her know that I couldn't walk and laugh, so we stopped a couple of times to laugh. On the way home, I saw the Full Strawberry Moon. This time I did my research ahead of time, so I knew the name was not based on the color of the moon.

The following evening, I attended an event at the Beacon Theatre. It was called "Jammin' in June" and was a scholarship performance for graduating high school seniors. It was in my birth city of Hopewell, Virginia. I have been driving past this theater for years, but have not gone to a performance there. The theater has been there since 1928. It was renovated and reopened in 2014, so it was high time I finally made it there.

I arrived super early to ensure a good parking spot. I ended up taking the second-best parking spot. The best spot was available, but was in the sun. Even though the AC was on, being in the sun makes a difference. It was 89 degrees outside. I had called ahead of time to see what time the doors opened to avoid having to walk back and forth to the car. I still had to walk about a half block to get to the entrance. I was the first person in the auditorium, aside from the photographer. By holding onto chairs, I made my way down the hill.

As I sat in my front row seat, I was entertained by advertisements on the screen. I like ads. A couple of employees asked me to do them a favor. I was asked to test out the visibility from the height of a couple of different chairs. It turns out they had recently raised the floor of the pit by 13 inches. That was fun. It was a few extra steps, but it was nice to feel needed. There were two comedians and three music acts. One of the bands performed with an instrument I had never seen. I don't know the name of the instrument, but it was an electronic wind instrument that emulates horn sounds. When the event was over, I headed up to the rear of the auditorium without holding onto chairs. Uphill is so much easier than downhill. I exited through a different door and my car was right on the other side.

On June 13, 2017, I went to Virginia Safari Park in Natural Bridge, Virginia. A couple of weeks prior I had seen Facebook pictures of my cousin, Frank Jr., there with his nephew. When I saw him at a family function, he told me it was something I could drive-through. That was right up my alley. Upon further research, I found out it was a 180-acre drive-through safari adventure with free-roaming animals.

After paying my admission fee, I grabbed a VIP parking spot, visited the restroom, and visited the gift shop. While there, I purchased a souvenir refrigerator magnet to add to my collection. My refrigerator is covered with magnets I have purchased or received as gifts. I had seen an advertisement for caverns that were close. A gift shop employee told me the closest caverns were only five miles away. I had collected a brochure of caverns from the hotel when I visited Roanoke, Virginia in February 2017. I had never seen caverns before and it looked like an interesting place to visit.

I started taking the driving tour. I had gotten audiobooks for the trip to Natural Bridge, Virginia, but I removed the disk while I was on the tour. I toured the park at the posted speed of 5 MPH. It was on a very gravely road that kicked up a bunch of dust. I didn't care. My car was not clean; it rarely is.

The animals walked right up to the car. I had not expected that. If I had looked at the guidebook as soon as they handed it to me, rather than when I was home sitting on my couch, I would have known the animals came right up to your car. I guess that's what's meant by free-roaming. The first time I was a bit frazzle dazzle and unable to take any pictures. There was also a petting zoo, but I did not visit that part of the park.

I opted out of feeding the animals. There was no way I was opening my windows. I was fine enjoying the animals from the comfort of my air-conditioned vehicle. Two vehicles that were stopping to feed the animals let me past them, so my tour was short. I saw bison, deer, and camels to name a few. I had gotten used to the animals by the end of the tour. I was able to get a couple of pictures of the animals. After driving through Virginia Safari Park, I headed to Natural Bridge Caverns. On the way there, I saw a sign for Natural Bridge Zoo, but I had already reached my daily allowance of animals, so I passed on the zoo.

As I was pulling up to Natural Bridge Caverns I took a picture of the sign. I decided against touring the caverns when the welcome sign read it would require some physically demanding walking and that descending and climbing upstairs would be required. Even though I had my walking poles in the car, I left after visiting their gift shop. I had a magnet and a picture so for all intents and purposes I went to the caverns.

On the way home, I pulled over to a place designated as a scenic view. What a great view it was. I parked and got out of my car and took a few pictures. It was a warm day, so I was only out of the car for a couple of minutes.

That day Taco Bell was offering free Doritos Locos Taco as part of a NBA Finals promotion. I had never tried one before, but I like Doritos and I like tacos, so I figured why not? With my outfit decorated in Taco Bell mild sauce, I headed to my polling station to do my civic duty by voting in the Virginia Primary Election. As you might imagine, I slept so well that night.

On June 17, 2017, I went to the Virginia Zoo in Norfolk, Virginia. They had their 15th Annual Day for People with disAbilities. This was the first year I had heard of this event. People with disabilities were allowed in free of admission and they were allowed to bring one care partner, also free. I had initially asked Sandra to take me, but I can't keep relying on other people, so I went by myself. I wore an orange shirt that read "Be Inspired. Get Connected. Walk MS." I also wore an orange silicone MS bracelet. I decided to leave my VIP card in the wallet attached to my cell phone after the Special Olympics. I had spoken to someone at the zoo a few days prior to confirm it would be okay for me to enter with my walking poles. I went early so that I could use my morning legs. VIP parking was all taken by the time I got there. I should have expected that, but I hadn't.

With a drawstring backpack and walking poles in my hands, I headed to the entrance. It started raining as soon as I left the car. Knowing they were calling for rain in the forecast, I was grateful that I keep extra ponchos in my car. I had placed one in the drawstring backpack I was carrying. Seeing me with my walking poles, the person at the ticket window nodded me in at no charge. Since the rain had gotten heavier, I chose this time to go in the nearby gift shop and purchase a refrigerator magnet. The rain stopped shortly after I made my purchase. The first animals I saw were orangutans, Sandra's favorite. I wasn't there long, but I was there and that's what counts. I'm sure if I had stayed longer I would have seen a menagerie of animals. I did not see anyone else using walking poles, but I saw several wheelchairs and other mobility aids. Just like when I was at the Special Olympics, I saw several people that appeared to have both physical and mental handicaps much greater than my own. As I headed back to my car, I got to see the water feature near the zoo entrance.

When I got back to Richmond, Virginia I stopped home for a quick bathroom break. I also wet my Chilly Pad, since it was warmer than when I initially left home. I then headed to Rockwood Park. A few months ago, a lady on an online forum talked about her and her kids busied themselves by hiding rocks. I had no idea what she was talking about, but I was intrigued. Upon further research I found out Richmond, Virginia has this whole RVA Rocks! painted rock movement. The purpose is to spread joy through random acts of kindness. I joined their Facebook group and found out that people hide rocks at Rockwood Park. I had never been before, but this scavenger hunt like activity sounded interesting. People decorate some real imaginative rocks, everything from animals to cartoon characters. Some rocks just display humorous or inspirational words. Others are decorated with some intricate designs. Rocks are decorated by both adults and kids and they take pictures of them, sometimes mentioning specifically where they hid the rocks or where they plan to hide the rocks. You are encouraged to keep a rock you find, re-hide it, post a pic, or do nothing. Again, carrying my walking poles, I started looking for rocks. I smiled when I found a colorful rock decorated with a flower design at the base of a tree. It was not one of the rocks I had seen online. After removing some debris that was on the rock, I decided to post a picture of it, stating where I had found it. I left the rock there in the same place, since I had not brought my own decorated rock to the park to replace the one I found. I later saw that some people paint both sides of the rock. I never considered turning it over, so I may

229

have missed out on seeing something on the other side. I slept like a rock that night. Again, pun intended.

The next day I went to the 5th Annual Richmond Bacon Festival. I hadn't been since I attended the first one in 2013. I managed to find a free parking space extremely close to the entrance. Just one of the benefits of driving a compact car. I walked to the festival without my walking poles. There was no required fee. However, there was a suggested entry donation of $1. The donation was to enhance Richmond's parks. I paid the suggested nominal fee. There was a live band. It was Father's Day so kids and their fathers were out in spades. I had Bacon Mac N' Cheese. In my opinion, everything's better with bacon. Again, I was only there for a short time. That was the end to a great weekend.

On June 20, 2017, I was looking on Facebook and saw that Kenny Wingfield and Suzanne of the MSAV (Multiple Sclerosis Alliance of Virginia) had taken a break near my house just two minutes prior. I texted Suzanne to ask if they were still on break. She replied that they had just finished. A few days prior, Suzanne had texted me saying they would be in my area and sent me their schedule. You see Kenny was riding a three-wheeled handcycle in order to promote MS awareness and raise money for MSAV. Thinking I missed my opportunity to meet up with them, I called Suzanne and she stated they could take another break when I told her I was close. In fact, they were on the road perpendicular to where I lived.

I was babysitting Kasharne's daughters, Kayden and McKenzie, so the three of us headed out. I explained to them we were going to see a bike rider that has MS like me. Suzanne asked me if I minded trailing a few car lengths behind Kenny, blinking my flashers, while she searched for a place to pull over. Not realizing I was there to help, Kenny tried to wave me past him several times. As we followed him, Kayden noted he would start going faster as we headed downhill. We didn't have far to go to meet up with Suzanne who was acting as his fill in SAG (support and gear). She was accompanying him by driving a car that read "MS Ride." The girls thought Suzanne's last name was Ride. The car also fashioned a poster that read "Multiple Sclerosis Awareness Ride across Virginia Kenny Wingfield MS Alliance."

Our meeting turned into Kenny's water, snack, and rest stop. I told Kenny that McKenzie asked me why his bike was so low. After telling her that was a good question he told us it rolled better and the bad part is that it is not as visible down low. He pointed out that he has a flag and lights to help be seen. Also the back of the car being driven by Suzanne has another sign that reads, "Caution. Slow moving bicycle ahead." I asked several questions myself. Kenny told me he was diagnosed in 1991. He also told me when he started biking on June 10, 2017, he had big hills the first couple of days. He said he had about 80 miles remaining of the 595-mile course and it was scheduled to end on June 23, 2017. What a coincidence, on the one year anniversary of my Throwback Thursday posts. I shared that factoid with them. Suzanne gave the three of us blue MSAV bracelets. She gave the girls a few extras to share with their friends. On the way home, I clarified that the poster stood for MS Ride, rather than Ms. Ride.

When I got home I realized I was wearing a volunteer shirt from Bike MS. I would have shared that had I noticed before. That just happened to be the next shirt in rotation. My t-shirt was blue like Suzanne's MSAV shirt, so people assumed I was riding with them when they saw the pictures on Facebook.

I listen to audiobooks, even if I am just staying in Richmond, Virginia. I started reserving audiobooks available at other locations and picking them up from my local library. Oddly enough, the audiobooks have actually decreased my episodes of getting lost. The CDs do not require me to be active in a conversation, so I guess I am more able to drive without any distractions. If someone was riding in my car with me, I would remove the disk and put the disk number and track number in my smartphone, noting where I left off. One time my brother, R-Jay, told me I could just hit the radio button to hold my spot on the disk. I'm pretty sure I knew how to do that before when I have previously listened to CDs in the car.

One time I was partially through a disk when I realized I had already heard that audiobook. The title did not jog my memory. I had to start keeping a spreadsheet of audiobooks that I listen to. Another time, I got an audiobook for a book I had actually read. I went ahead and finished that one because the visual I created from my own reading of the book was different than what I imagined from others reading the same words. The second time that happened I did not finish listening and wished I had a spreadsheet of all of the books I had read.

Chapter 16

Like I mentioned earlier, June 23, 2017 was the one year anniversary of my Throwback Thursday project. I made a Facebook post telling everyone it was the one year anniversary of my weekly Throwback Thursday posts. I told all of my Facebook friends that I hope everyone has enjoyed it because I plan on continuing. I was happy to see I only received positive affirmations.

I also updated my Facebook profile picture from 2014. This time it was not a temporary update. No one had seen this picture yet. It is the photograph I am using on the back cover of this book. Admit it, you flipped the book over when you read that last sentence. Don't feel bad, Facebook has caught me with a similar trick a few times. On March 8, 2017, I went to take this picture at the mall when I celebrated MS Awareness Week. I was so proud that I remembered to wear earrings. I was wearing a button-down shirt. Since I no longer try clothes on, I forgot how much of a challenge those little buttons are when I made that purchase. I didn't have my button tool yet. I didn't care that my wisdom highlights (gray hairs) were showing. I used a quarter to get a handful of M&M's from the candy machine. Okay, three quarters. Unlike Red Nose Day and dressing up for Halloween in 2016, this was done specifically because of this book. I used my morning legs for this trip. I rented a stroller from the mall. I had to plan which anchor store to park near to easily gain access to the strollers as well as researching the cost to rent a stroller. I was not able to go far, but I made it to the photography studio. When the photographer saw the empty stroller, he assumed I was waiting for someone else in order to take my pictures. I let him know it was just me and not to pay the stroller any attention. The photographer even made me laugh when he expressed that I was doing a fake smile. The final picture shows my real smile. I displayed a small copy of the picture in the item I got from the Pineapple Emporium in Alabama. It is on a bookshelf in my home office.

In addition to writing this book, let's see where things stand a year later in regards to Throwback Thursday. My most recent Throwback Thursday post from June 22, 2017 was a picture of R-Jay and I when I was in eighth grade. We are both lying in my bed, I have on a nightgown and a bonnet on my head, protecting whatever hairstyle I was rocking at that time, and I have rabbit ears behind R-Jay's head.

I was on level 795 of Candy Crush when I started Throwback Thursday. I am now on level 1425 and I haven't spent any money on the game. I probably could have gone even farther, but sometimes my brain and my hands are not on the same accord. I know getting this far was not all skill. Some of it was pure luck.

I had 209 Facebook friends when I started, I now have 409 and counting. I realize that not all of my new friends are related to Throwback Thursday. The additional friends will at least be made aware of MS. Some of the increase is due to people I have met along the regular course of life and have nothing to do with MS or Throwback Thursday. I continue to make Facebook friend requests, some based on people that have liked or commented on previous Throwback Thursday posts.

Not everyone I made a friend request to has accepted. I know some people have moved on to other forms of social media. Perhaps they saw some of my Throwback Thursday posts from their friends and did not want to be part of this ride. That's fine. I initially started taking six pictures at a time for my Throwback Thursday post. I have taken as many as 12 photos at a time because I get so caught up in enjoying looking through the photo albums. I still only post one snapshot a week, and I am skipping a lot of pictures. I got involved in some of the witty banter created from comments I receive from my Throwback Thursday posts. I ended up conversing with people I haven't talked to in a very long time or communicated with people I don't even know if their Facebook friend was tagged in a post. The interactive aspect of it all gives me such joy. Some of my Throwback Thursday posts have even created a back and forth dialogue between other people that may be in photographs together, but are not normally in contact with each other.

People that have been a part of Throwback Thursday have been surprised that I have so many old pictures. I let them know that I have every photograph that I have ever taken. Some of the snapshots taken during school were from field trips or other activities. Many were just taken during recess. A friend from fourth grade that was at my 2014 dinner in New York stated she wished Throwback Thursday was every day. That made me laugh. I let her know I had enough pictures to do it daily, but I wasn't going to do that.

Once Sandra's sisters created a Facebook page for her, I went back a little bit to add some photos of her. I still did a decent job of maintaining chronological order while alternating between friend and family photos. Sandra sure did spend a lot of money on film. That's what we used back then. Aside from the comments on my Throwback Thursday posts, people have called my cell phone to let me know how much they are enjoying the posts even if they don't know the people in the picture. I do not reveal which snapshot will be shown next. I just love surprises, even if I am not the one being surprised.

Some people have commented that Throwback Thursday makes them feel old. I just laugh, actually type LOL or select an emoji since it's online. There is only one alternative to getting old and I certainly don't want any part of that anytime soon. I am claiming becoming a nonagenarian. This 40 Metamorphosis has been so much fun and I am confident it will continue. I am looking forward to what 41 and beyond have in store for me.

As I look through pictures to post for Throwback Thursday, I laughed at the fact that I took some very interesting fashion risks, especially during middle school. I love that Ma let me be myself. I guess that was her invoking her right to choose her battles. Aunt Elsie had told me about that technique when her daughters, Jessica and Jennifer, were younger.

The post of my grandfather, Buster, with his 10 sons has been the most popular Throwback Thursday post to date. It was taken at my grandmother Agnes' funeral.

That was a very momentous photograph. It is the only one I have ever seen of all of the boys together. For all I know, it may be the only one that exists. So far, the greatest number of "Wow" emojis came from a picture of me holding a Boa Constrictor when I was about 11. It was an attraction from a weekend school fair. I hadn't held a snake prior to or since then. I would imagine I was too young and dumb to realize I probably should have been scared. After Uncle James saw the post, he reminded me I had called him to come over when I saw a small, dead snake outside of my house some years back.

In year one I did not miss any Throwback Thursday posts. I never forgot to put #tbt or tag the correct people on my posts. I guess my anal-retentive personality came in handy for this project. I was happy that no one sent me a message requesting I remove one of their photos, nor did anyone request to not be included in Throwback Thursday. If anyone unfriended me as a result of Throwback Thursday I did not notice.

Only one time, in January 2017, was I not thinking about my Throwback Thursday post when I got in the bed on Wednesday night. Again, reminders in the phone only work if you remember to check them. On that particular day, I had gone to exercise class at Sheltering Arms, I went to an afternoon MS support group meeting, I went to the grocery store, and I had a pharmaceutical company dinner. I was doing the most that day. No wonder I forgot. I made the post about 2:00am when I got up to use the bathroom. On one other very busy Wednesday night in February, I remembered Throwback Thursday when I first got in the bed, but I removed my glasses and prepared to go to sleep before I made my post. Even though I took Melatonin, I managed to stay awake until midnight.

No one other than my cousin, Leticia, made a request for me to show a specific photograph for Throwback Thursday. Some people have asked me to post more pictures of them if I had them. I plan on accommodating that request whenever possible. The only other request was from my friend, Keta. She wanted me to post her Throwback Thursday pics from VCU on her 40th birthday. I did not do that. I told her she had to wait until I got to that point.

A few unexpected things occurred as a result of Throwback Thursday. I did not expect to meet other distant relatives. Well at least meet through Facebook or Facebook Messenger. I love that Throwback Thursday is bringing people together. I learned that even folks that don't have a Facebook page want to be included in Throwback Thursday. I hadn't expected that since I can't tag them. I am happy to oblige and I will just tag a parent. People have made a Throwback Thursday picture they are included in their temporary Facebook profile picture. Some of my Facebook friends shared my Throwback Thursday post with all their other Facebook friends. Sharing is caring.

Since I have continued to post regular pictures along with my Throwback Thursday snapshots, people have seen posts of me at MS fundraising events and near MS signs. Because of this, people have shared with me in comments that they know someone with MS or they have a parent or other relative with MS. Some people that have stated they have never posted a Throwback Thursday photograph on Facebook are now posting them. I don't know if my photographs had anything to do with that or if it is just a coincidence. Either way, I like it. I really love pictures, probably only second to surprises (good ones).

I continue to learn how to do new things on Facebook. My smartphone has the capability to continue to watch a video as I scroll through Facebook, but I usually don't do that. I guess it's that whole multitasking trouble thing. I have to do one of those things at a time. My cousin, Leticia, told me about Facebook's Marketplace and showed me how to send a photo through Facebook Messenger. I even made my first video and sent it to my cousin, Leticia. It was a video of me doing a physical reenactment of a joke that I saw on TV. A Surry County High School classmate showed me how to "Check In" indicating your location. My friend, Regina, sent me screen shots showing me how to indicate what I was watching. I wanted to use that feature when I was watching the New Edition biopic. NE4Life.

My brother, R-Jay, had taken me to see them a few years ago as one of our Special Times concerts. It was my birthday gift, a few months before my birthday. That's just how we do things. I still have a lot to learn, I'm going to keep my IT Specialist, Janene busy. Anyway, play cousin, RonShai', taught me how to go Facebook Live. I haven't used that skill yet. Maybe I will use it to announce this book being published.

I heard that you can suck a popsicle to be more alert and energetic. So, I switched from my Italian Ice to

Popsicle as I sat on the porch, sometimes reading. There is a joke on the wooden Popsicle sticks, some of those made me laugh. I have shared some of the popsicle stick humor on Facebook.

On June 24, 2017, I started the day at a health fair at the local church. That seemed to be an appropriate way to start my day since I was wearing a shirt that read, "Living with MS. Together we are Stronger." I am all about bringing awareness to MS. There was not a MS table at the health fair. I left that feedback. I also left a piece of positive feedback.

After the health fair, I had to drive back home because I had forgotten my purse. It happens. I then attended a workshop on Installing Wall Tile at The Home Depot. I was interested in learning how to install a backsplash on the wall above my stove. I was supposed to take that class last month, but I woke up late and I did not want to rush. Let me clarify, I woke up in enough time to make it to the class on time. It's just that now I am unable to just hop out of bed, get in the shower, and leave the house right away. Those days are few and far between. There is usually a resting period that occurs between using the bathroom, taking my morning pills, and getting in the shower and then a second rest break after I have finished showering. Sometimes it feels as though I have just completed some strenuous activity. It can take up to five times more energy for a MSer to do the most menial task. I could have made it to the workshop if I were to forgo the rest breaks. I figured if my body needed the rest, who am I to deprive it of that luxury?

As soon as I entered The Home Depot, I grabbed a shopping cart and headed to the rear of the large store, as instructed by the greeters. I left the shopping cart just to the side of the tool table, so I would have it to leave the store. I sat at the table and had about 10 minutes to rest. Before class started, I was overwhelmed with the number of items on the table. The only thing I already had from the list of needed materials was a dust mask and rubber gloves. I thought, "If I buy all of those things, I might as well hire someone to do the work for me."

Class started with the instructor explaining the difference between wall and floor tile. It turns out that not every item on the table would be used for every job. There were vehicles driving by and I had trouble hearing the elderly man that was teaching the class. He apologized for the noise of horns and different vehicles driving by to move items and told us we were in a working warehouse.

We ended up taking a tour of a portion of the store. I was so glad I had that shopping cart nearby for our trip through the tile aisles. I was the only female and I was the only one to volunteer to put ceramic tile on the faux wall when we returned to the teaching area. I put down grout with a spackle knife. It did feel like putty with sand in it, as described by one person in class. After I was done, I had one of the other attendees take a picture of me with my completed work. The instructor asked for a picture of himself as well. He picked up a prop from the table and posed. That was funny. I was grateful I had hand sanitizer in my small purse. I made a mess. I made sure to measure the space with a tape measure and I put the size in my smartphone calendar on the date of the class. I'm just going to put a pin in that project for now.

I headed home for a nap. Okay, lunch then a nap. When I woke up, my friend, Kasharne, told me I had won a prize at the health fair, but you had to be present to win and I wasn't. Apparently, I had entered some type of drawing when I was there. The nap was way more valuable than whatever prize I would have taken home.

When I woke from my nap, it was time to start the second half of my day, I headed to Kroger to purchase grapes that were on sale. The overweight man putting the grapes on the shelf in the produce section said, "I want to be slim."

It was in response to my "I want grapes."

"We all want something," was my reply. He told me he grows the grapes in his backyard, but I don't know if he was serious about that part or not.

Once I made my way to the register, I attempted to hand the cashier my key card so that MSAV (Multiple Sclerosis Alliance of Virginia) could get the reward points. Turns out I handed her the wrong tag. She shuffled through my many key tags to find the right one. I am not making these kinds of errors on purpose or saying what I think happens to people just to have something to include in this book. Some of the adventures, yes, but not the errors. That actually happened.

I then headed to the fancy library. The person at the front desk had no record of the class I was there to attend. I even double checked the *Program Guide* to confirm I was at the correct location on the correct day. Plan B, stay at the library for a little while and check out the Comic Con exhibit. It was a miniature version of what I had only seen on TV. I saw several people dressed up as characters. I also saw a Wonder Woman poster. I even took a picture with a Stormtrooper from the Star Wars franchise. That is something I never thought I would do.

After the library, I headed home again to rest and get re-energized by the AC. I then headed to the Byrd Theater. I would not have been able to catch the movie that day if my original class was going on at the library. My friend, Kasharne, always says, "Everything happens for a reason." I guess she's right. The parking lot containing VIP parking was familiar to me from my many Byrd Theatre trips with my friend, Lona. It was about a block or so from the theater. I was early for the movie so I went to Bygones, a vintage clothing store next to Byrd Theater. I figured it would be perfect for the two Great Gatsby themed parties I plan on attending later this year. Also, I could use it for a Halloween costume at some point. The sales lady made that suggestion. I ended up not getting anything.

As I entered the cooled movie theater, I thought about the TV show *Adam Ruins Everything*. It is a show that dispels common misconceptions about various topics. On one episode, Adam talks about how movie theaters were one of the first public buildings with AC. Anyway, after I grabbed my seat in the theater I watched their advertisements on the screen. I saw an ad for Bygones and thought, "That's how I learned about them."

Before the movie began, a man rose up from below the stage playing the pipe organ. After he entertained us with a few selections, he prompted a "Take Me Out to the Ball Game" singalong. I participated. That was fun.

The movie I watched was *Boss Baby*. Yes, it's an animated movie and yes I went by myself. I used to not go to animated movies if I didn't have a kid to take with me. I am over that now. It was one of those movies with both kid and adult humor. As I left the theater, I heard a mother ask "What do you think about having a kid brother?" Spoiler alert. The movie was about an only child becoming an older sibling. I guess she used the movie as a way to break the impending sibling news. Or maybe not. I told you I make up stuff sometimes. The trip back to the parking structure was slow and difficult, but I made it to my car safely.

When I got home, I ended up ordering a 1920's flapper dress and a feathered, sequined headband from the Wish app. This is the first time I was trying Wish. I still order using Amazon, I just wanted to try something different this time. A member of one of my support groups told me about that app. I learn and hear about all kinds of things in the MS community, not only MS-related things. Anyway, that was a good day for me. I would not have been able to do that many activities in one day without taking a nap. I had a great night's sleep without the use of Melatonin or a sleep mask. I was worn out and stayed home all day the next day.

I attended both of my cousin Jennifer's graduation ceremonies and her graduation party. This time I was more social than I had been at the sister Jessica's graduation events two years ago and I am smiling in every photograph. Genuine smiles, not faker jaker smiles. At one of the ceremonies, my cousin, LaVita, suggested we take a sign language class. The funny thing is that I don't believe she was even aware of my fake sign language usage. I researched taking such a class and it was out of my budget.

On June 29, 2017, I went to Mariners' Museum and Park in Newport News, Virginia. My play cousin, Tasia, shared on Facebook that they had a $1 admission. It was a sunny day, so I put on sunscreen before I exited my car. Before entering the museum, I asked either one of two ladies, whom were also leaving the parking lot, to take a picture of me near the museum sign. After taking the snapshot, they headed towards The Noland Trail. It is a five-mile foot trail. I headed inside the museum.

The gift shop was before I even paid my entry fee. I got my refrigerator magnet before the trip through the museum so I wouldn't forget it on the way out. The docent pointed out the fact that I was limping like he was. Perhaps he thought I didn't know.

After taking a short tour of the museum, I asked where the restroom was located. I threw my hand up, when the lady at the information desk told me I had to walk back to where I had just left. She then offered me a wheelchair, which I refused. I would rather leave them available for people that have a greater need than I do. I was then offered a stroller, which I pushed to the restroom. Not only had I not noticed the strollers before, I had walked right past the restrooms. I then went back and took a longer trip through the museum. After I returned the stroller, I joked with the information desk lady that I wish I had asked about the restroom earlier. I usually do. We laughed and I headed to the car. A maritime museum would not have been my first choice of museums to visit, but it was in my budget. The walk back to the VIP spot in the parking lot seemed much longer than the trip inside. It always does.

After I was leaving Newport News, Virginia heading to Williamsburg, Virginia, my car started acting funky. It made a noise, the "Check engine" light was blinking, and it would not accelerate over 50 MPH, then 35 MPH. Due to construction on Highway 64, there was no shoulder available for me to park. The next exit happened to be where I was going. I was on the phone with my service technician while this was happening. When I got to the first red light, I did not know if the car would accelerate at all. It did, barely. I was instructed to pull over and turn the car off then on again. Why didn't I think of that? I had previously been taught that Step 1 in troubleshooting a computer or printer is to cut it off and back on. Anyway, the car sounded good, the "Check engine" light was no longer on, and I was able to pull back into traffic quickly. Even though the car started, I still wanted it checked out before I drove it out of the state. With the 4th of July holiday coming up, the car dealership in Williamsburg could not check out my car until July 5, 2017. My car acts like it doesn't know or care that I'm trying to write a book and trying to take it to New York the following week. I'm going to need a Plan B.

Since my car was running fine, I continued on to Jamestown Settlement. It was my first time visiting, so

I purchased a refrigerator magnet. It reminded me of the fact that I lived in New York for 17 years and did not visit the Empire State Building or the Statue of Liberty until I had lived in Virginia for many years. I guess places don't become tourist attractions until you leave.

I continued onto the Jamestown Ferry from Williamsburg, Virginia to Surry, Virginia. My first time taking this trip was a few months ago. Let me clarify, I have been on the ferry several times, but never by myself driving my own car. That part changed a few months ago. Thanks to directions from Uncle Ralph, I was able to seamlessly make the trip from a pharmaceutical company lunch I was attending in Newport News, Virginia to Surry, Virginia.

After riding the Jamestown Ferry from Williamsburg to Surry, I went to The Surry Seafood Company. It was right on the water and down a road I had never traveled. I could have sat outside, but the heat prevented that. I had a great view from the interior. There was a man playing a guitar entertaining those seated on the patio. The wait staff mostly had on orange and purple shirts. My waitress was wearing burgundy, but I did not hold that against her. The high bar stool was a challenge. Sure, I could have asked for a lower seat, but I didn't want to take up a larger table. My meal was topped with Monterey cheese and tomatoes. I love cheese. Tomatoes, not so much, but it seemed to be a good choice in my attempt to create a more colorful plate. I've learned that some more colorful foods have anti-inflammatory properties. My food was delicious. I couldn't eat it all, so I boxed up my leftovers. I noticed low, small tables when I exited the restaurant. I swear I did not notice those when I entered the restaurant.

I left there and went to Uncle Ralph's house. Shortly after sitting on the couch, I realized I had forgot my leftovers at the restaurant. Uncle Ralph even provided me with their phone number. I wasn't going back, so I just kept talking. Oh well, it happens. That's what I get for trying to do so many things in one day.

I spent the night at Ma's house. I did not leave her house at all while she was at work the following day. Nor did I turn on the TV all day. I made a few phone calls, but I mostly worked on writing in my sayings journal. I usually take screenshots or pictures of things I want to add to the journal. I took a late afternoon nap. It was mostly a lazy day where I was off the grid. I believe everybody occasionally needs one of those. Ma brought me a Filet-O-Fish from McDonald's for dinner. That is our Special Times when I spend a Friday night at her house.

I stayed with Ma a second night. The next morning, we went to a household items yard sale. That's the only kind of yard sale I attend. My cousin, Jamila, lucks up on some good finds at yard sales. Maybe I'll add attending a regular one to my next vision board. Anyway, Aunt Cat usually goes with me. I have even been by myself. The person that put on the yard sale even made me a gift basket once she found out from one of my cousins that I travelled from Richmond, Virginia for the sales. I told you I love unsolicited gifts. It is like a good surprise. After the sale, Ma dropped me off at Aunt Ann's house while she ran her errands. We joked that she was dropping me off at the babysitter's house. We later joked that Aunt Ann got fired for leaving me alone when she went to run her own errands. To be fair, she did ask me if I wanted to go with her, my cousin, LaVita, and her daughter. I refused. I stayed there and took a nap.

When we returned to Ma's house, I continued to add entries into my sayings journal. I stayed at Ma's house until it was time for my next activity. I went to my birthplace of John Randolph Hospital in Hopewell, Virginia and watched 4th of July Fireworks on the Appomattox in the parking lot. They were put on by City of Hopewell Recreation and Parks. Since I had stayed at Ma's house the previous night, I would have had to drive through Hopewell to get to Richmond, Virginia. I chose to see fireworks on the 1st of the month rather than the 4th of the month, figuring it would be less traffic and easier to navigate. I don't know if there were fewer people, but they had an ideal parking situation. I had a cold bottle of water from Ma's house. I put the water and snacks in a plastic bag. I keep those in the car too. I had a drawstring backpack in the car, but the chair was already going to occupy the spot on my back. After parking I put the folded chair, that has straps, on my back. I grabbed my walking poles and my plastic bag of snacks and headed to the seating area.

There was a nice breeze, so I did not need to have a cooling item around my neck. I stopped near the beginning of the area blocked off for viewing fireworks. I had claimed a viewing location before it got dark. Many people had folding chairs. I did not see anyone carrying them using two straps like a backpack. Some people put their blankets down on the pavement and others just stood up. Some people had entire coolers out there. Some families were dressed in matching red, white, and blue garb. I saw a kid's face painted. I did not see that set up, if he got it done there. Someone sitting near me was looking at my walking poles inquisitively, I just made eye contact, smiled, and said, "Hi."

Nutzy, the mascot from the Richmond Flying Squirrel baseball team was walking through the crowd. He had stopped near where I was sitting down. I let the kids have their fun first and after the crowd thinned out I walked over without my walking poles and got my picture taken with Nutzy.

After eating all my snacks, I made a proposition to a fellow spectator whose group was making a temporary trash pile on the ground. I agreed to give him my bag to collect his group's trash, but he had to dispose of the bag. He was happy to have a trash bag and that was one less thing I had to carry, so we both benefited from the arrangement.

There was a live band performing before the fireworks started. I wasn't moving to be able to see them, but I could hear them just fine. I just people watched and listened from afar. After the band stopped, I heard kids throwing snappers down on the pavement to make a popping nose. I remember doing that. By the time the fireworks began, the parking lot was packed. Turns out I had commandeered a perfect location, even not knowing exactly where the fireworks were being shot from. People were making the "Wooh!", "Ooh!", and "Aahh!" noises just the way I like to do.

That was fun. I considered waiting for the majority of the crowd to clear before heading to my car, but I decided against it. There were lights hanging from the rear of the building, so this helped when I was folding my chair. The trip to the car was fairly easy with the walking poles. That was a good day for me.

Chapter 17

On July 6, 2017, R-Jay started driving us up north in Ma's car. That was Plan B since my car was in the shop. Equipped with a sleep mask and a throw, I reclined the passenger seat with plans of going back to sleep. We left at 5:00 a.m. so it was still dark. I never made it back to sleep, R-Jay asked if I had gotten my E-ZPass from my car. Not only did I not have it, but the pass was never even on a list of things for me to bring. Oh well, there goes some money I hadn't planned on spending for this trip. Silver lining – I was grateful I had the cash money as an option to spend on the tolls. We first stopped in New Jersey to visit Uncle Vernis.

We continued to New York where I stayed with my friend, Regina, her husband Charles, and their family. Once again Regina had purchased my favorite snacks of Sprite, M&M's, and Doritos even though I told her not to this time. Before my trip, I tried to make plans with my friend, Aloma. She had to tell me she would be at work. It is so insensitive of me, but sometimes I forget most people work for a living. I was able to have my Special Times lunch with my cousin, Clyde. It was raining and I stepped in a puddle when I attempted to get out of the car at the restaurant. That's what I get for making up a parking space since all the VIP spots were taken. I moved my car to another location.

When I returned to Regina's house I took a nap in anticipation of a baseball game featuring Clyde's grandson. Okay, I took my nap after a trip to Zoe's Ice Cream Barn. While there, I took fun pictures outside of the ice cream parlor on the red tractor and with my head and hands in a pillory. I later found out Regina took a picture of me while I was napping with my green throw and my favorite sleep mask that read "Warning: Do Not Disturb, Disturbed Enough Already." That was a really good nap, but unfortunately the baseball game was cancelled due to the rain.

Back in November 2016, Regina and I had learned that the New Kids on the Block would once again be on tour with Boyz II Men and Paula Abdul would be joining them this time. Here is a nugget of information: The former member of Boyz II Men has MS. I used to think he carried a cane to be cool, it was presumably for the back pain he endured from his MS. Anyway, I quickly researched the performance locations. Unfortunately, the shows near either of us conflicted with unavoidable things Regina had at work. I thought we would not be able to partake in this Special Times event. In late February 2017, tickets to the concert in Boston, Massachusetts became available. Initially we had not considered traveling to Boston, but when Regina said she was going to purchase tickets as our 30th year of friendship anniversary celebration, I figured "Why not?" She also purchased me a copy of NKOTB's latest CD. I didn't even know they had one, but Track 5 is pretty catchy.

Two days after arriving in New York, with Regina driving her vehicle, we were off to Boston to see New Kids on the Block. I remembered to put the parking placard in her car for the trip. We got to Boston early to do some sightseeing before the concert. I had never been to Boston before and was excited about seeing NKOTB in their hometown.

I took pictures outside at the bar "Cheers," from the 1980's sitcom. We ate lunch at Wahlburger's, a restaurant owned by the family of one of NKOTB's members: Donnie Wahlburg. After resting at the hotel, we headed to Fenway Park, home of Major League Baseball's Boston Red Sox for the concert. I figured I would have to take additional precautions since it was an outside concert. The weather was great before the concert. I did not need sunglasses or a cooling item. I did wear a hat that read "Property of Danica." I'm pretty sure I'm the only one that thinks that is funny. The venue appeared to be sold out of their more than 35,000 seats. It started to rain and the people with floor seats were getting wet. Then they were made to move when they started calling for more severe weather. It delayed the concert about an hour. Silver lining – our seats were up in the Grandstand, so we were sheltered from all of the rain, nor did we have to move when they called for more severe weather.

Once the concert continued, NKOTB was definitely showing off for company to their city. There were fireworks and a NKOTBOSTON banner in the Boston Red Sox logo font that was displayed at the start of the concert. The whole crowd sang along to Neil Diamond's "Sweet Caroline." This is the Red Sox theme song and has been played in the middle of the eighth inning at every game since 2002. Even though I had attended several NKOTB concerts, I was fangirling. I can't speak for Regina. The next morning, we went to the pool. I didn't swim because the water was too cold, but I was at the pool and I was wearing a bathing suit, so that counts.

While I was in Boston, my friend Kasharne's oldest daughter, Kayden, attended MS Kids Day. It was sponsored by the National MS Society and billed as a day of fun and learning. Kayden told me she participated in swimming, archery, and canoeing. She learned that MS can affect any part of the body and learned about double vision in MS. She seemed to enjoy the event and told me they had pizza for lunch.

I remembered seeing some colored pipe cleaners from the TV show *Blue Bloods*. No, I don't only watch because Donnie Wahlburg from New Kids on the Block is on the show. After seeing the pipe cleaners, I purchased a pack. So far, the only thing I have done with them is make a "M" and a "S" out of a couple of the orange ones. These are pinned to the cork board in my home office. I may try and make some type of craft item with them in the future.

On July 17, 2017, I completed a Rubik's Cube! The void left by the yellow Lamborghini picture on my vision board was replaced by a picture of a Rubik's Cube. I scrambled it as soon as I received it. I thought it was something that would be helpful for mental sharpness and hand-eye coordination. From watching the movie, the *Pursuit of Happyness*, I remember learning the technique to beating it and I was certain I would have been able to restore the jumbled cube back to its original state. I am not embarrassed to admit I used YouTube. Even with online assistance, it was still difficult. I typed up the notes, in case I want to try it again. Due to my challenge with learning new things, there was a lot of rewinding of the video tutorial. Silver lining – I repeated the first few steps so many times, I was able to do them without having to replay the video or look at my notes. This item is displayed on a bookshelf in my home office.

Another item on the bookshelf is a new Koosh ball. It is mostly orange and purple. When I was a teenager, my cousin, Ta'Wane, dropped my favorite Koosh ball down a sewage drain. He claimed it was an accident as he was riding his bike, but I never believed him. This new one is a perfect replacement for the one Ta'Wane dropped. I'll admit I've been petty and have mentioned him dropping it many times over the last several years. I'm over it now. Compared to the life altering diagnosis of MS, a Koosh ball seems pretty insignificant. I have mentioned my home office several times. There is no office work done in that room anymore, unless you count ironing. That's where all the fun stuff lives. If my personality could be expressed in terms on one room, it would be my home office. There are puzzles and other fun, colorful tchotchkes all over the room. Several photographs are also displayed in the room. I even have a poster hanging on the back of the door, the kind that used to fill my walls as a teenager.

On July 21, 2017, I travelled to Clarksville, Virginia to be a part of LakeFest. The event was held at Lake Country Business Park. After parking, I put my folding chair on my back, grabbed my sunglasses, and my now lukewarm bottle of water and set up under a tree only a few feet away from my car. I attached my regular glasses to my shirt, figuring it would be dark before I left. I saw other people with their folding chairs or blankets, coolers, and some kids were playing soccer in the open field. I had a fireman take a picture of me with a fire truck. I saw a couple of hot air balloons being inflated. I did not venture to the part of the event where food and other activities were available. I was wrong about the glasses. I ended up leaving before it got dark. It was just too hot out there.

The main festival including arts and crafts was being held on Saturday, July 22, 2017, but they were calling for temperatures upwards of 100 degrees, so I planned to stay home that day. That was not the first time and won't be the last time the blistering heat kept me inside. Later that evening while at home, I noticed a mosquito bite. I had remembered to apply sunscreen, but forgot the insect repellent that was also in my car. Even though it is not one of the labelled uses, I remembered hearing that Vicks VapoRub was helpful with itchy insect bites, once applied and covered with a Band-Aid. Since I was no longer using Vicks VapoRub on my feet to help with sleep, I chose to repurpose it this way.

I was supposed to take a ride in a hot air balloon the prior week, but the pilot had unwarranted reservations. It is so sad that many people are scared of MS. My MS exercise class teacher even offered to go up in the balloon with me. I thanked her and turned down the offer, telling her that the whole experience had left a bad taste in my mouth. A member of exercise class suggested a hot air balloon festival as an alternative, so that's what I did. When I told my friend, Tichanda, I was upset after speaking to the pilot, she suggested I send him a MS pamphlet. I chose not to do that. I got the impression that not only did he not know about MS, he did not appear even interested in learning about MS. I chose not to use this experience as a MS teaching moment. Aunt Elsie suggested I look for a hot air balloon ride in the Hampton Roads area. Why didn't I think of that? The hot air balloon ride is something that started on my bucket list and is now on my vision board. We were supposed to go to a hot air balloon festival when I was in New York a couple of weeks ago. The festival was rained out. Maybe that was my sign that a hot air balloon ride was not meant to be. I will have to come up with a Plan B. Watching the hot air balloons get inflated would have to do for now.

I joined the Summer Reading Club at my local library in June 2017. I got a pencil and a bookmark when I enrolled at the library. I earned a drawstring backpack as a midpoint prize. I had to read a minimum of four books that I borrowed from the library to qualify for any prizes. Audiobooks and programs attended at the library counted too. I had lucked out, since I had already scheduled a class at my local library. The program ended at the end of August. Participating in this program had me going to the library more often, as well as visiting additional locations. I guess that was the point. My plan was to keep the nylon bag in my car and use it to transport audiobooks from the library back to the car. This plan made sense since I always order at least two audiobooks at a time. Unfortunately, I did not always remember to take the bag inside the library.

On July 27, 2017, I headed back to Roanoke, Virginia for the MS Conference & Retreat hosted by MSAV (Multiple Sclerosis Alliance of Virginia). This was the third year of the event, but the first time I had heard about it. I made sure to visit the drive-through oil change spot before getting on the road. Anyway, I was wearing the MSAV bracelets that Suzanne had given me the day I met Kenny Wingfield riding his handcycle. Another MSer was traveling with me this time and I did not listen to my audiobooks since I had a riding partner. This time the drive would be a collaborative effort.

I did not have to remember to request a room near the elevator this time since we were able to snag a room on the first floor right around the corner from all of the action in the lobby. My travel companion was also my roommate. Once arriving at the hotel, we checked in and everyone was given a nametag so that we could identify each other all weekend. My roommate told me about a long handled, easy lotion applicator. I ordered it immediately figuring it would be perfect for applying lotion to the middle of my back. No matter how much I stretch I can't reach that area and it usually stays ashy.

The first activity was an art exhibit. We were encouraged to bring items we had made while living with MS. People shared art, furniture, and other craft items. I took the painting I had created at Sandra's friend Eileen's birthday party in September 2016. At the time, I had no idea this item would be displayed at a MS event, but I had painted an orange background on my picture. I made sure to point out the line painted by the art instructor compared to my messy interpretation of similar lines. Most people that see the painting make fun of the picture, but "my people" complemented my artwork. Later that same day, I participated in an activity reminiscent of something from the TV show *Project Runway*. We had to make an outfit out of piles of random, nonconventional things. My roommate and I created a sarong dress out of an orange tablecloth. I created a hat out of a partially opened accordion paper ball. I did not realize that's what the item was when I made the hat. I decorated the hat with a Christmas bow on the side. I also made a necklace out of a ribbon and a button. That activity was so fun.

I had taken some dresses to donate to Cinderella's Closet. I had planned to donate them to a teacher collecting for kids to go to the prom. I chose to donate the items to a MS-focused organization. My dress this time was short, deep purple, and a size larger than it was last time. I was blaming it on the pizza, chocolate chip cookies, and soda I had for dinner. It probably had more to do with all of the Snickers I recently ate. I blame the marketing genius that came up with the campaign to put "Hot Mess" and "Oddball" on the candy bar wrappers. Okay, I had more than two, but they had some really funny sayings on them.

I'm losing the battle of the bulge, but I know how to get it back right and tight. For me the Cinderella's Closet experience was a chance for a 40-year old to play dress up. Other people have other reasons for wanting to participate. I forgot my dress shoes this time, so I wore my own black sandals that I had packed to wear with another outfit. I selected a choker and some earrings. I even got a manicure, I had not gotten one of those in forever.

At the dance, everyone was dressed up and people of all ages and at all disability levels were on the dancefloor. After being prompted, I got up for the

"YMCA" song and dance by the Village People. That dance turned out slightly better than my attempt to do the line dance the Cupid Shuffle at the hotel restaurant the previous night. Trust me, it was not pretty.

I was selected to be the roundtable facilitator for the topic of MS hugs. Suzanne the President and Founder of MSAV (Multiple Sclerosis Alliance of Virginia) had asked me to do this before I went to Roanoke. I shared the information I had researched on the topic. I told the attendees about how it is usually a tight feeling around your ribs or chest and how some people find they have trouble breathing. I also shared my personal MS hug experience and asked the other participants about their experience. I also participated in additional roundtable discussions on cognition problems, heat intolerance, and bladder and bowel issues. When people asked me about my charm bracelet, I was proud to tell them it was the gift I had received for winning the bingo marker competition at MS Respite Camp the previous year.

I purchased some raffle tickets and won a shirt that contained one of the sayings from my sayings journal and two cases of diapers. Not bad for only spending a few dollars and change I found at the bottom of my small purse. There was also a silent auction, but I did not participate in that. One of the new activities I did was Sound Healing with Angel Harps. I attended a Relaxation Therapy session that included not only harps, but a rainstick and wind chimes. There were additional sounds that I do not remember. I had my eyes closed so I wasn't taking any notes. I had never heard of it and that is usually not the kind of thing I am into, but it sounded interesting and it was. The harpist also did Inspirational

Sound Immersion. I did not attend that session, but others shared that they enjoyed the activity.

Kenny Wingfield did a presentation about his journey on the hand trike, the name he uses for his vehicle. He talked about the challenges he faced as well as the kind people he met along the way. He encouraged us all to dream and referred to Suzanne as an angel for stepping in to be his SAG (support and gear). Another MSer that I met at camp last year shared their love of the camera. I could definitely relate to that.

During this trip I learned that a DMT (Disease-Modifying Therapy/Treatment) has to be on the market for about six months before educational programs are offered. At one of the vendor tables, I met Stuart Schlossman, a fellow MSer and the President and Founder of MS Views and News. It is another not-for-profit patient advocacy organization that provides education, information, and resources to the Global MS community through their website and live events. I was already on their email list. One of the pharmaceutical company sales representatives from Richmond, Virginia had told me about this organization. I have already registered to attend their first live event being held in Virginia. This will require another trip to Roanoke, Virginia at the end of August.

There were 140 attendees at the event, not including pharmaceutical company representatives, Neurologists, and other vendors. Some were people I knew from my previous trip to Roanoke, some were from MS Respite Camp, and I made some new friends. Meals for the event were provided by the MS pharmaceutical companies.

One of the companies offered lip balm with a small hook. Something else I have added to my keychain. I even went to one lunch for a medication that I did not know much about. One of the Neurologists that spoke stated there were probably three possible reasons for attended the event that weekend. They were to reimagine yourself with a chronic disease, seek new information on the disease, and stay engaged with the MS community. For me it was all three. I did not participate in every activity that was offered. The event ended with a comedic presentation. A good, hearty laugh was a great way to end a fun and informative weekend. I got a partial mask from the comedian that looked like a twisted mouth wide open. She had regular lips, but taking a picture with that would not have been as much fun.

Neurologists, pharmaceutical company sales representatives, and others in the MS know stated they had never seen this type of MS event. I felt privileged to be invited. Though it was my first time attending, I'm sure it won't be my last.

Before leaving Roanoke, Virginia, I made sure to make my way to Mill Mountain Park, home of The Roanoke Star, which I had learned about on my initial trip to Roanoke, back in February of this year. The Roanoke Star was correctly billed as a must-see. I was able to take pictures of the star and the phenomenal view of the city from the observation deck.

On August 1, 2017, I attended the National Night Out. It was the 34th annual event, but it was my first time attending. I saw it advertised last year and made note to attend this year. I was able to get a parking space right in front of the festivities, so I did not grab my walking poles. However, I did have my folding chair on my back. I told a gentleman I had some physical limitations and asked him to help me step up the raised part of the ground for the event. I sat at my go-to place under a tree and listened to a man sing and play the guitar while a second man accompanied him by playing the bongos. Other attendees had folding chairs or blankets sprawled out on the lawn. It was a breezy evening, so I did not need a cooling item. It was a community building block party acting as a neighborhood watch event in Richmond's Museum District. Refreshments were provided by the Museum District Association. Neighborhood watch captains were present to address concerns and answer questions. They had drawings and I did not put my name in the hat since I was not a resident of that neighborhood. I made sure to introduce myself to the person who sent me an email encouraging my attendance prior to going to the event. Police officers were present to discuss ways to curtail crime in the neighborhood. Granted it was not in my neighborhood, but you can never be too safe. They gave away National Night Out 2017 hats. I had one of the ladies sitting near me take a picture of me wearing my new hat. I'm going to display it somewhere in my home office.

On August 6, 2017, I flew an airplane! No, for real, for real. I'm not making this one up. I've learned that if you want your life to be different, you have to be willing to try different experiences. Of all of the activities that I did not share with people, this was the hardest secret to keep. I was at Aunt Ann's house running my mouth for several hours the night before and was about to burst open with excitement, but I somehow managed to keep it to myself.

I first had some ground training with Andrew Jones at the New Kent Flight Center in Quinton, Virginia. While looking at the map, I even shared a trick that I learned in elementary school. It was a clockwise rotation mnemonic phrase of Never Eat Shredded Wheat, to remember the directions on a map. Mnemonic devices and acronyms are both very helpful when it comes to remembering things. I also use the acronym HOMES to remember all of the Great Lakes. That one I learned from the book *Improving Your Memory for Dummies* that my cousin, Leticia, gave me for Christmas a while ago.

Anyway, I made sure the instructor knew of my MS prior to flying. The diagnosis did not scare him at all. He even shared that he had previously worked with someone who had MS. Carrying a new pair of headsets, we headed outside for preflight inspection of the Tecnam aircraft. The cockpit of the 2-seater was small. Before the flight, the pilot... no I was the pilot that day. Andrew, the flight instructor, showed me how to get out of the plane in the case of a fall or other unexpected landing. I jokingly told him I did not want to hear things like that and he informed me that he had to provide me with that information before the flight.

Things started to get real when I actually turned the key to start the engine, but I had no trepidation about the flight. As I watched the propeller spin, it was time to taxi the airplane to the runway where I read items from the preflight checklist. I pushed the throttle before assisting with the takeoff of the aircraft. We went up about 3,000 feet and 100 MPH. I did a steep run maneuver over the James River. Flying over the water did not make me anxious like I thought it might. It was a clear day and Andrew stated that I had selected a perfect day for a flight. I was able to spot my VCU freshman dorm, the Richmond Coliseum, the Richmond Raceway, and other landmarks. The plan was to drive over my house, but those plans were thwarted and we had to move out of the way. Andrew pointed out the large church near my house. The same church I went to on my 40th birthday to donate school supplies. I found it interesting that he referenced the color of the roof to make sure he was pointing out the right place. I got to hear Andrew speak pilot, saying words like, "Tango" and "Alpha" as he spoke to the air traffic controller for the Richmond International Airport.

The flight was surprisingly peaceful and I so enjoyed the breathtaking view. I told Andrew, who was Chief Flight Instructor and the owner, that the landing was smooth like butter. I had the time of my life. After the flight, Andrew filled out the experience in my Pilot's Flight Log and Record. I felt so official. This flight was Plan B to the hot air balloon ride. This was so much cooler and I did not regret this selection for one minute. Andrew AirDropped videos he had taken to my smartphone. I was glad that Aunt Elsie had done that for pictures of my surprise birthday party last year or I would not have known what that was. Anyway, having a literal bird's-eye view, showed me which road to steer clear of on the way home and I was able to avoid some of the traffic. I treated myself to an ice cream sundae before going home. I had earned that.

Conclusion

It is still August 6, 2017, the final day of my 40 Metamorphosis. I will be 41 tomorrow. I just woke up from a nap. I put a lot of thought into when to stop writing. I considered stopping at the one year anniversary of Throwback Thursday, but I chose to continue since Summers are such a challenge for many MSers. I chose to include the ways I cope with different Summer activities. Soon I will be able to list Author as my employment status on Facebook. How exciting! I am elated with how far I've come in my MS journey compared to where I was when I was initially diagnosed. I had a rocky start, but I intend to finish very strong.

I have continued Throwback Thursday, but I decided to change it up. I initially started just posting one picture per week, but I just have so many pictures. After the one year anniversary, I started posting more than one picture each week if I wanted to select multiple pictures from the same event, birthday party, or other holiday gathering. I did this only for four weeks. I was only able to take pictures a couple of weeks ahead of time. It became too hectic to keep up with the multiple pictures and multiple people that needed to be tagged each week. I am now back to only posting one picture per week. So far, I have made it as far as the Summer after eighth grade. Even after more than a year of Throwback Thursday, I still look forward to making my posts. I have only had one Throwback Thursday regret so far. My friend, Regina's birthday was on a Thursday and I never considered posting a picture of her, but I had already scheduled the posting of a picture of her for the following week. I certainly could have switched those posts around. I felt so bad for that oversight.

Even though I started the sayings journals long before I started writing this book, I realized the inspirational sayings were helping me write, so I amped it up a bit. I am now on my fifth journal and refer to them as Journey Journals. In addition to rhyming, I like alliteration. The handwriting in the fifth journal compared to the first one is way worse. People claim my handwriting looks the same, but I am not convinced. The sayings make me feel so empowered. I wrote the entries using the date I saw or heard that particular saying or quote and the origin of the saying. When I realized I accidentally skipped two pages of the first journal, I decided to put stickers on those pages. That was fun.

The inside cover of each journal has MS related acronyms using the letters M and S. The second page of the first journal contains words from a card my friend, Tichanda, sent me. This card was included with my cake pop delivery from Walk MS 2016. The second page of the second journal displays words from a plaque that my cousin, Leticia, gave me when I received my MBA in 2008. That plaque is displayed on a wooden stand in my home office. The second page of all the other journals is still blank. As I peruse the journals, I noticed several entries were unintentionally duplicated, even triplicated. Silver lining – those sayings must be really important.

I try to remember to look at my vision board daily. I am no longer replacing things I complete from my vision board. The blank spaces left after I remove something make me feel accomplished. It includes some pretty lofty goals. I still want to ride in a helicopter. I'm still young-ish. Age is a state of mind. I'm at least young at heart. Another MSer I know has a goal of running in a marathon. My aspirations are not quite that high, but I do plan to walk a 10K one day. I need to include that goal to my future vision board.

I have not had another MS hug. I have continued to make fewer BM cocktails. I have not had any more hemorrhoid problems since that one time at the end of 2016. Though I have limited my Squatty Potty usage, I believe the raisins in my homemade trail mix are helping me stay regular. I'm used to the constant brain farts, but I believed the raisins were causing an increase in flatulence until I spoke to other MSers that had the same problem. That's okay, in reference to passing gas, Sandra says, "There's more room out than in."

Since I began writing, I have definitely noticed a decrease in intellect and my hearing has also gotten worse. I need to hone my lip-reading skills. My short-term memory and word finding have also gotten worse. I have forgotten what I am trying to say in the middle of a sentence. I find myself having to prompt people to refresh my memory more often. I believe I am suffering from some serious brain atrophy. What a great time to decide to write a book, am I right? Hopefully this is not reflected too poorly throughout this book. On several occasions, I have segued to another topic. Despite the cognitive deficit, I am more determined than ever to get this book published.   Again, competing only with myself.

There are other things that have changed since I started writing this book. If I see a car accident, instead of rubbernecking, now I pray that the driver and passengers are okay. That's new. I don't watch nearly as much TV as I used to do. Partly because I spent a lot of time working on this book and also because the ability to follow a movie and catch the subtle nuances of a program have become increasing more difficult. Sometimes I will text people during a show if I am unable to follow the storyline.   Also, when I am watching, the volume is lower than it used to be. I find that odd since I can't hear as well.

On my smartphone, I take a screenshot when I intend to select an emoji and select an emoji when I intend to make a comment on Facebook.   I have accidentally posted something to Facebook or put an item in my smartphone calendar, when I intended to send a text message. I used to take such pride in getting Facebook riddles and math problems correct. Now even though I recall the math mnemonic of Please Excuse My Dear Aunt Sally (you know, Parentheses, Exponents, Multiplication, Division, Addition, and Subtraction), I still can't properly calculate the math problem. On more than one occasion, I have totally forgotten what month it is, being off by several months. I have even forgotten how to spell easy words or easy names of people I have known forever.

I have mistakenly ordered duplicate items from Amazon.   Sometimes I hit the "Power" button on the washing machine, rather than "Start," turning off the machine, instead of starting a load. I can recall three times that I have returned incomplete applications and paperwork in the mail without ever signing it, even if the sender highlights where I need to sign. MS organizations are much more forgiving of this type of error.

In my opinion, feeling like I am losing my mind is worse than any physical problems I have had. People say it's just me getting older or they do the very same things. That may be true for some things, but I just don't think they get it. I make those kinds of errors several times a day.

Despite these issues, I try to pull out the silver lining in all situations. Okay, most situations. I think the optimism from my friend, Kasharne, might be rubbing off on me. I've noticed fewer occurrences of me having to say, "Why didn't I think of that?" Now on the occasion when I do get lost I just say I'm taking the scenic route. If I improperly prepare a meal I have made several times, I am first upset when I have to change the planned meal. Then I'm just that much happier when I prepare the meal properly on the first try the next time. Burnt dinner? I was preparing my food blackened. I now even have a couple of silver linings for that dreaded job I was working in 2010. They offered free health insurance benefits and I was diagnosed with MS while I was working there. I met a few people there that I am still in contact with, including my friend, Ta-Shima. She is one of the many people that has been on Walk MS team MS King both years.

I routinely get at least five consecutive hours of sleep. That used to never happen. Now that I am sleeping better, I require fewer naps. Another thing that should have been so obvious to me, but it wasn't. I purchased a neck support, contour pillow. This style of pillow had been suggested to me by a Sheltering Arms employee when I shared with them that I continue to wake up with a crick in my neck. That has certainly attributed to better sleep. I still take naps on hot days that take all my energy. On those days, it does not matter how well I slept the previous night. I started removing my glasses and wearing a sleep mask when I am napping on the couch. I learned that wearing a sleep mask during a MRI can relax you, even if you are not claustrophobic. I'm going to have to try that the next time I get one. I still am tired a lot and there is a lot of yawning. I have learned that MS is a marathon, not a sprint. I have not added any additional Post-it notes around the house as reminders, but I do have one in my car. I have started to venture out to attend support group meetings in other Virginia cities. At one such event, a MSer suggested I put a Post-it in my car when I shared that I forget about construction every time I am on 64 East/West, even though I am on that highway weekly. I now also interact with a few online MS support forums.

I used to think people could not tell something was going on with me if they just saw me walk. I also did not know I used to shake, so what do I know? Now my physical limitations are obvious to anyone that sees me walking. I find myself hip hiking (the raising of the pelvis) a lot when I am walking. When someone tells me that I'm limping I merely say, "I have MS." They usually respond by telling me about their affliction. It used to upset me so much when someone would point out my limp. I am over that now. Sometimes I feel better than I look, other days it is the other way around.

Being more aware of how temperature affects me, I drive with the AC on for any days warmer than 70 degrees. I also turn on the AC in my house earlier than I used to before MS. Trying to remain positive and reduce stress in conjunction with a good night's sleep has my good days far outweighing the bad days. Sometimes the bad days are random and not always the result of a busy week. I realize my body needs rest, but I don't always just stay in the house when I am having a bad day. Though I make every attempt to coordinate and manage my disease ahead of time, in some cases, I just hope for the best.

When I was working, I watched *Good Morning America* every morning. Robin Roberts would say, "Everybody's got something." Well MS is my something. It's just how you choose to respond to your something. Each individual has to take control over how they manage this or any disease. I am committed to taking an active role in my MS. I constantly learn new things and will continue to go to MS meetings to learn about new DMTs (Disease-Modifying Therapies/Treatments) on the horizon and other handy tidbits. DMTs offered today can now be distributed orally, as an injection, or as an infusion. I try to speak to both the MS ambassadors or medical professionals if I remember them from a previous speaking engagement. I have learned I have to be my own advocate in the management of my MS.

Please realize that what works for me, may not work for you. I hope you find hacks or come up with tricks or tools that work for you. It makes me feel so good when someone tells me they tried something I may have told them about. This book is specific to my MS, but maybe someone with another kind of challenge will read something that may help them. I just used this book as a platform to share my story.

This book started out just me telling about how posting pictures on Throwback Thursday was a welcomed distraction from dealing with MS. It became so much more than that. Writing this book was so therapeutic. As I search over the last 41 years, especially the last seven years, I see how all the people in my circle have helped me through this journey, not only family and long-time friends, but new friends as well. Hopefully, another MSer will be able to identify with some of the things I went through. Maybe someone will learn one helpful tip to assist them with navigating their own journey.

I am not trying to sugarcoat things. The MS struggle is real. Some days I still tell people, "MS Sucks," Okay, I say, "MS Sucks Balls." MS does occasionally cramp my style, can be downright disrespectful, and sometimes it won't let me be great. I think you catch my drift. Other days are alright. I haven't mentioned everything that I have done since I started writing. There are way more events in this book than available on Facebook. I have been very busy with both MS related and non-MS related activities. Though I like to remain active, I make sure to squeeze naps in amidst the hustle and bustle. If I don't get a nap in, sometimes after a long day, I collapse on my bed, and with no TV on, I do a couple of rounds of a 4-7-8 Yoga-style breathing technique. I often joke that I stay in the mean streets, but I am usually home before dark. I keep so busy because I have no idea how long I will be able to do all of the things I do. None of us do. I'm going to make the dash between my birth and death years count. YOLO (You Only Live Once). I have had some spills but I am still smiling. I am hopeful about my future. In a nutshell, I got this! I am a work in progress, but I think I am evolving and on the way to becoming the best version of myself.

I encourage everyone reading this book to find something that brings you the kind of joy that Throwback Thursday continues to bring me. People have told me their pets bring them that kind of joy. Even though I stumbled upon some real treasures as I was selecting photos for Throwback Thursday, the thought never crossed my mind to use my massive collection of photo albums to help me write this book until I was almost finished writing. I certainly could have gone back and made changes after going through the photo albums, but I wanted to show how I wrote organically. I wanted to show how my mind actually jumps subjects and how my thoughts are all over the place. I have learned the best project you'll ever work on is one's self and that is what I'm trying to accomplish. This has been a journey of discovery. I have learned some real pearls of wisdom and not all things are MS-related. I am embarrassed to admit that I used to think that most people in wheelchairs had some type of decreased cognitive ability since I have both physical and cognitive challenges. I did not know you could have physical limitations and no cognitive impairment. I thought the brilliant Theoretical Physicist,

Stephen Hawking, was an anomaly. You don't know what you don't know.

Thank you so much for taking this journey with me. I hope you have enjoyed it. I believe MS is part of my larger purpose in life. Perhaps this diagnosis is part of my destiny to allow me to be a champion for the MS community. Maybe it is so I could write this book and share my story and hopefully even inspire others.

By the way, the last entry in my Journey Journal from August 6, 2017 reads, "Your story is not over!"

For questions or comments email
FigureItOutMS@comcast.net

Made in the USA
Middletown, DE
02 June 2019